Dreaming in Hindi

DREAMING IN HINDI

*Coming Awake in
Another Language*

Katherine Russell Rich

HOUGHTON MIFFLIN HARCOURT
BOSTON ◆ NEW YORK
2009

For information about permission to reproduce selections from
this book, write to Permissions, Houghton Mifflin Harcourt
Publishing Company, 215 Park Avenue South,
New York, New York 10003.

www.hmhbooks.com

Library of Congress Cataloging-in-Publication Data

Rich, Katherine Russell.
 Dreaming in Hindi : coming awake in another language /
 Katherine Russell Rich
   p. cm.
 Includes bibliographical references.
 ISBN 978-0-618-15545-3
   1. India—Description and travel.   2. Udaipur (Rajasthan, India)—
 Description and travel.   3. Rich, Katherine Russell—Travel—India.
 4. Americans—Travel—India.   5. Hindi language—Social aspects.
 6. Hindi language—Psychological aspects.   7. Psycholinguistics—
 Case studies.   8. India—Social life and customs.   9. Udaipur (Rajas-
 than, India)—Social life and customs.   I. Title.
   DS414.2.R53 2009   954.05'31092—dc22   2008053295

Printed in the United States of America

Book design by Victoria Hartman

DOC 10 9 8 7 6 5 4 3 2

The author gratefully acknowledges permission to use the poem
"The Cruel Festival Time" by Nand Chaturvedi.

Stuart Paddock Rich,
in memoriam

✦

Contents

Part III

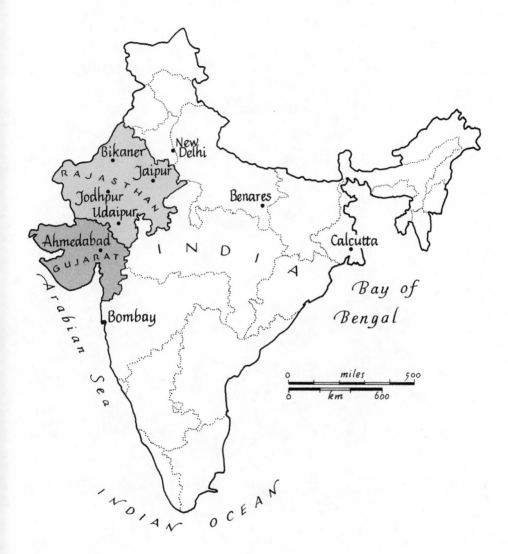

Prologue

One time in India, I appeared half-naked in a temple, just up and flashed the worshipers. This was not something I'd been planning to do; I surprised myself on the Lord God Shiva's birthday. Surprised the celebrants, too, I'd say. They hadn't been expecting it either.

This would have been a long time in, for by then I could make out what the people around me were saying. I knew, for example, what the woman in a coppery sari had squeaked to the man pressed between us on the bus ride up to the temple town. *"Gori! Gori!"* she'd exclaimed: "Look! A white woman!" The main reason I'd come to India, in fact, had been to learn the language. Originally, I'd thought that if I could, it would be like cracking a strange veiled code, a shimmering triumphant entry, but by now all it was was someone talking.

By the time of that trip, I knew a lot of things easily: That the peeling dashboard sticker of a goddess on a tiger meant the bus driver was a devotee of the goddess Durga, for instance. Or what the Hindi was for *"The langur has no tail due to an electrical accident,"* one of the things a man in Western clothes, an engineer, said when we struck up a conversation outside the town's main temple.

"There used to be beautiful gardens here," he said. *"The Palace of the Winds at the top of the hill was once the summer residence of kings. Would you like to join us for Shiva's birthday worship?"** Not one word jammed, the talk was purling, though every so often the man would excuse himself and slip into the temple, then reemerge. The last time he did, he was in a bright red lungi wrap, transformed from an engineer. A grizzled old man in a white lungi followed him.

"You may join us, but you must change your clothes. We don't allow pants inside," the old man, a pandit, a Brahmin priest, said. I said I'd be honored to be included.

"See, Pandit-ji! She speaks good Hindi," the engineer said, and the priest handed me a bundled white cloth, the makings of an impromptu sari. I eyed it warily. Anytime I'd tried to wrap myself, the results had been unfortunate.

He directed me over a high step, into a sanctum containing statues of gods, where five men and a woman with grape green eyes were seated in a circle. Farther on, in a back room, I gave the cloth a try. I took off my jeans and draped myself, I thought, rakishly. But when I reappeared at the door, the Venus de Milo effect unraveled into strips, leaving my *gori* flanks exposed. The men gaped. The green-eyed woman barked out a reproof. Western women were known to flagrantly exhibit themselves. The pandit abruptly ordered me out of the room, commanded the woman to follow and lend a hand.

I worried I'd irrevocably disgraced myself, but once she'd snugly fitted me, the priest waved me back to the circle. He was solicitous throughout the ceremony, through the hours we kneeled on the cold stone floor and my knees turned to points of stabbing pain. He

---

* Throughout the book, conversations that took place in Hindi are given in italicized English, to avoid taxing the reader's patience with repeated translations.

guided my hands onto copper bowls, onto my neighbors, at the necessary moments. We washed the gods in milk, honey, curds, water, and ghee. He continually chanted their names, and I blinked to find myself sinking into what seemed like a far center I'd always known. This place was greenly translucent, soothing, universal, like the water in the pool where as a child I'd nearly drowned and hadn't, till I surfaced, been afraid. But the sudden merger with the infinite skewered my earthly activities. Lulled, I tipped a bowl of water onto a deity's head.

"*Dhire! Dhire!*" the devotees cried: "Slowly! Slowly!" "*We are giving the god a bath.*"

Incense spiraled up like djinns. We rubbed the gods with sugar. We garlanded them with marigolds, as people gathered on the steps outside. They leaned across the stone threshold to the temple and peered in. The gawkers lit more sandalwood sticks, left oranges as offerings, asked what was going on in there. There was a foreigner?

"*Her Hindi is good,*" the devotees informed them the first hour.

"*Her Hindi is very good,*" the devotees said in the second, though my known repertoire had not expanded much beyond "*What was that?*"

The third hour, a new man joined us, glanced over, said something. "*Haan,*" the priest said: Yes. "*She is fluent.*"

"*That was Sanskrit he was speaking!*" the devotees exclaimed after each of the priest's rumbled chants. "*Very old,*" the priest concurred, holding up a text the size and shape of a comic book, breaking to provide me with some tutelage in the classics. Then the green-eyed woman produced small outfits hemmed in tinsel, and we carefully dressed the gods.

Afterward, with the grainy smell of ghee in our hair, the worshipers clamored to explain that the ceremony was older than Buddhism, than Jainism, than Christianity. "*It is only once a year,*" a man said, adding that I was lucky to have arrived here on this day. "*And after, you feel so peaceful,*" another man said of the four hours of pure devotion. *"By doing this, you keep the world happy,"* he told me, though the exact verb he used was more like "set."

What follows is a story about setting the world happy, about the strange, snaking course devotion can take. It's about what happens if you allow yourself to get swept away by a passion. The short answer is this: inevitably, at some point, you come unwrapped.

It's a story about a stretch of time I spent in India, learning to speak another language. Since that year was an exceptionally violent and fragmenting one, both in India and throughout the world, it's a story that sometimes turns savage. This book, the way I'd conceived it before I left, was going to be solely about the near-mystical and transformative powers of language: the way that words, with only the tensile strength of breath, can tug you out of one world and land you in the center of another. By the end of that year, however, the story was still about transformation, yes, but it had become one about the destructive power of words as well—the way they can reshape people, can leave them twisted, can break them. It's about language as passport and as block.

Since the book is concerned with language, with one person's attempts to learn another, and since the person in question, i.e., me, is not a blazing talent in that department, I think I should probably allow this right up front. I'm not that great, naturally, at learning other tongues. I simply love the process. When my mother traveled, she liked to eat her way through a place. Her trip journals were all about meals, never sights: *Got up at eight. Went to the French Quarter for beignets. At eleven had shrimp remoulade at Christian's.* "I speak menu," she'd say. Me, when I travel, I just want to speak. I've always been fascinated by language in any form, the more unintelligible, the better. When I get on a plane, I lose myself in the vocabulary section of the guidebook, not excluding the sentences for businessmen. I can cite favorite lines from various books. *"Is vakt sattewalon ne is chiz par kabza kar liya hai,"* from the *Cambridge Self Hindi Teacher,* is a good one: "Speculators have for the moment seized on this article." *Cambridge* stands out because it breaks form, which requires that the travelers' sentences be kept jaunty. It allows a measure of melancholy, even existentialism. "Unfortunately they are in such a bad condition we can't accept them." "The date of the arrival does not matter much." This is a quality that I think sets it apart, though others might argue.

I love a lot of things about language study—the way it can make you feel like a spy, the covert glimpses it provides into worlds that were previously off-limits, even the confounding difficulties, the tests it puts you to. For the purposes of this book, I interviewed a former Fulbright scholar, a linguist named A. L. Becker, who knows Burmese, Thai, Old Javanese, and Malay well enough to teach them. "I sometimes think I study these things," he said, "because I have such a hard time with it," and I nodded emphatically. Also for this book, I interviewed a number of neurolinguists and people who study the science of language acquisition, for at the same time that I developed a passion for Hindi, a corresponding obsession kicked in: to understand what learning a second language does to the brain. The process, for me, was frustrating and exhilarating and at times transcendent, all in a way that felt deeply corporeal; I could only believe it was scrambling my brains. What I learned was that to some extent, a second language does. It makes you not quite yourself, your old one.

This might explain the pattern I observed when I first began taking Hindi lessons. People would exclaim, "My daughter's doing that! She was having trouble at Smith and had to drop out for a semester, and so she's decided to study Mandarin!" Someone had retired and was learning Basque in a chatroom. Another, recovering from a breakup, was hot in pursuit of Greek. Conjugants, I began to think of us as. I'm sorry to have to report to the Modern Language Association that in monolingual America, no one much past school age seems to take up a language when their lives are going gangbusters, that it's a preoccupation of the disoriented. I've a feeling the same principle might apply to any pursuit that demands you start over as a beginner, given all the other stories I've heard—of the divorces and dislocations that resulted in people learning, finally, how to swim, or play chess, or play the piano. Mandarin, mandolin—in a way, same thing. You embrace pursuits like these as an adult, I think, as a transfer of focus when your life has shifted you into another place, when you've had to begin again in some way. By immersing yourself as a neophyte in a realm that's more controllable than your now unwieldy and sorry whole existence, you keep yourself in one piece, at least in this one area. The impulse is probably a perverted survival mechanism, but so what?

In my own case, I took up with Hindi at a time when it seemed my life had buckled out from under me. I'd been fired from a magazine job and come to a reckoning: I wasn't sure I wanted to do that anymore. And since, other than early counter work at Burger King, magazine editing was all I'd ever done and, past the age of sixteen, ever wanted to do, I was disoriented in the extreme. The business, first in concept, then in fact, had been my fueling passion since high school. As a kid in the most straitening suburbs of Philadelphia, the Main Line, I'd hoped to be either an archaeologist, a circus performer, or a poet. Magazine work, when I hit on that idea, seemed like it might combine the best of all three. You'd dig deep into culture, perform high-wire acts with deadlines. And you'd be immersed in lyricism of a kind, wouldn't you?

Not necessarily, or not at the glossy journals where I ended up, or not so far as I could see, twenty years on, when a chant had begun to loop through my head: *I want to lead a more artistic life.* I looked around then and saw how my life, long set in this direction, was turning out. At thirty-seven, I had an extensive collection of giveaway moisturizers; as the second most geriatric person on staff at the magazine where I worked, I'd been required to test them. I had stacks of review copies of books I never read. My evenings were taken up with the rounds of business parties and merchandising events that can blur whole years in New York City, where I lived. I had a closetful of shoes that were unnervingly expensive and a cat with bizarre proclivities—a kind of foot fetish, I'd say. The cat liked to eat the toes off leather high heels, but only the finest ones, only the Manolo Blahniks. I'd come home and find him on his back in the closet, cradling one half of a gnawed pair, a sated gleam in his eye. I couldn't say what psychological derangement was spurring him, but I could see this was a sign.

By the time, a few years later, when I was fired from the place that required on-the-job moisturizing, my life no longer made any kind of sense to me. Not bedrock, regenerative sense. Compounding this state of feeling uprooted from my existence while still in it was the fact that in the decade just passed, I'd had several encounters with a serious illness, had been sick with cancer twice. The last time of full crisis had been three, four years before, but I remained perpetually on half alert for a third siege.

That, then, is the place where I'd arrived first time I took a Hindi lesson:

I no longer had the language to describe my own life. So I decided I'd borrow someone else's.

Part I

"To go"

 The whole year in India, I was never confused, though often, for days, I thought I was. "Vidhu-ji," I asked the teacher with the angular face, remembering to attach the "ji," an honorific that could also mean *yes* or *what?*—point of bafflement right there. "Vidhu," I repeated, promptly forgetting to. "How do I say 'I'm confused'?"

"Main bhram mein hoon," he said: "I am in *bhram*," and for the rest of the year, I used that sentence more than any other.

"Vidhu-ji! Wait! I am in bhram," I'd say, flapping my hand, interrupting Grammar, Dictation, till he must have wished I'd yank myself out of it, must have regretted the day he ever told me.

I was in *bhram,* off and on, at the school and beyond: when I'd try to ask a shopkeeper in Hindi if he had this thing in blue, while he stared at me with his mouth half open, as if he were watching a trick. When India later on became like an opiated dream; when the poet Nand-ji bent my senses using words; when I sat and watched the deaf school boys flash language on their hands—all those times, too. And in bhram, but a dark, pernicious kind, when soon after I arrived, the world was exploded; when months after that, India went up in flames; when people by the hundreds then were slaughtered.

Many times throughout that year, I was in full-press brahm, in nonstop confusion, or so I thought. I wasn't till I returned to the States that I learned the exact meaning of the word. Illusion. The whole year in India, I'd been in illusion.

MY FIRST VISIT to India had been a chance encounter. I'd wandered in by accident. Took a plane, to be exact, but I hadn't meant to go, hadn't meant to lie and tell a newspaper editor who was phoning with an assignment, "I can't. I'll be in India."

This was three years before my unveiling in the temple, at a point when I'd been contemplating becoming a full-time writer. I'd had a lot of time just then to consider what, exactly, I was supposed to do with the rest of my life. Four months before, I'd been fired from the magazine that was able, psychically, to prompt my cat to eat my shoes. It was the eighth one I'd worked for that had either folded or snapped me suddenly from the work force, and I was coming to a belated conclusion: I'd had enough of this whiplash. When the editor called, I was tottering between two lives: the old one, the one where I loved the execution of my work but where the practicalities of the workplace could inflict slow soul death, and this unimaginable one that kept trying to take shape, the ferociously uncertain one where I'd cut the tethers and become a writer.

I'd already made forays in the second direction. The last year on the old job, I'd written a book during evenings and weekends and accumulated sick days, one of the reasons I'd gotten bounced: divided attention. A chant in my head that had been prickling me had gained voltage. *I want to lead a more artistic life.* Though the book was now completed, and though it had initially seemed like proof of the direction I should claim, as time went on, it could with harsh clarity be revealed for what it would likely be: a stone, one that would sink without sound. Thousands of books did each year. This possibility would flare to mind, then I'd lose my nerve, then I'd talk myself back onto the dividing line, say, *But you can do it—have a voice, come into your own.* And I would think, for a time, yeah, I could.

But when the newspaper editor called, he called my bluff. The dividing line vanished along with my resolve. India seemed like a foolproof out, the most distant place I could think of, and I wasn't expecting him to say "Well, why don't you do something for us there?" Or for me to say "I will."

Two weeks later, India was flying by in tumbled glimpses. Turquoiseorangelime, the color stream of saris. Monkeys, black-faced in trees. A flat dun highway that shot straight ahead with the force of an exclamation.

"Have I changed yet?" I'd asked my traveling companion as our bus idled on the edge of midnight in the dank New Delhi bus station. On the plane over, I'd told her what a writer I'd worked with had said: "India will change you forever." Having just managed to blow up my life, I was thinking that might be appealing.

"Completely," she said as passengers filed by and took seats. "Totally now," she said and laughed as we started into the night.

On the bus, when people squeezed in beside us, she asked them about the next stop. We didn't need to know. She was practicing Hindi from a book. Mostly Hindi sounded like you just repeated the word *swaga,* but *swaga* was taking us a long way. *"Swaga,* how do you say that, *swaga,"* and next thing we'd be at the movie theater, so called but really someone's living room. *"Swaga,* oh what's the word, something, *swaga,"* and we'd learn that the monks brushing past us on the mountain path were hurrying to get to the temple before sundown. *Swaga,* we could find out things, we were about to learn more, and then it was over, we were back.

"I did not realize then that this sense of an enormous revelation

about to occur is simply fundamental to the Indian experience,"
Anthony Weller wrote in his travelogue *Days and Nights on the
Grand Trunk Road,* and he'd been going on English alone. We'd had
a number of revelations—foremost, that contact dharma is a powerful high. And if my friend—or I—had been better practiced in the
language, we could have had even more.

On my return to New York City, I decided to keep one dusty
shirt unwashed to preserve the olfactory memory, then accidentally
threw it in the machine. Didn't matter. A dun smell had settled in
my skin, along with a desire: to put it into words.

ONE MONTH INTO Hindi lessons, with a moonlighting Co-
lumbia professor named Susham Bedi, and the language was making my head smolder. One misplaced *m,* and you were no longer
saying "weather" but "husband of maternal aunt." You had to learn
to think in sentences whose verbs went at the end, which had the
effect of producing vertigo: *"to the house the mother the child is
taking."* There was the fact I couldn't pronounce it, plus I couldn't
write it. The beautiful letters, like stick trees that had bumped into a
ceiling or a revue of performing snakes, came out shaped like cows'
heads in my hands. I was frustrated, and fascinated.

Susham was handsome, with eyes like black ice and a manner so
languid that sometimes when it took me a while to answer, I'd look
to find her dozing. Relatives darted through the room, and once she
asked a visiting sister to take over the lesson, but nonetheless she got
the job done. Two months on, the snakes had become elegant script
that, if pressed, would release words. I was reading Devanagari now
and cranking, nursing a sensation like falling in love. In love with
what? With the snakes, and the Sanskrit and Persian words they preserved, records of distant migrations. Whoever names something
has power over it, and with the subcontinent's multitude of tribes
and sects past and present, there have been numerous rechristenings
in the Indo-Aryan languages, one of the subsets of Indo-European,

which makes them distant cousins of English. Hindi, Rajasthani, Punjabi, all the close relatives in the north, echo with names that were staked in different tongues and beliefs—by Aryans and Hunas, Hindus, Muslims, Buddhists, Jains, Christians, Sikhs. And, of course, by British colonialists, 350 years' worth, who left the linguistic terrain mottled with Victorianisms: *svimming kaustyoom* for "bathing suit," *motar gaadi* for "car." Just as South America is littered with antiquated cars, Hindi is strewn with words no one in America had used since Agatha Christie's time, and for that alone I loved it.

On a tape that came with the textbook, a mystery man sounded a little like he was making obscene suggestions. He recited the consonants with a regal insistence, and I was floored to find, three months on, that I couldn't tell the difference between *tha* and *ta, ra* and *rha. Na* was like he was clearing his throat, a sound from another world.

"If you speak English, you have one world. If you speak Navajo, you have a another world," a linguistics professor said in an article I'd found. And if you are able to have two worlds, I wondered, does that mean your original one has doubled?

I'd come across his quote as part of the research I was doing for a magazine story I'd pitched, on learning a language as an adult. "It doesn't make sense to write about French or Spanish," I'd argued in the proposal letter. "We've all muddied them up in high school. I want to try a more distant language in order to get a more precise view—a bas-relief—of what goes on with the neurons than I can obtain with a Romance language." The editors said go ahead, even though they couldn't have had any idea what I meant, as I didn't, other than that I'd screwed up French and Spanish several times in school, Turkish, too, at Berlitz. If the drive to acquire a first language is instinct, as many linguists think, perhaps the urge for a second is, too—at least that was the best explanation I had then for why I kept throwing myself at the wall. Mostly, all I produced were spider lines. Once, I'd caught sight of a door. It was, strangely, in an interview with Mick Jagger, who said he hadn't been able to crack French till he got himself to admit he didn't truly believe the French were speaking a real language, whereupon he was able to take a leap of faith: barriers fell; he was in.

I'd filed that idea away then, because at the time I had other leaps I had to make. In Hindi class now, it came back to me. The language was hard. All I had to go on was faith and perversity. Always before with languages, I'd started out with the conviction that I was hurtling toward fluency. I'd just sit down and learn French, but then French would collapse into unnecessary complications. Spanish would take on a crushing weight that had not been detectable in those first, friendly exchanges between *chicos*. Enthusiasm would wither. My interest would die.

Hindi was such a losing proposition going in, though, I didn't have expectations, which meant that every word gained was a bonus and small thrill. The word for green made me feel invincible. Since there was no way to explain this to anyone without looking tetched, I came up with an answer for when someone asked what it was I thought I was doing. I was doing this on a lark. I consciously believed that myself for a good two years, till sometime in India, the real reason became clear, and then I saw it had been obvious all along.

When one day on my arrival, Susham said she had no more time for private lessons, I was despondent. I'd grown to love the sunny Morningside Heights apartment: computer on the dining room table, shocking tiger skins on the wall, a lingering incense that merged with the alien words on the far plane I could reach. I'd been using all senses.

WHILE I LOOKED for another teacher, I burrowed down in research for the magazine story. In my apartment, drifts of papers torn from journals covered books with titles such as *The Neurobiology of*

Affect in Language. In the way passions can, this one had spawned an offshoot—a sharp desire to learn what science thought a second language did to the brain.

Anyone with this curiosity will soon find themselves snowed under, for the study of second language acquisition, or SLA as it's known around the hundreds of conferences convened yearly to examine it, has become a vast field that's given rise to numerous professorships, fellowships, books, and journals. The speed at which the field has grown is astonishing when you consider that as recently as the early 1980s, it simply did not exist. You could find publications on language learning aimed at helping French or Spanish teachers back then, but that was about it. No one was debating where second languages were lodged in the brain, or what permutating crossover effect a second vocabulary can have on your first, or whether background TV sound messes with your Spanish lessons, or any of the thousands of topics, ranging from the silly to the momentous, that are now routinely thrashed out.

The rapid expansion of second language acquisition in the United States seems peculiar when you consider that it has occurred during a time when the state of foreign language study has never been bleaker. Thirty years ago, sixteen of every one hundred college students were taking French, Spanish, or some other language. Today that figure's roughly half. On the elementary and high school levels, there are a few bright spots—Mandarin classes for kindergartners in Oregon, for instance—but only a few. Despite all the fervent warnings about how monolingual nations will be eclipsed in the global market, in reality the government's cut back. The government has repeatedly trimmed funds for high school language programs. It has shuttered the Office of Bilingual Education and Minority Language Affairs, thereby helping place the United States in the odd position of being officially monolingual, while also being the fifth-largest Spanish-speaking country in the world. One count, in fact, puts the number of languages spoken in the English-only United States at about sixty, including Kansa, Ho-Chunk, Burmese, and Louisiana French.

What you get, then, when you look at the state of language study in the United States is mixed-up. On the one hand, you see what seems to be a spike in interest among adults. UCLA continuing ed has had to add levels to its language offerings to accommodate all the new applicants. The Concordia Language Villages, in Minnesota, has seen a zoom of 40 percent in enrollments in its adult division. (The average age range there is 47 to 67, though one of the matriculates is 92. He's decided to get cracking on German.) At the same time, you see kids, as a result of government policies, being dissuaded from studying languages at a time when their brains are most equipped to absorb them. "We spend eighteen years knocking language out of our kids, then spend hundreds of thousands of dollars putting it back in when they hit college," Dora Johnson, a researcher at the Center for Applied Linguistics, says. You see a thriving industry, SLA, positioned to study a population that's falling off. Which is not to complain that the industry is there, only to remark on the irony.

If half the energy that fuels SLA could be shunted into language study itself, we'd all end up bilingual. SLA studies is a spirited, exploding, and explosive field. Arguments break out over a host of concerns: Does a second language alter how we take in the world? Does the language instinct exist, and if so, does it apply to seconds? Is language ability, with both first and second, a special function in the brain, or is it part of wider cognition?

One of the more contentious pieces of SLA theory is the notion of a critical period. The question there is, Is there a window of opportunity that briefly and magnificently opens, allowing grammar, syntax, all necessary linguistic knowledge, to flow in till about puberty, when lateralization is complete? Lateralization is the period when functions set up in the brain. For most right-handers, the language systems end up being housed in the left hemisphere. Ethologists have come out in favor of a critical period, observing that the same kind of cutoff can be observed among animals. Goldfinches can grow up with accents. Teachers sometimes take a dim view of the critical period, having seen too many exceptions, while brain guys (occasionally referred to as "neurophiliacs" in the other circles), some of them, contend that it's not one window that shuts, but four or five, in sequence. Michel Paradis, a neurolinguist in Montreal whom I flew up to interview for the story, is of this belief.

"Prosody is the first to go," he said when we met in his quiet gray office. Files were lined up precisely behind him. Paradis, in a fitted light gray jacket, had an air of exactness about him, too. He was basing his argument on the idea that language is a function of multiple subsystems in the brain, each one a command station that depends on a network of cells firing thousands of synaptic impulses per second. One is in charge of prosody, or intonation, what Andy Kaufman made extreme use of on *Taxi*. Another is set up to control phonology, sound patterns. Separate systems govern morphology, the combination of small sound splices — "can" plus "dy" — into words, and syntax, or the ordering of words into sentences.

Most of them, Paradis believes, are subject to their own critical period, which concludes about the time myelinization occurs — that is, about the time the dendrites and axons, the whiplike connectors in cells, grow insulated enough to carry electrical impulses. This critical sequence, as the entire extended wrap-up is called, begins at about eighteen months of age and continues in phases through around year seven, setting all aspects of speech except one. Lexicon, vocabulary, is exempt from maturation. You can learn new words forever, or until your memory is shot, which is why in French or Spanish, vocabulary is easy for adults, compared to knowing what to do with it. Otherwise, once the cells that produce the cant of a sentence are firing straight, "you're stuck with your intonations and stresses. You can always tell a foreigner by the prosody. It's very hard to change," Paradis said.

For the past thirty years, Paradis has been studying bilinguals with aphasia, speech damaged by cerebral insult. Working backward from their silences and shuffled words, he's gleaned insight into how the brain processes languages, first and second. I'd come because I was curious about his deductions. All aphasia leads to provocative calculations. If language is what makes us human, then what happens when our humanity is suddenly altered through the violence of a stroke or an accident?

What happens with bilinguals, Paradis observed, is that people can lose one tongue and not the other, for a time, to a degree, or completely. His textbook *Readings on Aphasia in Bilinguals and Polyglots* contains numerous examples. Following a head injury, an Austrian commander, once fluent in German and Italian, was able to speak to his wife only in the remnants of his Italian, to his doctors only in what was left of his German. A terminally ill woman of "unreported age or handedness" could no longer speak English, which she'd used for the past twenty years, and reverted to Dutch, her mother tongue. For a long time after I read the book, I thought about these language ghosts, made to wander the debris of worlds they'd constructed, worlds that would sometimes flare back to life, then just as suddenly sputter out.

One patient, a Moroccan nun born to French parents, had slammed her head when her moped crashed into a car. Afterward, she could still speak French and Arabic, but only on alternate days. "On the days when she couldn't speak French, where did it go?" Paradis asked. He has many deductive theories, well regarded in his field, about why this might happen, though not about where the French goes.

"All knowledge divides into two types," he said, by way of introduction. "Procedural, also called automatic, is acquired incidentally and at a very young age: the ability to tie your shoes, walk up stairs, speak English, for those born in the States. Why do you make a word agree with the past participle? You don't know. Neither do five-year-olds, but they do it all the time." Five-year-olds naturally absorb whatever talk is around them. Mandarin, Slovene, Yoruba—it doesn't matter. It becomes procedural and wired into one stretch of the brain—gathered through the cerebellum, basal ganglia, and corpus striatum, he posits, then stored in neocortices in the left hemisphere.

All native languages, then, are a form of procedural knowledge. Procedural knowledge is a world apart, practically, from declarative knowledge, the other variety. Declarative knowledge is what you learn later in life: math, the combination to your gym locker, Italian in a night course. For the most part, new knowledge, Paradis said—and this explains a lot, if you're wrestling with a new language—is stored diffusely, all over the brain. Hence the space-bump feeling when you're trying to recall something recently learned: *How do you say "farm" again?* It's right there, on the tip of your hippocampus.

The reason, he believes, that a blow to the head could mangle your English but leave your sparse high school French intact is that first and subsequent languages—procedural and declarative knowledge—are processed slightly differently by the brain. They're handled by microscopic and varying pathways. A contusion or illness can affect one route and not the other, similar to how tornadoes in the Midwest sometimes level the houses on one side of a street but spare the ones opposite.

In navigating another language, then, you're not using precisely the same brain you do when employing your first. With a second one, you're flying through different combinations of circuits, drawing more on pragmatics—sense guessed from context and gestures—in the right brain, less on the limbic system, which is located near the base. The limbic system churns emotions, the gel for memory. The first time around, emotions help language set: "Bird? Bird? Can you say bird? Good boy!" your mother exclaims, to your gurgling delight. The limbic system, however, doesn't get revved much in language class. *"Où se trouve la pharmacie?"* the French teacher asks, but unless you've got a headache, who cares? Need and fear are what stamp words in the cortex. Heartache's an iron press. So's desire. A lover who speaks the language is a faster route to fluency than any tapes or courses, but perhaps more expensive.

As the interview was coming to a close, I inquired whether Paradis thought that a second language learned in adulthood could ever reach a par with a first. Even before the question was out of my mouth, I knew it was a mistake to have asked. As dazzling as that second world was already becoming to me, there could only be one right answer, and Paradis, I could tell by then, wasn't likely to give it. He didn't. "There's doubt as to whether, when you learn a second language late, you can gain procedural competence," he said. You can speed up your processing, he added, but you will always, for instance, have an accent. You will always be off by a beat, by a stress, detectably from someplace else.

Other investigations I conducted then were similarly dampening. Foreign language studies are a rigged operation, I learned. An estimated 95 percent of students "fossilize," the linguistic term for hardening at a certain level. Ninety-five! So accent's a given, perfection's impossible, and odds are you're on your way to becoming a linguistic fossil: good work. At some point, then, the question has to become, Why would you even try?

IN HINDI, YOU drink a cigarette, night spreads, you eat a beating. You eat the sun. *"Dhoop khaana?"* I asked Gabriela Ilieva, a moonlighting New York University Hindi professor, first time we hit the phrase. "Sunbathe," she said smiling. "To bask in the sun." My mind, alert for ricocheting syntax, was momentarily diverted by

the poetry of idiom, the found lyricism that's the short-form answer
to the question of why you'd try.

"They really say 'Victory to Rama' when they answer the phone?"
I asked a tutorial later, reporting what Chirag, a computer student
I'd enlisted for practice, had told me. "Oh, it's no different from you
saying 'Good God,'" she said. Gabriela was originally from Bulgaria
and conversant in eleven languages. Her mother was the most famous actress in her country—"like Sophia Loren," she said—which
somehow gave the fact that she knew Sanskrit, Punjabi, and Old
Church Slavonic an even greater gravity. Seeing that I still looked
incredulous, she tsked: It's just what they said! She was practiced in
knowing when to convert the extraordinary to ordinary, when to let
the extraordinary stand.

It was the pull of these conversions that kept me returning now,
their mimicry of transcendence—ordinary to extraordinary, then
back again. Invariably, once a class, the assumptions of one language
would collide with the other's, shaking me from the certainty that
Aldous Huxley called "reduced awareness." Boosted, I could skid
across syntax so alien that if translated directly, it would read like a
computer shorting out. "India returning of before to us right here
stay" could remain "Stay with us before returning to India" only if
you didn't look down.

"*Hindimein! Hindimein!*" Gabriela would call when my energy
drained and I took a spill: Think in Hindi. "Come on! No English!"
she'd chide. "*Haan,*" I'd snort, meaning "yes," meaning "Why don't
you just speak it?" and she'd burst out laughing at the look on my
face. I doubted that she laughed maniacally at her regular students,
but a while back we'd become friends, and anyway, they were kids,
we were adults.

"Did you hear? Did you hear?" she'd ask at the beginning of each
class after I'd applied for a Hindi program in India that Susham had
mentioned. I'd done this for complicated reasons, not one being I

thought I'd get in. I didn't fit a single entry requirement, didn't, for one thing, have two college years of the language. But I'd needed just then to see myself as someone who'd do something on this order, who'd throw "my whole life up in the air for a passion," as once or twice I'd floridly declared, a desire that stemmed from my truculent medical history.

The second time I'd gotten sick, they'd given me a year or two. The disease I had, cancer, was breaking bones from within, had turned vicious and insistent, when one night I dreamed I was fighting with a woman over a piece of cloth. The fabric was sleek and blue, beautiful, weft pressing warp in a way that caused ripples, and she was trying to take it from me. "But it's mine!" I shouted. "I made it." The woman grew somber. "You may have made it," she said quietly, "but that doesn't mean you get to keep it." A friend had to explain that the cloth symbolized my life.

I'd accepted that I was losing mine, when the illness went into one of those astounding reversals cancer sometimes does. It skidded and turned, leaving me in a perpetual state of spooked awe, with an impulse to keep my life narrowed. Though I'd fallen in love with a man when the disease returned, once that affair ended, I avoided romantic entanglement: too much anchoring to the slipshod processes of life, too much touch. My life became fortified, safely latched down, though I was left with a small, lingering need: to tell myself I was unafraid, of anything. Not because I was. In case I had to summon fast courage again.

"You're prepared to live in India for a year?" Gabriela stopped one class to ask. The week before, my oncologist had stared at me when I'd said I wanted to. Stared, then smiled. He and I had a longstanding congenial accord, unusual in a relationship in which one member had had to nearly poison the other to death four times not that long before. That was, essentially, the protocol with bone marrow transplants, a now abandoned desperation treatment for a desperate group: stage four breast cancer patients, women who, on average, had two and a half years to live. If a little chemo was good, then earth-scorching amounts would be better, the thinking went—mistakenly, it turned out. But stage four is subject to experimental approaches, being, by and large, endgame cancer. My own illness, in the four years since the transplant, had been kept in check with lightweight hormone treatments, with pills that were portable if someone were to request permission to leave the country for a stretch. "India, huh?" my doctor said. "All right, but you'd have to be watched closely." He said this after a pause. In the annals of medicine, I was guessing, there weren't many case studies of patients with this diagnosis expressing a desire to light out for parts unknown. But he and I were in terra incognita, and besides, he'd helped keep me alive all these years. He wasn't going to keep me from living.

"In Bulgaria, they think that's lucky!" Gabriela cried after a bird spattered my textbook as I was hurrying down to tell her the acceptance e-mail had come. "Welcome aboard for a world of experience!" the attached leaflet said: twenty hours a week of pronunciation, grammar, and film discussion ahead, with time off for holidays with names like Makar Sankranti and for chatting with the Hindi-speaking host families. Tips were included for cultural navigation, for engaging in life without toilet paper. I scanned them from a growing distance of disbelief. I was in, and stupefied to be. But they'd said two college years, and I wasn't even in college. How could this be?

"We could have been speaking Swahili and they'd have taken us," one of my co-academics, a metalhead turned Indology major, would remark upon our arrival. In the wake of several scandals, it seems, applications were down.

As the months sped by and departure hovered, I could have used a more encouraging omen than sudden bird shit from the sky. There were days I couldn't believe I was doing this: Throwing my life over? Why? About to jettison it, I saw with clarity that it was finally where I wanted it. And days when I saw that was the reason to go.

The last month passed in a whirl of inactivity. I postponed a visit to the foreign-diseases doctor till I was begging for a case of malaria down the line; made lists I misplaced; ordered novels there wasn't room for; knocked off from these activities to see a psychic, a bon voyage gift from a friend. His predictions were fanciful—I'd be taken up by kings and queens, would teach in a school on the outskirts of town, would witness a spectacular healing—but I succumbed to suspension of disbelief and for several days occupied myself lazing around, imagining how I was going to talk my way into the heart of India. I sent out a mass e-mailing asking if anyone knew of someone who'd sublet my apartment and look after the cat. I decided that if I couldn't find anyone, that would be a sign I shouldn't go. I heard from a husband-and-wife team willing to clean the litter box and pay the rent. With the fellowship's monthly stipend, my expenses were covered.

Coming down the homestretch, I had a dream that the girls in the host family I'd been assigned staged nightly porn films once their parents went to bed. The day before I left, I packed and repacked and, when the driver rang, repositioned things some more. I dragged the suitcase to the elevator, pressed the button, grabbed the handle.

And then I took a flying leap.

· 2 ·

"To speak"

 Orientation was held in Outer Space. It followed on the heels of the warm-up welcome-aboard sessions we'd had the first day in Delhi. Those had taken place at the guesthouse of the governing institute and were attended by ten graduate students who were setting off for various language programs around the country. One woman was about to embark on a year of Tamil study in the southern state of Tamil Nadu; one young man was aiming to immerse himself in Marathi in Maharashtra, to the southwest. The Hindi students numbered four—the largest group, given that Hindi, being the country's official language, was the institute's flagship program. We did not make a great showing. When a grad student taking off for Urdu in Lahore introduced himself as "Iqbal," one of our contingent, the only guy, snickered audibly. "Sounds like 'one hair,'" he said under his breath, grinning: *eek* = "one" in Hindi, *bal* means "hair." I regarded this person closely, considered that he and I would be spending an entire year together. In the northwest state of Rajasthan; that's where we were headed, to a school in a blocky mid-rise, judging by the brochure, with a sign that read ANTRIKSH FLATS. "Outer Space Apartments," in translation.

At the front desk in Delhi, old men with kind faces cocked their heads when I asked questions. They didn't speak English, and contrary to what I'd thought, I didn't speak Hindi, and the situation continued in Udaipur, the city, size of Cincinnati, where the program had recently resettled. Apparently, there'd been some problems in the school's former locale, Benares,* though it never became exactly clear what they were. *"During the festival of Holi, bad men threw cow patties,"* the local headmaster, Swami-ji, would periodically recall throughout the year, face darkening, and that was as close to an explanation as I got.

I'd heard about Swami-ji once on the South Asian studies circuit back in the States, again the first day in Delhi. He turned out to be a small man in his forties, with a small round face and a boyish mop of hair that throughout the year never perceptibly changed length. After years of teaching hormone-addled students, he'd adopted a defense of looking simultaneously concerned and surprised. His nervous air of watchfulness was understandable, as a number of scandals had occurred on his watch. The year before, a (male, Western) student had run off with a (female, Indian) teacher—such an unthinkable breach of hierarchical order for India that news of the transgression washed up on the shores of every South Asian studies department in the States.

"Rumors go around about Swami-ji," the director of the institute, a man with the defiant jaw of a bulldog, had said during one of the seminars in Delhi. "But I have investigated and learned they

---

* Called Varanasi in its most recent rechristening, but as no one in the town where I lived referred to it that way, I've used the older name, Benares, throughout. I've done the same with Mumbai/Bombay and Kolkata/Calcutta.

were all a matter of misunderstanding." He mentioned an assistant cook who'd been hired perhaps unnecessarily, but at a cost of only 1,500 rupees per week. Thirty-five bucks—a demonstrably mild offense, we could see.

"I have investigated," the director had said growling, then caught himself. "They were all just misunderstandings."

TWO THINGS I knew about Udaipur before arriving: One, it had been a featured locale in the James Bond film *Octopussy,* a fact every news wala, every news vendor, I'd quizzed back in New York had mentioned. Two, it was a curious choice of location for a Hindi program, in the news wala consensus. "Why are they teaching you Hindi language there?" as one put it, though no one articulated the reason behind the sentiment.

Once we arrived, I got it. The inhabitants, in fact, preferred to speak Mewari, which had been a language until 1967, when the government voted to recognize only eighteen official languages in the constitution, and it wasn't one of them.* Now it was a dialect. Mewari has an illustrious history—it was the devotional poet Mirabai's tongue, for instance—but what it didn't have was "a senator in Delhi to push for it," as a local Mewari writer later told me, a variation on Max Weinrich's remark, "A language is a dialect with an army and a navy." In India, thousands of languages go unplatooned.

As it turned out, though, Udaipur was so romantic—two marble castles rising from a lake like floating mirages, others soaring grandly on the hill above them—its crenulated beauty so staggering, that I'd acquire a thick Mewari accent and be happy about it.

The town was located a night's drive south from the Great Thar Desert, a day's drive east from Pakistan, and off the main rail line

---

* Later, the official number was boosted to twenty-two, and it still wasn't one.

from Delhi. This last fact cut down on big-city grifters, though not on tourists: for years Udaipur had been a featured stop on any travel excursion that touted "the Raj." Before that, it had reduced Victorian adventurers to babbling. On our first day at the Quality Inn downtown, we caught sight of the splendor that had sent a Miss Norah Rowan Hamilton into paroxysms in her 1915 book, *Through Wonderful India and Beyond.* Rapture mounted as she related encounters with "temples gleaming white through the green gloam," "blood red flowers flaring insolently against the molten sky," and the "story book palace, . . . where fighting elephants, tusks tipped with metal, were kept." When, toward the end of my stay, I found the book on a dusty back shelf in the palace library, I was struck by how little things had changed. There was still flaring and gloam all over town, though the elephants now functioned more as wedding limousines than as tanks.

The area was only forty years out from being a princely state, the kingdom of Mewar, with its own language and king, or maharana (a lexically enlightened concept of government: "rana" — "raja," too — comes from the word *ranj,* "to please": it is the ruler's duty to please his subjects, through right actions.) Every other princely state in the area had a maharaja, but Udaipur had a maharana. When I asked one of the other students, a girl with a southern accent, what the word "maharana" meant, she said, "A bigger deal than a maharaja."

"Udaipur, I am thankful to say, is incurably medieval," Miss Hamilton wrote, and downtown, this was still true. The spill of palaces dominated life and thoughts locally, to the extent that a number of citizens seemed unaware that they were no longer living in a feudal principality. The fact that Indira Gandhi had stripped the Indian royals of their titles in 1971 was widely regarded as a technicality here. Hurrying through the winding lanes in the old town, you'd pass wall paintings of maharanas in saintly nimbi, wall paintings of maharanas astride tasseled elephants, and in one montage on a hot-pink balcony, oval portraits of both maharanas and Indian film stars ringing a lurid Durga.

Out in the suburban stretch where the school was located, however, a cure for the medieval had been found. Fifteen years before, when Udaipur's population had numbered 100,000 and television in the home had been only a rumor, the neighborhood had gone by another name, Hiran Magri, or Deer Hill. Then the economy had swelled on technology, and a local boom in mining and education tripled the population. A couple of canny builders realized that pretty, wooded Hiran Magri was just fifteen minutes out of town by rickshaw, five by Maruti, if you had a car. They quickly descended and carved out tight subdivisions, then gave the acreage a more alluring name, Sector Eleven, which sounded like a *Star Trek* fuel stop only to Western ears. The old one was no longer accurate; there were no more deer around, and besides, no one wanted to live in a place with a Hindi name.

Including Swami-ji, the head of the Hindi school where I now found myself, who'd happily moved his family into the apartment next door. To the Indian eye, the homes in Sector Eleven trumpeted "arrived," though to my untrained one, they looked bulky and showy, as if an architect from Ursk had been ordered to design for expanse and lay off traditional details: no peacock arches, no fanciful cupolas, ever, ever. What the people wanted in the new environs was Western, and they got it, a Miami–Eastern bloc blend. At the Paras Hotel, behind the school, the pool was shaped like a mango. The Paras Theater next door was geometry in concrete.

The school itself, in a fifth-floor unit of Antriksh Flats, was furnished in functional décor: gray rugs, black sofa with thin wooden arms, metal shelves with books that had titles such as *Rural Indian Development: 1971 to 1982*. The first morning, the layout reminded me of a suburban cooking school I'd seen once in a Japanese film, but that was early, when my overtaxed brain was still trying to process details and frantically making them familiar.

The first morning, Swami-ji instructed us to call him by that name, at what seemed like some length. The word means "teacher," he repeated several times. Later, I'd learn that fate had bestowed a trick name on him at birth. His given one literally meant "Beloved of Vishnu," but when it was mispronounced, by a thick American tongue, say, it came out sounding like Achut Anand: "He Who Loves to Be in," um, "Women's Privates." This startling dual property had not become apparent till his first restaurant outing with students. "Hey, Achut Anand-ji, how do I ask this guy for salt?" one of his charges had called out. The whole place fell into stunned silence, and from then on, Swami-ji was Swami-ji.

Orientation continued. *"To you rajanpathinehiunkahi downtown market lugikimarudiran,"* said a teacher named Vidhu, whose long angular face made me think that his ancestors had swept in from Turkestan. The other students wrote it down. Vidhu was in his thirties and was Swami-ji's right-hand man. His pleated black trousers and spotless white sneakers lent him the air of a hipster, an impression deepened by his laugh when he laughed: reverbed, cosmically amused. More often, though, he kept the polite and gracefully fawning demeanor of a majordomo.

"Because you have said korengiratko," Vidhu added. Orientation in Udaipur was hours of Hindi, so hours of flickering sentences. In the draining heat, only every fifth word penetrated my brain, every twentieth when the fan cut off and words thickened to a glaze. At normal speaking rates of 3 to 7 words per second, you could calculate, and I did, that was between 171 and 390 words each minute I wasn't getting.

Occasional warnings came through in English. "If you see a group of sacred cows, we ask that you not disturb or frighten them, as that can make them rush this way and that and possibly brush you. Last year cows strained a girl's leg. And she was a dancer," Vidhu warned, and then I was desperate to know what else they'd said.

Probably things like, "Udaipur is the city of lakes, but lack of rains means lack of water," one sentence that cleared the wall. There was a drought on, year four. I got that, even visually, even with my limited knowledge of the town, just two buildings at first: the school with its side lot of dust and weeds, and the Quality Inn, where a speckling of dead bugs starred the half-empty pool.

In a diarrhea lecture, I was identified as a troublemaker. "Bored? I am boring you?" the guest speaker, a doctor, suddenly rasped. It was hot and late in the day, and my gaze had gone unfocused. I hadn't meant to let my attention wander from the subject of stools, but it had. Dr. Sharma stared. The other students waited. *"Nahin, nahin,"* I said: "No, no." "With a subject like this?" No one sniggered. We were in India now, where irreverence was unfathomable. With 333,000 gods to revere, irreverence was outnumbered.

The lecture was in English, the only one that was. After days of disappearing sound, I was grateful for discourse on the consistency of stools. They should not float. If you don't feel like defecating by yourself in the natural way, then it's known as constipation. The Indian teachers looked rapt.

Sixty-two percent of the country's desert is in Rajasthan, the lectures continued. Eighty-four percent of the marble is mined here. Percentages were easy, they wrote those on the board, but never dates, not even during the architecture talk. In India, I recalled, time is circular, a perception that's been shaped by the concept of reincarnation. People go through rebirth after rebirth and always end up back in the same place: here. "Yesterday" and "tomorrow" are the same word: *kal.* "The day before yesterday" and "the day after tomorrow" are both *parson.* The concept of "weekend" here is an imported one. All days in the spin are the same: *aaj,* "today." In the

West, in English, by way of contrast, time is linear—the speakers move ahead, they put things behind them—while in China, in Mandarin, it's vertical. Even when Anglophone Chinese switch over into their adopted tongue, one study found, they continue to imagine the minutes rising up to the sky. But in India, in Hindi, it's always right now. In the right here and now, flattened by jet lag, I tried to get used to swirling time.

The women teachers were appointed to take us shopping for supplies. There were two on staff, opposites in all but caste, Brahmin. Samta was tall and in her twenties. She had the extreme good looks common to Rajasthan: the high defined cheekbones, the long, heavy-lidded eyes seen in miniature paintings, the full mouth that made her appear voluptuous, though she was in fact slender. The effect was striking, but offset some by the daunting amounts of sunshine in her personality. "I am com-ple-te-ly fine!" she'd chirrup each morning, an objectionable sentence when you had jet leg.

Vanita, tiny, a year or two older, had the worried air of a titmouse. Her thin, intelligent face was pinched, the result, perhaps, of studying night and day for a master's. Whereas Samta's saris were rippling, languorous, Vanita's were starched to within an inch of their lives, even the *dupatta* scarves. Her scarves never lay down on the job, but remained frozen in a fluff, giving the impression that a hooded snake had reared up behind and was about to swallow her.

Four teachers, four students: it was a neat one-to-one ratio for a while—till fate, or karma, or the rebound effects of poor judgment began picking off numbers on either side.

For the shopping expedition, we hopped tootling little buses. At every stop, more passengers squeezed on, till boys were clinging to the sides. In the bazaar, the sun was so hot, it sapped all energy with its brilliance. I bought a shortwave radio to catch the news, a plastic alarm clock that played a Hindu chant and had Vishnu the protector on its face. With each purchase, in that sun, my new language eroded more. When I stopped for a pale green blow dryer and Samta made a teasing remark, I was too drained to say, *"I don't understand."* I pretended to laugh along, but she read my reaction as forced. *"I was joking,"* I heard her apologize through Hindi. *"I make jokes a lot."* What, I wondered, had she possibly said? "Now you will be able to style your hair"?

Photographs were taken, for identity cards. "Why did he pick these?" one of the students complained in a whisper when she saw the photographer's choices. In the black-and-white squares, we all looked shocked; we were the picture of culture shock.

"Maybe he sent the others to the paper for the marriage ads," the girl with the southern accent cracked.

"Yeah, you'll get a lot of offers with those," the one male student, a guy whom I will refer to as Harold, said with a chuckle that ended in a *hyuck.*

A placement quiz consumed half a morning. "That exam really showed me the direction this course is going to take," Harold said afterward. He was portly, with robust red spots on his cheeks, and wore black Metallica T-shirts and tight khaki shorts. His combination of pursuits was also unlikely: deciphering Sanskrit texts, quoting Rush Limbaugh. In the States, he'd been in telesales till he saw he could parlay an unfinished South Asian studies major into a year-long stipend in India.

Harold had come to my attention in Delhi with the "one hair" comment, and again when he'd been led weeping from a first-aid talk, sobbing that he missed his wife. He'd gotten himself out of Sexual Harassment, too, a symposium that took up half the afternoon. To the Indians at the institute, sexual harassment was a terrifying concept. Even its name, with its clacking, hissing sounds, was ominous. The idea behind it, actionable sexual attentions, was purely Western, and so no one understood precisely what it meant. But academic advisers who materialized throughout the year had made it clear that in America, whence most students came, this was the most serious of all offenses. Lawsuits from across the seas could come flaming down on any staff member who abetted the behavior. Careers could be singed to charred stumps. In Delhi, an afternoon of role-playing was planned, to armor the students. *Your teacher is requiring you to stay after class to discuss the test you failed. What will you do?* Harold, getting a load of the agenda, had had to make a phone call.

Now in Udaipur, he was back up and running. "Direction?" I said. The test had been simple translation, no big deal: "Five chickens are on the table," that kind of thing.

"You didn't notice how many words were Sanskritized?" he said. I was, in fact, familiar with the concept of Sanskritized Hindi. This is when words, often ones of Persian or Arabic—that is, Muslim—origin are excised and replaced with others that have Sanskrit etymology. Since street Hindi contains a fair amount of Sanskrit words to begin with, Sanskritization isn't an overhaul so much as an intensification. A purification, by some lights, the extreme right wing's. When the language has been Sanskritized, it's called *shudh* Hindi. *Shudh* translates as "pure," but it can mean "uncontaminated," and in a xenophobic sense.

Sanskritizing often signals refinement. Even to those who can't understand it, Sanskrit sounds elevated, majestic, its long looping words like scented poetry. It conjures incense and devotion, as it's the language of the Vedas, adds a sonorous beauty when it's folded into Hindi. Cultured gentlemen speak this way. But there's another kind of Sanskritized Hindi as well, this one ugly. Hindu nationalists also like their Hindi Sanskritized, and in their case, the desire is to establish Hindu dominance, to purge the language of foreign elements. Like fundamentalists everywhere, the right-wing nationalists exalt a mythologized version of the past: an India that was *shudh,* without Muslims. They subscribe to *Hindutva*—loosely,

"Hinduism above all"—and want Muslims to either get out or accept their inferior position in society. Whenever the right-wing Bharatiya Janata Party (BJP) is in power, as it was now throughout the country and in concentrated numbers in Rajasthan, you hear a lot more Sanskritized Hindi. Persian words then become all-too-tender reminders of past Muslim incursions. Linguistically, the invaders have to be routed. In India, language has always been a battlefield.

I knew all this at the time of the placement test. I just didn't know what direction the chickens meant we'd be taking.

Orientation stretched on, till late the second afternoon, I began to hallucinate speech. Summoned to a back room, I found the four teachers posed stiffly in a half circle for a conversation quiz. *Won't you please have a seat?* Swami-ji said with his hand, gallantly sweeping the air. The more panicked I became, the more I convinced myself I was understanding words and not, as was the case, reading gestures. *We are delighted you could join us,* Vidhu said, judging by his broad smile. *"Thank you,"* I ventured. *"I'm glad to be here."* No one frowned, and I was emboldened by having discovered the technique of psychic language acquisition. Samta leaned forward and asked a question. *"Are you enjoying the town?"* seemed likely, to which I gave the likely response: *"Yes, yes, it's very nice."* The teachers' smiles stayed fixed even as the talk degenerated and I seized on any word. *She surely did not mean to say her father lives in a brothel,* one said with his darting glance. *I am certain your assumption is correct,* a colleague replied, also ocularly.

Orientation proceeded, through several turns of the karmic wheel, till it threatened to become a fifth *yuga,* a fifth mythological epoch. Till it became its own world in which even I understood that if you were female, you were asked to keep a distance from host family males; that at departure, clearance from the Indian income tax authorities would be necessary. That traffic sense here was poor.

It continued, through tangles of contingencies, two discussions of Indian language groups, a visit to Foreigners Registration, till the student with the whispery voice said that she would not fill out bank papers one more time and the year lurched forward. We began.

· 3 ·

"The new house is big"

 Orientation finally wrapped up. Immediately after, we were moved in with host families, the three of us who didn't have one. Helaena, the student with the southern accent, already did, or she did in a way: the maharana.

Helaena had made an impression on me in those first days with her easy knowledge of India. One morning, on tea break, I expressed puzzlement as to why, when I'd gone to investigate the Shaping Sense gym across from the school, the slope-browed proprietor had scowled when I'd asked about the yoga he advertised. Mr. Ahmad, I related, had been too busy overseeing the hammering of huge holes in the wall to answer questions about the StairMaster, of which there was none anyway. "Because he's a gangster," Helaena explained from the couch where she was stretched out. In Hindi and English, she had a drawl. She also had wide green eyes, a fine, straight nose, and a mouth that at rest naturally pouted, all of which combined to drive the Indians to distraction. To them, she looked exactly like the

Lord God Krishna, who, though male, is considered the embodiment of female beauty.

In the States, Helaena was pretty, in a milk-drinking way. In India, she was an avatar—the cause of stampedes in the streets and, before she dyed her blond hair brown, frequent deliveries of gifts from unwanted suitors. Kings fell at her feet. The local one, the maharana, had taken one look when she'd arrived several weeks in advance of classes and moved her into the palace. Personal assistance might be needed at receptions, he'd hinted. She'd wasted no time dressing for the possible job. Already American Express was compounding interest on the fifty entry-level saris she'd purchased at the snooty Mansai Plaza boutique. They were tacking on late fees for the biweekly arm waxes she'd been getting in order to look *pakka,* proper, an aesthetic that for women also called for a headscarf, neatly gathered hair, a gaze kept modestly on the floor. "I like being pakka," she'd said earlier. "Back home they assume I'm a flirt just because I'm a little outgoing. Here they assume I'm good." Other than grooming and stopping by the school, she spent her days watching *Friends* on palace cable, being driven around in curtained palace cars, and analyzing the mystical effect the subcontinent had on her looks and vice versa. "Ramu, my teacher last year, said, 'No, you *are* a god'," she'd said. This was her third Hindi language program.

"They should call that place Shaping You Senseless," she said now, gingerly tapping her newly pierced nose. "Gyms in India are hangouts for gangsters. Muslim gangsters go to one, Hindus go to another.

"Hey!" she said, introducing a change in topic. "When we get our place, we could rent you a StairMaster from Ahmedabad." She'd been campaigning for everyone to get a collective, off-the-record apartment, "so you could have privacy from those Jains," she offered, referring to my clamorous new host family. And so she could be shielded from prying eyes, for she was in the middle of an astonishing subcontinental Daisy Miller maneuver. Two weeks after the maharana moved her in, she'd begun enacting plans, matrimonially speaking, to nail his nephew.

"I'm fine at the Jains'," I said. I was. The only trouble I'd had so far was calculating how many of them there were—they always appeared in either fives or tens—and trying to keep up when they talked at once. Over dinner, they'd ask questions simultaneously or in round robin.

JAIN 1: *How much did you pay for the radio?*
ME: *Five hundred rupees? No, I think it was six.*
JAIN 1 (to the kitchen at large): *She is telling us she paid five hundred rupees for the radio.*
JAIN 2 TO JAIN 1: *Five hundred?*
JAIN 1: Haan. *She is telling us five hundred.*
JAIN 3 TO JAIN 1: *Five hundred? I think she is telling us six.*
JAIN 4: Haan. *Six.*
JAIN 5: *She is saying six. No. Maybe she is saying five hundred sixty rupees.* (To me) *Are you telling us six hundred rupees?*
ME: *I think that's what I paid: six.*
JAIN 5: Haan. *She is saying six.*
JAIN 1: *Six hundred rupees? She paid too much.*
JAINS 2, 3, 4, 5: Haan, haan, haan. *She paid too much.*

The dinners I'd attended had been women and children only. The men ate separately, or they came home late, sometimes not at all. I saw the men so infrequently at first, in fact, I thought they had the same first name.

"I'm living with two brothers called Raj in the state of Rajasthan," I gleefully wrote a friend, then learned they were actually Rajesh and Rajkumar. "Kingly" and "Prince," which, since Kingly was younger than Prince, led to further confusion. I tried appearance mnemonics, Jerry Lewis Raj and his younger brother Art Carney Raj, before settling on Jain Dad 1 and 2, their religion being easier to pronounce than their last name.

The Jains were a joint family, a typical Indian arrangement wherein several nuclear clusters join together to form one sprawling household. With the help of the girls, I diagrammed them on Post-its. The family took up three squares, two more with identifying notes. Jain Dad 1 and wife Alka, bedroom upstairs; one boy, two girls. "Rajkumar: straight arrow"; "Alka: self-possessed, face like heart." Jain Dad 2, married to Meena, room off the kitchen; one boy, one girl. "Meena: rolls her hips when she walks, spirited," by which I meant tart.

Meena's marriage, Alka's too, was arranged. "There are no love marriages here anymore," one of the girls explained, in a tone that let me know they were a poor idea, that's why. Meena's husband, Rajesh, was goofy and gangly and wore cherry red shorts. He was making a lot of snorting fun of my cultural exchange attempts, according to a fellow student who'd moved in upstairs. I kind of got that.

"You bought a mobile?" he asked one afternoon, sliding the phone from my hand as I stood in the driveway trying for a connection. "How much did you pay?" he said. "You don't know? You don't—*hey!*" he shouted into the kitchen. *"Hey! You have to hear this."* Although Swami-ji had put them under orders not to, the Jain Dads, Jain kids, too, often broke into English with me. Relieved, I'd answer in kind. Only the women, married out of educations, were sticking to the student-immersion plan, only because they had to.

"Hey," he yelled. "She doesn't know how much she paid for her mobile!" The wives rolled out from behind the screen-door, stopped. *"Haaan,"* they said, tilting toward me like sea branches. *"Nahiiiin?"* They tilted back. Just then, the other student emerged and supplied the figure. Four thousand rupees, one month's rent, and the damn thing didn't even work.

Generally, though, the men were otherwise engaged, at the marble mine they either owned or worked for. *"You are naukers?"* I'd asked, trying for "workers." No no no, they said hastily. "Servants" I saw when I looked it up. "Upper management" would have been a safe bet, for their house was a testimony to the fortunes of marble, charting the family's rise.

One half, the first half built, was modest with scuffed floors and a few tiny bedrooms. Then ten, fifteen years back, the family had clearly lucked out, for the newer half was a Sector Eleven fantasy: gray-veined marble floors, zebra-striped marble baseboards, a serpentine marble staircase that spiraled above a sitting room filled with plastic flowers. The bouquets, candy-dye pinks and yellows, were arrayed in marble vases. And the showstopper—a marble drive. The driveway, though hazardous to pedestrians when washed, possessed a peculiar grandeur: inlaid circles set against squares, rich browns fitted into mossy greens; a display fit for a museum, a board game leading out to a street of pigs.

My room was in the newer half and therefore august. Just off the sitting room, it had white marble floors, a sunken marble bath, spacious built-in shelves. It was grander than any place I'd imagined myself living here, but all the same, it made me antsy, particularly when I wasn't permitted to venture out, which occurred for a time early on. The surfaces of the room were unyielding. Neon light rods jutted from the walls and turned my face a sickly green. The first night, I discovered that, amplified by the marble, the clicks from the Vishnu alarm clock were lethal to concentration. *Chulha-chakki,* "routine chores"—tick, and the words would fragment. Tock: *Chulha fumkna,* "to keep busy with cooking," gone. Crack: *Bunaa-i,* "knitting," another homework word splintered.

"You will ask five questions," Swami-ji had said earlier in the day, handing out a vocabulary list. A weekly guest, a representative member of the community, was coming in tomorrow. We'd had one guest try to stop by that day already, but the visit had had to be aborted. This man, a cobbler, had been lured up with promises that American students were eager for information on stays and lasts, but once he'd arrived, he'd been struck mute by the incomprehensible outbursts, the scowling attendance on his every word, and had had to be allowed back to work. Now we'd be having another conversational go, with a young housewife who'd been corralled from two flights below. "Later there will be dignitaries," Swami-ji promised.

The vocabulary list hinted at a life spent in drudgery, but the actual housewife, when she appeared, did not look downtrodden. She had the pep and lip liner of a talk show host. Her sari rustled as enthusiasm edged her forward on her seat. Only the braying of a donkey outside gave her pause. Her smile held till I tried my question, *"Dowry to your husband of family is? Paying you think?"* Four times, and then her face assumed the tight, polite expression I'd come to know well. *Here's an idea,* it said. *We could all just speak English.* She could have, no doubt, except she was under orders, along with the teachers, office aide, and cook: Hindi only.

Swami-ji was an advocate of total immersion, not one of the popular contemporary approaches. As a science reporter who'd done a college stint in Borneo told me, "We called it the aural-anal method. If you didn't get it by ear, they shoved it up the other end." In the States, where immersion, no boosts, has fallen out of favor except in language chains like Berlitz, it's called now, tellingly, "submersion."

With total immersion a Catch-22 sets up: If you don't have coaching, it's hard to have exchanges. No exchanges, no memories formed. No memories to draw on, more disjointed conversation about big books and small chairs, interrupted by persistent questions about whether that man was here yesterday. Is a banana blue, or is it yellow? Out of context, this would be talk that called for Haldol. "Never fully to understand and constantly to misunderstand," A. L. Becker writes, "are linguistic pathologies that characterize a wide range of phenomena from the strategic understanding of the schizophrenic to the persistent confusion and uneasiness of one who is learning to use a foreign language."

On a study abroad, though, don't you naturally absorb, say, Italian, the way watery breezes plump your hair on the Emerald Coast: by osmosis? The truth, though it sounds cynical, will be: You wish. "The data shows an immersion overseas is not a hell of a lot better than staying home with a fast-paced course," the psycholinguist Brian MacWhinney said on my return. He ticked off reasons. "In the field," he said, "you've got the adult problems. They want to speak English with you. You go home and want to listen to English news. They're not talking to you like a child. They're talking over your head or beneath you."

You've got the communal talking problem, you've got the inability to concentrate in a strange place, but all the same, all the data in the world can't measure the irreproducible pleasures that come as well, from being left, for a time, speechless. Of being blasted into a world that, because it's not yet named, is limitless. "The delight of defamiliarization," Becker writes, exuberance breaking through the fusty vocabulary of philology, "is one of the genuine pleasures of languaging." Forcing yourself back to the start, finding names again for everything, requires you to look at everything fresh: sky, dirt, air, your feet. In bhram, in the sweet illusion you get without words, nothing in the world can remain what it was. Nothing can possibly stay ordinary.

Around the end of the second week, I'd light out from the Jains' and go on long, observational walks, trying to take in all the alien sights so that later I could apply the right names. "You can't learn a language without noticing," the linguist Richard Schmidt said, and while he was referring to morphology, the argument can also be applied to the place that gave rise to it. Certain words make sense only in context: the things they describe have to be seen. A *haveli* in the Hindi-English dictionary is only, flatly, "a nobleman's townhouse," no mention of the walls that are high and crumbling, of the massive front doors studded with pikes to block the marauders now dead for centuries.

On those walks, I was voracious for new sights. The hunger propelling me was nearly greedy, for at this time, I was busting loose. At the end of the first week, there'd been an incident in what was now the far world which had spawned rumors of violence here. For a number of days, we'd been confined inside. In the room with white marble, the walls bounced my anxiety back to me during this stretch, when my brain stayed turned on all night. Clicks became cracks at 3 A.M. Words I was trying to read would form, then revert to snakes. Once they did, my mind was free to try to imagine what the world outside was like now. Between the rumors and the neon light made cold by marble, I imagined the world around me gone white: an India turned ghostly and covered with ash, drained of color by the echoes of violence. White India, still and spectral as the room.

Afternoons then, once we were free to, I'd head out the gate and into a kaleidoscope of distractions. Posters were the best: HIGH STATUS ELECTRICAL ACCESSORIES, on the corner by the school. A HUMBLE REQUEST FROM SURESH CHOWDHURY, the pop-eared Mr. Chowdhury having several years ago hoped to be made vice president of Bhupal Nobles' College. DECENT ASS. SOLVING PROBLEMS; whatever it was, I'd take it.

Flatbed spilling bananas as light green as if they'd been bleached, old poster board rippling on brick wall, signs for courses, fading green house, rubble, litter, limping pig: each day, my mental notations got flatter as my English began to thin down.

The landscape that came into focus was dusty and matter-of-fact, but as my sight adjusted, it brightened some. Sky blue shard of pottery; butterfly wing, brown velvet with a red eye. On a dirt pile. But still.

EVEN THE FIRST WEEK, time begins to slow, thickened by the Rajasthani sun. In the classroom, our bodies are musky by ten, all last night's spices exuding from our pores. By noon, we're no longer answering *haan*. We slouch and say *hmm*, conservation of effort. At school and at home, only confusion can lift me above the torpor, imbued as it is with the promise that if I focus hard enough, on the point of fuzziness, some revelation will follow. Bhram, then, is a little like speedball: about to be elation, about to be thunder, about to let me get what the junior wife in the new family has just said. *"What?"* I frown. She repeats it.

"She is saying do you like the soup," one of the girls translates. One of three. I know the numbers exactly now. Five children, four parents, one tiny grandmother with a thin gray braid, an ill-tempered Pomeranian named Taffy. Two boarders, too—me and another student, who's living upstairs and who is not, currently, at the table. She has large, hard eyes magnified by glasses, but her voice is tremulous, little-girlish, breathy. She's the whisperer from orientation. That's how I've come to think of her: the Whisperer. At school, she asks questions into her dupatta scarf, as if she needs protection from the big, bad oblique case. No one can understand her. At home, she'll suddenly bark out orders at the Jains, and her Hindi then is revealed as turbocharged. She grew up in the States, but her parents are from India.

"The soup is very good," I say, estimating how many adjectives I know for "good." Three. I'm down one.

"Oooooh, really? You like the soup?" the senior mother says coyly.

"Very much," I say. *"The soup is very tasty."* Two.

"She is saying the soup is tasty." They repeat the sentence down the line like "telephone," though I've said it in Hindi and they can all understand. Now the wisp of a grandmother hops up from the floor,

points at my bowl, says something glottal. The old lady, a Mewari speaker, seems to mistake my bad Hindi for bad Mewari.

"*Haan, haan, haan,*" I say, fixing the soup with a wide smile of delight. "Please tell your grandmother it is very good," I tell the girls. A discussion in Mewari follows.

The grandmother circles back. The junior wife is up again. "*This soup is tomato,*" she begins, leading with logic, then slyly nudging the point around. "*You like tomato?*"

"*To me tomato soup is very good.*"

"*And you like* this *tomato soup?*" Her tone is triumphant.

"*This tomato soup is magnificent!*" "Magnificent," *kamaal:* I'm out on the edge, and we haven't even had the okra.

Dinners go like this till one day, playing badminton in the drive, I give an automatic high-five. The gesture startles everyone, shuts down the action. From then on, I high-five often. Did I like the soup? High-five! Did I like the lentils? High-five me more! They laugh so hard when they slap my palm, it ends all further discussion.

AT THE PALACE when I visit, the air is sweet with jasmine. Even in stolid Sector Eleven, there are sudden whiffs of perfume; of sandalwood; of something shadowy, violet. At school, two weeks on now, we fight indolence, push on to headier realms, though no matter how high the plane, the conversation is stilted. "*Yes, I like the film very much.*" We never just like anything, we like it very much; extra words. "*But to me, the ending was not a surprise.*" "Surprising" is a vocabulary stretch, plus you risk using the wrong suffix or infix, turning out "surprised person" or "person who causes surprises." Hindi has a vast series where, by adding a short *a* in the center of a verb, you make it causative. "To eat" becomes "to cause something to be eaten"—that is, "to feed."

"*Yes. I see—no, I saw . . .*" The teachers, who all deserve acting awards for animated enthusiasm in the face of continued babbling, smile and nod vigorously, make the *Come on!* gesture, curled fingers. *"I see—saw—the ending in forward."* Slight frown. *"In advance?"* Precise nod! Delighted smile!

"Kathy-ji is saying she did not like the ending, that it was, can we say"—introduction of new word—"stereotyped, *ghisa-pita.*" Vidhu turns and writes the word on the board. He's been planking sentences with English on the sly, thank God. *"Stereotyped. To stereotype someone. Stereotype"*—the Hindi word—*"means* 'beaten and rubbed.'"

Occasionally, they throw in an idiom without alerting us. *"To beat someone with shoes?"* I repeat, puzzled. *"To beat someone with shoes—yes!"* the small teacher, Vanita, replies, thinking I'm unsure of the script. *"It means?"* *"Oh! It's an expression,"* she says, but before I can ask for what, the class moves on.

Words rain down on us all day. A monsoon of words, so furious that I pull away sometimes, pull down. I hear the tat-ting at night and can't decipher it, *aane-jaanewaala,* bits of phrases from the day coursing through my head. At night, I dream in Hindi I can't understand. The language has to stay fixed, or I'll lose the nuance: *Aap,* not *ap. Ghar* not *gora.* I know it when they say it, then two days later, it's gone. My English sometimes now feels spotty, as if, in preserving the new words as long as possible, my brain keeps the old ones tamped down.

At night, in white India, the Hindi snatches keep me awake, chittering sometimes till dawn. During the day, I'm safe in the slow dream. At night, a terror comes on, steals in through the window from a distant place, from over deserts and oceans, past the squeal of a million sounds. "With each new language, you acquire a new soul," a Slovakian proverb goes, and for this rebirth, I've chosen one of the most inauspicious birthdays possible, in any calendar, Indian or Gregorian. For I arrived in India on the fourth day of the dark quarter of Bhadrapada, Hindu year 2057: September 6, 2001.

Five days later, when I went to collect Helaena at the palace for dinner, a uniformed man at the front desk held out the phone. "I think you better come up and see what's on television," she said, her voice so strained it made me check his face. The man looked away. And that, always, will be my first memory of the day when bhram savaged the world: a man turning his face to the wall.

In New York, it was ten in the morning.

"I AM YOUR SISTERMOTHERFRIEND," the pretty Brahmin teacher, Samta, said, wiping tears from my face when we met up at the school, in the hour before it shut down.

· 4 ·

"What time is it?"

 Time spun so fast then, past and future converged. Yesterday was tomorrow: impossible to say how long we'd been at the palace, holed up with Helaena. Two days? Five? Tomorrow was yesterday: parapets and citadels, crows cawing from towers, implacable ancient white stone—in the palace, it was always the seventeenth century. Murals of elephant fights ran the length of the walls. In the Diwar Gallery, the eyes of framed maharanas followed us as we moved, a trompe l'oeil perfected over 566 portraits.

Sharp studs in doors to pierce attack elephants' breasts, lintels set low to crack barreling intruders' heads—the architecture of defense was reassuring. Murderous men had clearly been thwarted here, though they'd swept down on horses, not from the sky.

At the front desk the first night, a late arrival thundered, "The Philistines have done this thing." When I couldn't sleep, I'd slipped out of Helaena's room, hoping for news. At daybreak, when I padded back, spots of orange lights in the high tower windows gave the impression of startled eyes.

On the second day, the palace employees held a peace march. Cooks and chauffeurs and receptionists in saris, a ragtag band with hand-lettered signs. Helaena and I joined them outside the maharana's quarters. ANYONE WHO COMMITS A TERRORIST ACT CANNOT SAY HE IS RELIGIOUS, the posterboard beside me scolded.

The door in front of us snapped open. The maharana in sweatpants and a yellow polo shirt delivered a speech from the step. He was short, with a fuzzy white beard that made me think of a hedgehog. In the middle of his speech, Helaena cut short a giggle. "I bought Sri-ji that shirt in Bombay," she said out of the side of her mouth, using the honorific everyone at the palace did. Sri-ji, "venerable lord," pronounced tightlipped and southern, came out like "squee-gee." The door clicked shut. Someone handed us white candles. Helaena hoisted hers, and I followed as she led the line through the bazaar. AMERICA, INDIA IS WITH YOU, the front banner declared, in English, though most people in the throngs couldn't have read it. By now, most Westerners had fled.

On the third day, there were tiffs. The Whisperer complained about having to watch the CNN loop again. "I just don't want to prepare anymore," she said when we voted to postpone school a few days more. She'd spent the downtime studying verbs. "I just think it's unhealthy to stay in this. All my friends back home are starting to get over it, okay?"

All my friends, in e-mails, had the slow tone of witness. "It's four days after, and everything below 14th Street is still closed," one wrote. Hearing about this thing from so far away sharpened worry, the way when you can't see a loved one who's ill, your distress grows more acute. But when friends asked, "Shouldn't you come home?" I said I couldn't. My truculent, sweet-talk city, tricks of will exposed: I couldn't look. "But the attack was there," I answered. Or I explained how the decades here were rearranged, were like barriers. "In Udaipur, we're muffled from events. This town is in a time warp, though it's hard to say which time. When neighbors wave and ask, 'Who was that who walked you home?' I think the fifties. When rickshaws whiz by, looking like Model Ts from the back, it's the mutated Indian twenties. But when I go to the doctor and find myself next to a tribal woman with an enormous gold nose ring, or when I talk to a Rajput, a member of the aristocratic warrior caste—the men have knife-straight backs and villainous handlebar mustaches—I can see the links to the Middle Ages so clearly, it's startling."

I was muffled, true, but not so swathed I couldn't perceive the shape the twenty-first century had taken here. Anti-Muslim sentiments were running high. Down by the Clock Tower, boxes scrawled with slogans denouncing Pakistan had been set on fire. In Bapu Bazaar, they'd burned Osama Bin Laden in effigy. George Bush afterward, too, though. Osama Bin Laden, I heard for a fact, had ordered all Americans abroad killed on sight. I heard that the year before, they'd caught a member of a terrorist Islamic organization living just outside of town, and this was a fact. The man who told me repeated the name of the group, something like "Ul-ka-da." The borders had closed, all flights to the States had been canceled. You couldn't get out now if you tried.

Worry gnawed holes in illusion. For a time after I moved back in with the Jains, I'd watch Alka as she went about her chores and wonder, *Would she harbor us if it came to that? Would she, they, remain kind?*

"What if we can't leave?" I asked the other students on a weekend when we all went away to Kumbhalgarh, a mountain resort run by the maharana's nephew, Aditya. This was when we were all still speaking. We were slouched down then in Helaena's room, watching *Star Wars* as she got ready for Aditya to get off work. "What if we're stuck?" I said. "Where would we get money?"

"The institute," Helaena told her reflection in the mirror. She turned, freezing the mascara wand in an exclamation. "Or we'd go to the embassy. They'd fly us out." But the marine who answered at the embassy when I later called to register our presence didn't sound like he was gearing up for evacuation. He couldn't take down information then; could I call back? "Well, ma'am," he said when I asked what we should do till his schedule cleared. "I would not go into a dark alley. Don't wear a shirt that says TENNESSEE or anything. And just don't act like an ugly American."

"I always make a big deal out of things in my mind, then they always turn out all right," Harold said in a pointed singsong. On the screen behind him, Darth Vader was choking a guy using mental telepathy. Earlier, on the terrace, a waiter had been flipping through broadcasts on the television above the bar. Hindi, English, Urdu, he made the news stutter as the same image showed on every channel. Men in white robes, their faces contorted, were kicking at a burning straw man. Its grinning Western head had been painted to look obscenely simian.

Harold had sighed then. He sighed again now. "I always get all worked up, and then nothing ever happens," he said in a calm, instructive voice. He'd had it with this whole belabored business. The Whisperer winched her face in commiseration: *What did he think? So had she.*

Kumbhalgarh was tony in the extreme: silver chandeliers in the great room, where women offered rose-scented goblets; a gray stone staircase threading up a hill through greenery so wild, it concealed all but squares of the cottages. On a late-afternoon jeep tour of a wildlife preserve that Aditya had arranged, we cut through swarms of butterflies the color of morning glories, rocked past lavender and pussy willow under a sky streaked with violet. "What's the word for 'sky,' d'ya know?" I asked Harold on the seat beside me.

"Aakaash," he said with a bored sigh; *who doesn't?*

"Aakaash," I repeated. *Aakaash*—from the Sanskrit, I could tell. Already, bloodlines were showing. Elegant or jawbreaker, the word was Sanskrit. Gravelly or plangent like a sarod, Persian. The ability to distinguish had developed so fast, was so sure, I mistook it for a portent of mastery. But in fact, rats have exhibited a similar talent in the lab, are able to demonstrate, by pressing levers for pellets, that they can tell the difference between Dutch and Japanese in just weeks.

Aakaash—as he said the word, we were bumping through high grass at sundown, a time when cooling breezes would have made me lightheaded anyway, even if the driver hadn't just said that at this hour, leopards could appear; even if I hadn't been tipping my head back to examine every passing branch. Forever after, "sky" for me in Hindi is less a color than a charged sense of devouring revelations about to come. Or that word for sky is; the language has a dozen.

Soon after, back in town, the other students reached a tacit agreement: what we'd seen on TV at the palace had been sci-fi. Some FX movie like *Escape from New York,* probably on the Murdoch channel. Among ourselves, if someone, me, mentioned this thing, conversation would falter, then we'd return to the subject at hand: Hindi. Days went by without discussion in English, till sometimes when the e-mails from home came in, it was like I was learning about it all over. But that was also the effect of ripple shock.

One afternoon on the street, I heard unholy screams and saw that two men outside a house had a pig lassoed by the neck. The animal was crying frantically and choking itself as it raced circles against the rope, while other pigs squealed and fled. I knew I shouldn't watch, but I did, as one man grabbed the doomed pig's legs and flipped it on its back, and the other, flashing metal, leaned down, and the cries grew more terrified, as I raced from it, too, my fingers pressed into my ears. When I stopped at the corner and turned around, the pig was no longer struggling. In my room, I couldn't stop crying. *You're a spoiled American,* I thought. *What do you think you've been eating all these years? Lovingly culled meat "products"? Happy cows? Happy pigs?* "I've never seen anything be killed before. Never," I said out loud, which brought the next thought. "Oh, God, those people," I said, and cried harder.

"AMONG THE MAITHILS, time is like a spider's web," an Indian anthropologist named Baidyanath Saraswati writes; the Maithils are a subcaste of Brahmins. "Like a tree with branches spread out; like a river with tributaries progressing relatively in relation to the surface of the earth; or like a lamp flickering; but *not* an arrow like movement."

In the center of time's web, in the sly tugging present, I watch a fat woman standing in front of a Birla Cement sign. Her sari is the same birthday-party yellow as the Birla ad—and the Oasis mobile ad, and the Rupa Macro Man Briefs ad, and the "straight-dial" phone booth signs. Apparently, there's only one loud yellow paint available here. Bara tempos, oversize mass-transit rickshaws, also all canary. An ox cart rumbles past. On the ox's horns, a ring of fading yellow around a ring of fading blue.

Evenings on the mountain above Fateh Sagar lake, the lights leading to the Monsoon Palace glitter, a crooked line of diamonds in the dark. Even in these circumstances, India can't stay white for long. At night, when it can't fill itself in with colors, it adopts the glitter of jewels.

"WE ARE SHOCKED and saddened by this dastardly attack," the e-mail from Delhi headquarters had said, adding that it would be better if we didn't go out alone. Soon my social life consisted of field trips. On the first, we toured a Styrofoam gallery where the Leaning Tower of Pisa, the Eiffel Tower, and Vishnu's-head-complete-with-snakes had been rendered in polystyrene. At a folk performance, a man who looked like the performer Prince in a dress balanced ten clay jugs on his head—on a metal cup—and walked daintily around the stage by rocking on the edges of a metal bowl. "The dance represents a lot of time in the desert with nothing to do," Helaena said.

At a renovated *haveli,* a manse built for a nobleman, she showed me where to find the erotic art painted low on a wall for newlyweds to see. "I can assure you," she said, laughing, "no Indian man is that well-endowed." Previously, she'd described her investigations. In Jodhpur, site of her last study abroad, there had been several scandals, she said, adding in a contrite tone, "And I was at the center of all of them." Two teachers' marriages had been undone by enthusiastic investigations into the oblique case. There'd been a scrape with a Rajput prince, romantic torsion with his Rajput cousins, an ill-fated excursion with an older Rajput man to Bangkok. "I have a weakness for Rajputs," she'd said.

Outside the Lord Ganesh wing, she reported the latest piece of palace intrigue. "I think your puppet has become smitten with someone else," a courtier had told the maharana, alerting him to what the palace spies had discovered—that Helaena appeared to be on the verge of committing some indiscretion. But the grapevine was clueless about the extent of the perfidy—that the maharana's own nephew was involved—and therefore, the maharana was still oblivious too. On hearing the report, he'd only laughed and said, "It won't get very far." In fact, neither had he, yet.

Each time we emerged from another informative folk exhibit, Swami-ji announced the latest international development, usually a dastardly act by Pakistan. "Pakistan is going with Bin Laden," he informed us when we returned to the bus for the next leg

By the end of the day, China was rolling toward the border, Israel had bombed Afghanistan, and I'd figured out Swami-ji's news source: the bus driver, who was getting his facts from other drivers when we stopped. If Swami-ji noticed this, it didn't deter him. "India is on red alert," he announced as the bus pulled out of the Garden of the

Maidens. "Within twenty-four hours, America will bomb Pakistan." The teachers all shook their heads gravely.

AROUND THAT TIME, I was perpetually flummoxed, one reason I was fond of an ad that ran in the *Times of India,* urging readers to enroll in a course that would, by means of "three simple truths," leave them "one hundred percent English-Fluent." Its tone conveyed the hysteria I felt. "<u>And remember this,</u>" it insisted, "You can't pick up fluency in English thro' any other language. NO! Course designed by the eminent scholar Mr. Kev Nair. Don't wait for an emergency! Ask for prospectus now."

I liked the concept of a language emergency in theory, till an afternoon following the mountain getaway, when I returned home to find one in progress at the Jains'.

I'd brought my shortwave radio into the kitchen to use as a conversational prop. Everyone had gathered round to see it. "You have bought this downtown?" Ekta, Alka's thirteen-year-old and the designated translator, was asking when Alka had barked at her, *"Hindi-mein bolo":* Say that in Hindi. Turned out, we'd all been busted. At school I'd say *"Oh, yes"* when Vanita asked if I ever spoke English at home. Her tone had been so offhand, I never imagined the question was investigative. But Vanita was in charge of student-family relations, and she executed her duties with the utmost gravity. She'd been by on her motor scooter, not an hour before.

Till then, I'd assumed Alka was shy. Now she became a Hindi commando. Returning home from a hard day at the mine, the poor Dads, in an attempt at conversation, were forced to ask four different ways if I believed in God. *Did I like Indian food? Were there arranged marriages in America? NO? Was I really forty-five? Why wasn't I married? Had I never been married?* The wives leaned forward, incredulous at the thought, while I lied and said no. But being divorced in India is suspiciously similar to being widowed, and widowhood here is a deeply reviled state. Widows must have done something so foul in a past life, the thinking goes, to have caused their husbands, their sole means of support, to die in this one. With sins that black, who's to say any overflow of bad karma won't go on a frenzied spin through the family? Given their radioactive pasts, widows can be stripped of all jewelry and cast out to beg. The social reckoning with divorcées follows the same line as with widows—they're both subject to a bad fate they brought on themselves. All around, better just to say "never married," which implied only "so ox-face ugly your parents could not buy you a husband" and not "past-life felon."

Evenings, the Dads sprang pop quizzes. *"You ate what?"* Jain Dad 1 asked after dinner, and when I had trouble following, he answered: *"You . . . ate . . . daal."* Lentils.

"I ate daal," I repeated.

"And . . . also . . . chaaval." Rice.

"And also chaaval."

"And what is this?" No go. He was holding one of those thin wafers they always throw down first in Indian restaurants. No one ever orders them by name. *"And you ate papadum,"* he said when I shook my head. There were five children racing in and out of the house, batting a cricket ball in the drive, shouting over music videos. I marveled at his patience. But he was willing, and for once I was able.

"I ate daal and I ate rice and I ate papadum," I concluded, and everyone cried, *"You did!"*

Afternoons, I'd make my way across the drive to the kitchen, where the wives were always amenable. The kitchen through the screen door would look beckoning, with Meena in her housecoat shelling peas on the floor and Alka by the sink chopping fennel. They'd look up when I entered; we'd have a companionable talk. Except I was a companion with one active verb tense, a language ed student tearing forward on one gear. The talk would rev, then I'd screech through an intersection, then we'd all fall quiet again. I hated the silences, reminders of how powerless I was, though had I only known, silent was exactly how I needed to be then.

"If you take a child, six or seven, and put them in France, the child will go through a silent period," says Martha Young-Scholten, a professor of second language acquisition studies at Newcastle University in England. "They won't use the target language, then suddenly, after several months, they'll open their mouths and start speaking fluently, and everyone's amazed. Adults and teenagers often struggle against doing this. They think they have to try right away. But listening without speaking is important." Only months later did I find that the dread silences had allowed words to set.

The Jains rallied, and soon in the manufactured infancy I'd entered, I was acquiring vocabulary at five, ten times the rate I had in my first. Words settled at the bottom of my brain in aggregate, they fermented, and not always to good end. *"Brash pati,"* I'd call to Alka, up on the balcony, where she waited nightly for me to come in: "Goon tight." *"Shubh rati,"* she'd correct: "Good night." Through the force of rapid acquisition, the press of so many words at once, actual structures of words were being changed.

THE ACADEMIC YEAR stumbled back into place. Classes resumed—empty exercises, for the most part. From time to time, scientists conduct investigations into what effect sleep has on language learning. In one study I read, test subjects were seated before a speech synthesizer that added distortion to the words it reeled off. After a while, everyone was able to make the words out anyway. The group was then divided and one half sent off for a good night's sleep. The others had to keep their eyes open all night. The next day, when the groups reconvened and listened to a second staticky round, the rested could still decipher words; the exhausted were no longer able. This showed the "sleepers retained the ability to generalize," the team leader told a science journal.

This showed they'd only kept it up for one night, I'd have added. Had they gone longer, there would have been plenty more the deprivation group would not have retained. Running on two, three hours sleep a night, too blasted from nerves and diffuse fear to go under for long, I found that most new words might have been Mandarin for all I recognized them twenty minutes on.

My brain could digest nothing ordinary, not *"high," "stand up," "I must be going."* It blocked the list of animal comparisons we were given, though normally those would have made an impression for the differences in anthropomorphism they revealed. But each time I saw in my notes that *"cowlike"* here was a positive quality, implying life-giving, or that *"doglike"* carried the implication of "dirty, goes about the street snatching food," I was like Chauncey Gardner in *Being There* again, mildly surprised and, for one brief flash, curious.

Not every word crumbled on impact. Neurons that fire together, wire together, neurologists say, meaning that repetition is how the new gets fixed in the brain. "Evidence suggests words first acquired when you're learning a second language are responded to much more quickly, perhaps because they've been repeatedly used," the British psycholinguist David Green says. There are Hindi words from those days I used so often, they're hardwired for all time: *"terrorism," "fanaticism," "safety," "exploitation," "war."*

"There is a deep bitterness in the minds of the Indian people. If the Muslim world disappeared, no one would heave a sigh," Vidhu, the teacher with the planed face, said in a monotone. The previous week's theme in conversation had been village life. *"You cannot know what a Muslim is thinking. Muslims act as one."*

"One side American exploitation is whose democracy's cloak come dressed in. One side fanaticism is. War is inevitable." In a homework assignment, I labored to unscramble a newspaper story that, once I had, made it clear that American capitalism was as pernicious as Islamic fundamentalism.

Chuli: "palm hollowed to collect water." I missed the gentle language from before, the one that fussed over when to drop the auxiliary verb. The Hindi I learned now was a Hindi of dark impulses and invasion. "We know how to say 'Terrorists killed the man.' We don't know the word for 'side table,'" Helaena said.

I missed full language of any kind. During these months, I existed in half language. Early on, I'd made an effort to swear off English, and the results had been astonishing. In no time, my English had become lumbering. In the Cyber Planet café, I'd construct and discard the same e-mail again, frustrated by my lack of surety about anything. Was the man who sat on his haunches out in the driveway all night a servant or a marauder? Was Meena angry because I accidentally used the bathroom hand at dinner? It was as if the loss of cultural certainty I was experiencing was being reflected in my language. Was the way you said that in English "lively"?

In Hindi, of course, I was a moron, and would have to be for months. But as much as I'd coach myself—"I'm prepped, I'll just plunge in"—it all got wearing.

In half language, I couldn't make full sense of the world. I'd note and accept the inexplicable: Each morning, Alka would answer the red phone that rang all through breakfast, her voice crisp and official. It was as if she was engaged in helping to run a business, though she never reported any messages to the men. By nine, when the phone was silent, her tone was once more hesitant; she had now only ever been a housewife. In half language, it's the shape-shifting that gets you, the casual mutations in yourself and others.

To learn a second language, you have to be willing to give your self up, the self encoded in your first one. You are no longer a person who speaks with facility and authority. You are less than what you were as a child: You cannot transact a phone call without help, discuss matters more complex than the color of fruits and vegetables. You cannot signal who you are. Most of us, by the time we're adults, speak in so many words. We convey information through tone: *I am sad,* or *I am displeased,* or *Is it not clear? I am important.* Our speech acquires layers so that directness, when employed, has power through force and rarity: "I don't like what you did." But at the beginning in learning a language, you can only be direct. You can say *"Tea is required here,"* not *"Can I get a cup?"*—a vast difference in terms of your popularity.

In half language, you're half what you were, half an overgrown child. You speak like a child, are received as a child. In this other state, you lose abilities.

"I was amazed at how quickly my English . . ."

"Fell apart?" a cognitive neuroscientist named Arturo Hernandez, who'd also done time abroad, said, and laughed. This was a year or two after my return, and we were comparing notes. "There's this very weird thing that happens where your language starts to bust apart. It's because there's language in your head and there's language in the environment." The one absorbs the other, he explained, the external one filters into your thoughts, becomes, to some extent, your inner one. "We think of language as ours," he said, "but it's not. It's on the news, and we speak it with people. We use other people's language all the time. It all makes you question, What is knowledge? What about that—is knowledge in our heads or in our environment? And if it's in our heads, how fast can it break down?" He mentioned that overseas, when you're aiming for fluency, you try to suppress your first language. "You don't want to use it," he said, then paused. "It's interesting. Language is a lot more fragile than we think it is."

Those weeks of white India are stamped in babble in my head, in Hindi, mostly, in Hinglish, in American, Indian, Victorian English—a problem when you consider, as David Green says, that "there's an intimate connection between language and memory. If you cue people in one language"—that is, people who have more than one—"you get memories from the times they were using it." If you ask Russian immigrants to the United States about their lives, as Cornell researchers did, you'll likely hear stories from Russia if you speak to them in Russian, from the years after if you speak in English. Bilingual patients in therapy, bilingual therapists note, often dodge feelings by relating painful events in the tongue they weren't using at the time of a particular incident, a muting effect that provides safe distance from what they're attempting to stare down. Though "people who speak about trauma in the language it occurred in get a sense of relief they don't in the language it didn't," Green says.

But then what if something occurred when you were between worlds, when you were in a fragile language that was still evolving? If you can't re-create that particular half language you understood it in—and how would you reproduce the exact tangle of errors and misperceptions and understandings?—do you not get relief? Maybe those weeks can't ever be faded.

Though maybe that first concentration of wonder can't be either. So far, that's still full color.

LATE ONE AFTERNOON, toward the end of September, we brought the shortwave radio out into the drive, the wives, girls, and I. We arranged ourselves in a line along the curb, under a pink-flecked sky, and I placed the radio in front of us. Tensing for English, I fiddled with the dial, but all I got was a spin of sound, metallic screeches dropping to moans, the restrained tones of argument or confinement. In the faded voices from other worlds, I could hear I was very far away.

I'd caught a scratchy band of BBC, was frowning to listen, when Alka said something I couldn't understand. I glanced at her oldest daughter. Alka nodded permission. "She says you shouldn't get married," the daughter said as Alka watched me with a faint, amused smile. I had the strangest sense she knew I'd lied about being forever single.

"You have a good life," she said.

"Haan!" I said. *"I'm not lonely. I have a lot of friends. And hus-*

bands . . ." I paused, not sure if New York wisecracks converted here. *Oh, hell,* I thought, and went ahead. *"And husbands are a lot of trouble."*

Her face broke into a grin as the meaning went through. *"Haaan!"* she exclaimed, and held up her palm.

Meena stared at me dully while we waited for her to catch up. *"Haan! Haan!"* she cried suddenly, as she got the gist. The night before, Jain Dad 2 hadn't rolled home till 1 A.M. Then we sat on the curb saying *"haan, haan, haan"* as the sun began to drop down.

The sky had turned the bright honking pink of a cut-rate sari when the front gate opened and the Whisperer walked in. She gave me the smile of a fellow sufferer, nodded curtly at the wives. The Whisperer regarded the entire consolidated Jain family as shifty characters who needed watching, for reasons I couldn't understand but she often tried to explain. "They wear evil faces when they think we're not looking," she said one night when we were hanging out in her room. Her voice was knowing, controlled.

"They do?" I said. Mine was light, ready for the joke when it came. She stared grimly at her desk. "Do you know the grandmother calls you the *niche wali*?" she asked. The downstairs dweller—I was. "Do you know that can mean Satan?"

In the drive, we waited till the Whisperer went inside, then resumed talking. How was Helaena? Alka wanted to know. Helaena had been a topic of conversation since she'd stopped by one night to pick me up. *"Tell her your family says she's very beautiful,"* the wives had said after, fawningly.

It was looking like the nephew might marry her, I said. *"Sex ke bare me, Ameriki auraten stress-free hain,"* Alka observed: "When it comes to sex, American women are stress-free." With *Baywatch* on eternal replay here, with Hollywood imports, centuries from now American women would still be known as vacuous high earners who'd go down on you on a dime. Alka's sparse English was salted with bits of American advertisements. "Tension-free!" she'd say, an ad plug that had been left to float forever, divorced of its product but still sell, sell, selling.

A slate-colored ink was spreading across the sky when Alka looked at me and said, apropos of nothing, "You are a good woman." In English, the one time she ever allowed me the indulgence—to be sure I understood. The reprieve was brief. When I returned from the cybercafe that night, she was leaning on the railing, captain of the house. *"Shubh rati,"* she called down. *"Shubh bratik,"* I replied. *"Shubh rati,"* she said, and we went inside.

SWAMI-JI ANNOUNCED THAT the school would close again, on October 2, Gandhi's birthday. *"We are having a chutti,"* he said: a holiday. With India's many religions and Swami-ji's spontaneous inclinations, we had chuttis a lot. This time when the school closed, we were allowed to roam free. Locally, this thing was receding into the past, though the occasional bus driver rumor still whipped through the town.

"I heard American troops bombed Pakistan and Afghanistan," Harold whispered one Tuesday afternoon in film class. We were watching a hyperbolic Bollywood movie, and life was far eclipsing the plot. Or what I could make of it. Swami-ji banned subtitles. Most weeks, though, he'd post himself behind us and, getting choked up, break his own veto. "I know now he is my father," you could hear him mumble above the music from back near the kitchen. *"Va!"* he'd sometimes exclaim, beside himself.

Between assists, I'd frown at the screen. Had the unfaithful husband really said, "Boys will be boys"? He looked too sensitive to have pulled that.

Hindi films were unendurable—horrible honking songs, bleary cinematic clichés—till something clicked and I became a convert. Punch for punch, I saw, you couldn't beat them for high drama. In one we'd watched, there was an illicit pregnancy, a hinted-at abortion, a suicide, a wedding, and repeated shooting of a groom on horseback, all before the opening credits. *"The film demonstrates what Shakespeare could have done had he had access to automatic rifles,"* I wrote, or some facsimile thereof, in the movie journal we had to keep.

After a while, I'd watch, rapt, and try to employ a technique a translator, a polyglot of extraordinary natural talent, had told me about back in the States. At thirty-eight, the man was up to speed in twenty-eight languages and occasionally, for work, had to rev up in others. Then, he said, he knew a trick. "You do?" I breathed, leaning in for the secret. "Yes," he said. "You want to find a soap opera from the country, find someone on it who looks like you, then watch it every day and imitate her. Like this," he said, and reeled off a line in Hindi to show how the technique would work for me. I was floored—not by the tip, but by his accent and syntax: perfect, though Hindi wasn't in his top twenty-eight.

After meeting him, I grew curious to see if there was a profile of the virtuoso language learner, discovered that the entire linguistic community is, too. Everyone knows there are people with stellar abilities, the ones who absorb Italian or Spanish as if they're breathing it in. But no one can figure out what accounts for this. In the 1970s, an Israeli researcher proposed what might be called the "low self-esteem theory of language learning excellence." People with permeable ego boundaries have an advantage, he claimed, possibly because it makes them more like children. To test the theory, he plied a group of subjects with alcohol and Valium. Their pronunciation did improve, but this wasn't quite the blockbuster evidence needed to put him on the map.

Through the years, all sorts of contributory traits have been proposed and discarded. In the 1980s, two Canadian researchers tried to argue that people with poor visuospatial skills are better at languages. They aren't. A gift for music isn't linked to language ability, not in any way that's ever been proved. Intelligence doesn't have much bearing. Language savants exist, the best known being "Christopher," who, despite an IQ of between 42 and 76, has partial mastery, at least, of Danish, Dutch, Finnish, German, Modern Greek, Hindi, Italian, Norwegian, Polish, Portuguese, Russian, Sign (British), Spanish, Swedish, Turkish, and Welsh, in addition to his native English.

You can be smart and hopeless in French, both. "It doesn't have anything to do with intelligence in other areas," A. L. Becker says. "It has to do with changing your mind. Frequently, very bright people don't like having their mind changed. If language learning means building a new subjectivity, changing your inner polarities, it makes sense that smart folks might find this task threatening. Often lesser-grade scholars are wonderful at languages because they're able to get that new mind quickly."

The (very brief) list of what it does have to do with: Motivation. Good phonological working memory—the capacity to reproduce and retain sounds. Knowledge of other foreign languages. (The more you have, the easier it is to add on.) A propensity for being a ham, or, as second language dean Elaine Tarone puts it, "a willingness to play, to pretend to be someone else."

The best films pull you out of yourself, make you, briefly, someone else. Hindi movies, I'd have argued, were right up there. Tuesdays, I learned to form the sounds with the actors, hoping to take the words into my mouth.

SOON AFTER, THE BUS driver rumors died down altogether. When for a while it'd looked as though the world was going to understand what they'd put up with from wilding Muslims all these years, people here had remained sharply focused on this thing. Pakistan, surely, was going to get it, but when that didn't happen, people returned to complaining about the Mughals. "Those damn Mughals," you'd hear, "they knocked the faces off our statues." Four hundred years before, sure, but the evidence was still visible on temples. In this place where most people had never been to Delhi, Aurangzeb's sweep was more real than something that had occurred in a far floating world. New York is in New Jersey or in France, I'd heard someone say, sounding like an American kid being quizzed in geography.

Though a small group in town was, in fact, from that floating world. "Is it safe here?" I asked at a gathering of expats in the otherwise deserted Sixteen Chefs restaurant.

"For the most part, yes," said Piers, the publisher of an events magazine in English. Piers was a Brit, in his forties, with dwindling straw-colored hair and ruddy boyish features. In five years here, other than acquiring a fondness for multiple gold rings, he hadn't gone remotely native. He and his ailing mother lived in a mountaintop villa with a collection of Mr. Bean videos, a number of fringed lamps shipped over from the Midlands, and three Nepalese houseboys who'd learned to cook lasagna. What Hindi he had dated to the Raj: *chota*-peg, "Oh, just a small one."

"You're safer here than in the States," said Renee, who had a steel gray pageboy, a perpetual cough, and some basis for comparison. A Brooklynite by birth, she'd directed theater in Minneapolis until she was in her sixties, when the calls for work had stopped coming in and she'd discovered how bleak growing old in America could be. After five years of contemplating the view from her front window, she sent herself to India for her seventieth birthday. On the stop in Udaipur, an unplanned detour, a voice said, *You're home.* The return trip had lasted long enough to sell the house. Now four years into this unexpected incarnation, she'd acquired a second career as a photographer, an apartment near the Chandra Prakash hotel, and a handsome swain named Hukam Raj, a Gandhi freedom fighter two years her senior.

"The biggest danger you face here is stepping in cow patties," a jowly Australian journalist about to ship out assured me.

"I heard that's lucky," Renee said.

"The one thing," the Australian said, "is how often you get propositioned by men. Oh, all the time! In the bazaar." Prostitution, he meant. In sleepy *Udaipur?* I thought. It was the hundredth reminder I'd had that day that I couldn't be sure what I was seeing, couldn't know what I was hearing, that I was unattached to surroundings by familiar sights or words. "You have to be able to tolerate ambiguity if you want to learn a language," my teacher Gabriela had said, and now I saw this extended beyond sentences.

All night, I'd had a peripheral sense of Piers watching me. I'd wait till he was in conversation with someone, mistime my glance, catch his eye. *Interesting,* I thought, but as the evening broke up, a slim Indian man appeared beside him at the table. "Shubra Singh?" I said to Piers, reading the name on the card the man handed out.

"When you see me, you'll often see him," Piers said. "He's my *jigri.*"

"Jigri?" The word sounded a little too onomatopoetic.

"A jigri is—what did you say it was?" he asked the man. "Right. A close friend."

"Very close friend," the jigri said.

"Not *that* close." Piers laughed. At the curb, he hopped onto the back of the jigri's motor scooter. He put his hands on the man's shoulders. They sped off into the night.

Hundred and first reminder: in New York, I could have read the scene with both eyes shut, but here, where men stroll the streets holding hands and male friendships strike Westerners as erotic when they're not, I stood frowning at the tailpipe.

When my rickshaw pulled up at the house, the Jain wives tumbled out the door. Back in the kitchen, they held a debriefing. Where had I gone? What had we eaten? Rice, lentils, bread, I answered—about what I ate everywhere. *"Haaaan?"* they said wondrously, as if they'd never heard of this combination before.

"What do you cook at your house?" Alka asked. I didn't bother running across the driveway for the dictionary. "Take-out" was not go-

ing to be in there. I said I went to restaurants. *All the time?* they cried. Okay, then, I didn't.

"Rice," I said, stretching the vowels. *Riiii-iice.*

"Haan. Rice. And?"

"And vegetables."

"And?"

"And lentils and bread."

"And?" But I'd covered the acceptable bases. Steak and chicken were out of the question. All Jains are vegetarians, so strict that the devout avoid root vegetables for fear that an insect might have been crushed in the harvest. The family, modern businessman Jains, did eat garlic and onions, all except the grandmother, but any answer more respirational than that was pushing it. In Hindi, I considered, how did you say "tofu"? You didn't. There went my one specialty.

"Mexican?" Alka offered.

"Yes!" I said. At home, many times, I had heated up rice. Other times, microwaved beans.

"So you can cook Mexican for us here?" she said, glancing at the stove. Damn.

"No, I need the book," I said.

"Book?" She looked puzzled. No one used cookbooks in India. They learned the repertoire by the age of eight.

"Haan. I need the book of the kitchen in order to cook Mexican," I said.

Alka gave me a nice-try smile. *"Good answer,"* I swear she said.

When I finally made it back to the room, I looked around for the dictionary. "Jigri. Having to do with the liver," it said. More rocking enlightenment coming out of India: Piers and the man were just livers.

"ARAMSE SONA," Meena says, strolling into the darkness to lock the gate, as I stand at the door and fumble for the key and let the language break over me: *Aramse sona:* Sleep comfortably. Before I could detect the women's kindnesses through tone; now they take form: I can hear them. "Sleep with ease": that's it precisely, and she says it with ease. It's the first time I've heard it, the thousandth time at least she's said it in her life. It's just something you say, but it has the effect of curling me into the family. *"Do baje,"* she reminds me: "Be back by two tomorrow," for the *mendhi* application. The festival of Navratri is coming up. We're having our hands painted with henna, a holiday ritual.

Do baje. Alka and I sit on scratchy jute mats as Meena and the girls look on. We hold our hands out to the mendhi wali. Flowers, thatched hearts, paisleys bloom on our palms. *"Thandi?"* Alka says: "Cold?" I panic. It is. It's the same sensation as a nurse swabbing lidocaine on skin for a biopsy, for a catheter, for another catheter, for a fourth. Neurons that fire together wire together; it's not my fault; that's how I've been wired, am wired; everything that happens to us changes our brains, I was just telling Helaena. "The machine is continually repairing and remaking itself based on experience," a neurologist I'd interviewed had said. In India, I'm replacing hatches on my chest with arabesque swirls on my hands. Rips turn to hearts turn to flowers.

"Mendhi looks so good on white skin," the youngest girl, Meenal, observes.

"But if I'm white, what are you?" I ask. Our skin is nearly the same.

"Uhhh." She thinks. "I'm okay."

Meenal looks just like the grandmother, exact same face, only smaller and unlined. They're like points on a diagram of Indian cultural history. The grandmother sits on the floor to eat. She wears the same yellow sari every day, does not have a fixed birthday. When it's the full moon in the second week of August, it's her birthday. Meenal in jeans in a chair at the breakfast table speaks perfect English, lightly accented in a way that sounds British, though she's never been a hundred miles from Udaipur. Except once, they went to Kashmir. "When we were there, then we were so white," she says. Her birthday, without fail, is March 9 every year.

The children feed us grapes while Alka and I lounge like nautch dancing girls, waiting for our hands to dry. We talk about everything, except *this thing* that has happened. The wives never ask how I feel, and I don't want them to. I'm in India, where, right now, I've always been, where I'll always be, till I'm alone at night.

At night, I lie in bed and worry that we've become a little like the Raj, the other students and I: dumb to the ways the homeland's been altered, loyal to old notions, too floridly assured now, out of sync and out of time. In the right here and now, we're citizens of the America we left at the beginning of September, a country still blessed by sheltering geography, a country that's impregnable and will always stay fortified. Until the hissing neon light fades the henna on my skin. Then my veins go white as the walls fill in with the exact and obliterating images.

"Let's stay longer"

Remarkable how much can hinge on a syllable. One afternoon in early October, the Jain wives appeared at my door with news: something was on for the night. Something big. *What,* I tried to make out. "Sudesh Bhosle," Meena said, then she and Alka spoke so fast, I had to squint to understand. At length, the meaning went through. A Bombay recording artist had come to town. The Lions Club, or "Loins Club," as it was pronounced locally, was hosting a concert.

"Every song in Bollywood," Rajesh, Dad 2, shouted from the doorway. "This man has sung every song!" From the way he stabbed the air on "every," it was clear we were talking glitterati crowds.

"Jaayegi?" I heard Alka say: "You will go?" The prospect of three hours of Bollywood crooning was about as appealing as a polka weekend, but feeling guilty because I hadn't been around much, I said, *"Jaungi":* "I will go." I was slightly surprised when an exchange of glances followed, and Rajesh bolted for the driveway. When later

in the day he presented me with a ticket, I was puzzled to see it was stamped "1,000 rupees," not the 500 Alka had quoted me earlier.

Alka and Meena in full jewels looked smashing when we gathered in the driveway at dusk. Rajkumar's hair was oiled to liquescent beauty. Anticipation ran high in the car as Rajesh, wearing a new orange shirt, reminisced about Mr. Bhosle's hits.

At the concert grounds, near the palace, Rajkumar handed the usher their tickets. Then all four Jains shooed me away.

"Go, Kathy," Rajesh said, scooping air toward the stage.

"There!" Rajkumar said. He smiled as he gesticulated. "There, Kathy. That way. Tonight you are first." As an usher led me toward the front, I deciphered the situation. I'd screwed up on an *"egi."* Alka hadn't said *"Jaayegi"*: *"You* will go?" She'd said, *"Jaenge"*: *"We're* going." She'd stopped by to tell me they wouldn't be around, and I'd said, essentially, *Yeah, well, you're taking me.* I should have known something was up when, on handing me the ticket, the usually snorty Rajesh was sweet. "You are VVP, Kathy," he'd said. "Not a very important person, a very, very important person. Free cold drinks are." After scrambling into last-minute prices, he was not getting stuck with the seat.

Now here I was, by myself in a sea of men in kurtas, of women in saris and their best thick gold, staring at a stage empty except for a banner, LIONS CLUB UDAIPUR: SUDESH BHOSLE NITE, and a smaller sign, YOU CAN'T BEAT A BAJAJ. THINK OF BAJAJ AUTO. Over the next hour, I thought of Bajaj often as I read and reread the sign, slapped at mosquitoes, grew more and more lonesome. There's nothing like blocks of India's firm family units to make you feel absolutely alone.

But yet, even so, until a dry-ice machine began to fumigate the stage, there was a certain dark charm to the scene. Bats flitted overhead. The palace rose like a Halloween mask behind me. Then the smoke-master twirling-light effects began, turning the proscenium into a pulsating swamp, making it hard to brood, though I tried. I could assemble sentences if people would just give me time, I thought, but how was I supposed to assemble and talk simultaneously? Oops, now twirling and spinning lights, two separate sets, quite an effect on dry ice—like a desperately signaling spaceship in a cloud. I gave up the black mood. But if I squeezed my brain and hung on, I considered, cheering, I could last three, four sentences now before getting bumped. And I was getting a kind of pidgin going that the Jains were down with. And—up ahead, shapes were moving in the gloaming. You could see the tops of heads.

The swelling clouds flattened. Band members found chairs. The wet-sari, hair-flipping film sound began. And this, I reflected, is what can happen if you miss so much as one thin syllable. You end up at Sudesh Bhosle Nite.

MY DAYS THEN were shaped by these absences. What language I did have was still too slight to let me assemble much of anything, though with each word learned, a world was coming further into view. My gray-haired friend Renee, the expat from Brooklyn, no longer lived near a hotel called the Chandra Prakash. Now that I knew what the name meant, her apartment was by *The Moonlight*. But entry into this world was slow and blocked by negative forces: The phonemes, the sounds I strained to hear but couldn't. The words that wouldn't cross over (literally; the word "translate" means "to carry across"). That would be 90 percent of the total, in the philosopher John Locke's estimate. "If we . . . exactly compare different languages," he wrote, "we shall find that, though they have words which in translations and dictionaries are supposed to answer one another, yet there is scarce one of ten."

In any new language, you discover missing words, as revealing as the ones that exist. In Hindi, I soon learned, you couldn't say "appointment" or "minute" or "second," except with the English loan versions. In Udaipur, where only 50 percent of the homes had phones then, you didn't need to. "If a people have no word for something, either it does not matter to them or it matters too much to talk about," the sociologist Edgar Z. Friedenberg said, and here appointments didn't matter. People stopped by. "They'll come to your house at six-thirty in the morning. Once I came back from dinner to find a friend sitting in the living room reading a magazine," Renee told me.

Each missing word was a shock to discover, one thing more that had become a figment of my imagination. For if you can't express something to anyone around you, doesn't it exist only in your mind? Each missing word was a loss, a piece of the old world falling away. I began taking note of all the fragments that had vanished: "handsome," "paint," the verb "to wonder," the verb "to own." It was now literally impossible to own anything. In Hindi, new shoes, bread, your car could only be "in your direction": *ke pas*. I loved the construction's nod to impermanence till I used it so often, it became just a figure of speech. And one perhaps best left unexamined, though Helaena did from time to time: In India, there's no female orgasm, not to speak of. "Orgasm" applied only to men. "Interested" was not a word. There weren't separate terms for "marriage" and "wedding." Your *shaadi* was your wedding and your marriage, a small distinction, but in the early days of my marriage to Hindi, I was acutely aware of what was missing. "Privacy" most of all.

Once, on contracting a bug, I hailed a rickshaw to take me to the doctor's. The driver was uncertain of the address, so he waved over a pedestrian, who looked at the slip of paper, looked at me, leaned into the back. Was it my head? the man wanted to know. Just a slight fever, I answered. What about my throat, did that hurt? No, that was fine, I replied. Had I taken anything for it? he inquired. I gave a quick nod yes. Allopathic or naturopathic? he asked. *"Mujhe jaana hai,"* I said, which loosely translates: "I know this is a silly idea, but I was thinking we could leave some questions for the doctor."

"There's no word for 'privacy' in any of the Indian languages," we'd been told during orientation, though I surely would have figured that out pretty fast on my own. A month into moving here, I'd begun to suspect that the whole town belonged to the Central Intelligence caste. "Madam, you are living in Sector Eleven?" a rickshaw driver asked. "My friend said he took you there from the bank two weeks ago." "Madam, who was that man who walked you home last night?" the candy shop owner inquired. I had to think, then remembered—just Swami-ji. "He is my teacher," I said with an extreme annoyance that went unnoticed. The guy was too busy nodding, as if calculating implications.

"There are three things you can't hide—happiness, a cough, and love," a Hindi proverb goes, but I think the list got truncated in the retelling. In Udaipur, in any Indian town, the list could be amended to include where you are going in this heat, how much you paid for that lamp, why you were wearing a fancy sari two nights ago, whether you've put on weight. The notion of off-limits is alien. Perhaps this has to do with the fact that here, as Indologist Diana L. Eck writes, "the 'individual' as we think of it in the West does not exist. A person thinks of himself or herself not as a singular entity, but rather as part of a larger interdependent whole, in which parts mirror one another in an infinite, intricate pattern." Or maybe it is because, as a friend said, "in India we share everything, even privacy."

Eventually, I'd come to like it when a cybercafe wala would boot up the computer and automatically log me on to my server. I'd grow accustomed to strangers on the street giving me updates on my appearance: "I am thinking your skin is looking dry?" a man I'd never seen before said, as I was waiting at a corner to cross the street. "You have not been applying oil?" Though I continued to draw some lines, as on the evening I came home to find the Jains debating how much money I had in the bank. "No, you misunderstand," Dad 2 said when I refused to answer. "We don't want to take your money.

We just really, really, really want to know," he said, as all ten family members nodded emphatically, in complete unison.

MUCH FARTHER OUT along the spidery web of time, long gone from the Jains' now, I begin a list of words missing from English: *Leelaa:* the acts of a deity performed for pleasure. *Vidya:* translated as "knowledge," but which a friend explained as "having characteristics of knowledge but not itself knowledge. It's symbolic of God's world. A person who knows *vidya* knows everything." And *advait:* roughly, non-duality; and *aanand:* broadly, joy or bliss; and then I toss the paper away. Departure's looming. I can't bear to see, spelled out in black and white, what will become unspeakable once I cross back. Transcendence: that's what I'm going to have to lose.

RENEE PHONES TO see about an outing. She's been invited to a performance at a deaf school at 3 P.M. Do I want to go? My afternoon plans so far extend to sitting in the kitchen and exclaiming over the neighbor's baby, so yeah, I say; sure, I'd like to.

The rickshaw guy who drops me off scolds me when I thank him: "You should say *shukriya*." I'm momentarily confused. *Dhanyavaad*, what I'd said, is perfectly fine in every "Speak Hindi" book, but then I realize: he's Muslim. I'd used the word from the Sanskrit. He's insisting on the Arabic-based one. All year, every time I give thanks, I end up putting someone off.

A block from the Chandra Prakash, on the corner by the Titanic Travel Agency, I manage by the determined unfocusing of my eyes to avoid the attentions of the overwrought cybercafe owner who wears a zoot suit. He has a business proposition he wants to discuss. I can scientifically guess what it is: I should come to his place only. I'm worn-out from his other business proposals, sympathetic nonetheless. There's a drought on, all the tourists have vanished, the merchants are desperate or dulled.

I pass an elephant standing on breakfast, curling sweet-smelling chickpea greens up in his trunk. A round old lady, head hennaed a silly orange, pulls a little girl across the street. Four old men in red and purple turbans lounge at a table, watching me, *videshi* television, foreigner TV, and that's it for the block. Even when you turn a corner and suddenly encounter a crowd here, it's never the full-press crush of people in Benares or Calcutta.

At Renee's, she yells, "It's open," when I knock. "Almost ready," she calls from her bedroom. "Just using your bathroom," I say in reply. What I'm after is her scale. The needle shows another pound gone. I'm down six, the Jain vegetarian miracle diet. Sometimes I stop by after school just to check. The count is compelling, proof of what I suspect: I'm no longer physically quite myself. These days, my hair looks electrocuted no matter how much conditioner I apply, a mystery that won't be resolved for months, till Helaena says, "Oh, no, you've been using the green shampoo? Oh, God, you want the red. The green strips your hair. It's made to take out coconut oil." My hair, still light brown from the American summer, is going dark at the roots from the blasting sun here, from the need to keep my head covered. My feet are cracked: constant exposure in sandals. My English is somewhat, too. A weird crossover effect from my studies has occurred. Hindi pollutes my English and vice versa. I construct clunky Hindi sentences using English syntax; total groaners, all wrong. The courtly politeness of Hindi filters into my English, "by your kindness," "I am obliged to your honor." It leeches my American personality, makes me feel I've gone pale. I never realized before the extent to which we reside in language. We are how we speak.

The way I speak, my pronunciation, is sometimes different now. Just as the formalities of Hindi have begun to appear in my English unwanted, unexpectedly, when I go to phone home. I open my mouth and notice that my vowels are tighter, the start of an Indian accent. It's odd, automatic, like spirit possession. It brings to mind a remark the linguist Jenny Saffran made during a discussion we had of how first and second languages most likely share the same neural systems, as opposed to, say, being separately lodged in the brain. "There's evidence a second language begins to cannibalize your first," she said, a revolutionary rethinking of transfer.

Transfer, as it's been conceived for years, is the way a first language, an L1 in the vernacular, interferes with a second, an L2; the way you inevitably try to press foreign words on an English template and end up sounding like the local version of Peter Sellers on a roll. "Individuals tend to transfer the forms and meanings . . . of their native language and culture to the foreign language and culture," the linguist Robert Lado writes. L1 imperialism, but just recently several researchers have observed transfer goes both ways.

A second language can, weirdly, start to revise the DNA of the first. The implications are rather remarkable: study French intensively enough, and you're no longer speaking the same English you were. (But only if the effort's intensive. Experiments with students in Hungary found that at two to four hours a week, no real permeation occurred.) Study French long enough, you're no longer speaking the same English as your countrymen. In their book *Foreign Language and Mother Tongue,* linguists Istvan Kecskes and Tünde Papp argue that a German-English bilingual speaks a German that's different from that of a monolingual German speaker and an English unlike that of a native English speaker. "You can tell a French speaker who also speaks English," the British linguist Vivian Cook says. Or an English speaker who also speaks Hindi.

"We'll see you at seven," I told Renee one day. Confused, she snapped, "Who else is coming?" Only me, and I didn't realize till I'd hung up that I'd adopted the Hindi habit of using "we" for "I" in English—more humbling, a quality that's become pleasing for how it makes me feel more connected to the world.

Study French or English or Hindi long enough, and the way you perceive the world will change. Or so the case can be made.

In Renee's bathroom mirror, I twist my mouth to see if, aided by weight loss, my cheekbones will stand out. Somewhat, though on the whole, my face is no different: green eyes rimmed in black, an aunt's bump on my nose, a long space above my lip. It's the same, will remain the same two weeks from now when I'm jolted from bed by the conviction it's been terribly altered: Why not? Everything else has been. But even as I get lucky—ordinary face in the mirror, just pasty at 3 A.M.—even as relief beats in my veins, I'm waiting for the day when I look and I see that I'm no longer there. A day that, when it comes, will be no less unnerving for being expected.

In Renee's living room, it's peaceful and airy, India and sanctuary from India. Cool blue walls, dark wicker chairs, day bed beside wicker stools. Cool light, like morning no matter when I stop by. Prints of the Hindu gods, Haitian art, jazz. Afternoons when she puts on Cleo Lane, for an instant I think we'll have brunch. Instead, we drink spiced tea, and I tell her gossip from the school. Each time in the stories, everyone's a little crazier.

"Gopal should be here in a few minutes," she says, lumbering in. Her arms appear to be so long, her fingertips nearly brush her knees, effect of old arthritis. The handsome Gopal is her rickshaw driver, but she calls him her son, a complicated affair of the heart they have going.

"For you," she says, handing me an article on teenage suicide, text in the ongoing tutelage she's conducting with me. "They're having a real problem with that here." She sighs and takes a seat.

Renee, late in life, has discovered her one true passion: the anthropological study of India. Sometimes her love borders on the fanatic if you don't agree with her interpretations, and then Helaena says, "Renee thinks she owns India." We both believe our proprietary stake is greater, that the language has crashed us farther in, that we pay for what claims we can make to greater knowledge by being unshielded.

Renee, in English at all times, can start all sentences with a distancing "they," the anthropologist's pronoun. When another story of a kitchen fire appears in the paper, she can say, "They're not allowed to leave the new house once they're married. It's the culture." Kitchen fires, a particularly gruesome kind of death, occur here each year in the thousands. A new bride's in-laws, retroactively displeased with the dowry, furiously demand more—another refrigerator, more rupees—till the girl's parents balk. When it's clear the parents won't pay beyond what they already have, the husband holds the girl down while the mother-in-law, above her, tips the kerosene jar. Afterward, he'll be free to collect another dowry.

"They aren't allowed to return home," Renee can say, expressing sympathy, but "they" aren't "me." In the study of a new language, you use all the pronouns. You say "I," you say "we," and knowledge slams you sideways. When Friday quizzes, say, are dark muttering haiku. *For three points each, you will write the following in Hindi:* "Beautiful songs will be sung at my house / Would you like some oranges? / My sister is often beaten." As time and my immersion go on, I'll press my lips when Renee gets didactic.

Gopal is taking more than a few. "Tell me again about Pauline and the uniforms," I say to kill time. The phrasing's the lead-in to a family story, though just then I don't notice. My own mother died three years earlier. Renee has a kid about my age who hasn't been in touch in years, perhaps, she thinks, because he's in the CIA. In this place where the days are all circled by the past, it's easy to blink and incarnate someone.

"Oh, yes. The time I wrote about her for Piers," she says. Pauline is a seventy-eight-year-old Christian-Brahmin buddy of hers who, with church lady backup, makes trips to the villages to dispense medicine. "When the story came out, I got a call from the palace. They were sending a donation. The next day, thirty-nine packages big as bales were at my door, all old uniforms. The palace had cleaned out their closets." We're grinning in advance of the ending.

"So we loaded up taxis, and Pauline took them with her. Now

there are four or five villages outside town running around in City Palace uniforms." Liveried villagers in fields, by huts; the image is as good the second time around. Then Gopal knocks, and we bolt. We have to get to the deaf school in time to meet Piers. "It's way the hell out," Renee says nervously in her carbureted Brooklyn voice.

Twenty minutes later, we pull up to the gate. A tethered goat tries to stand, reconsiders, sinks down. Like a mascot: everything about the school suggests a slide. The small yard in front is dirt, not grass. The pink trim on the khaki stone buildings has faded. Even the name on Renee's invitation, turns out, suggests decline. Viklang Vidyala. *Vidyala*, I know, is "place of study." *Viklang*, I assume, is a word for "deaf," till Vidhu explains: "It's translated as 'handicapped,' but it comes from *vika*, 'something defective.' *Ang* means 'part.'" Viklang Vidyala: "place of study for defectives." With each word learned, a world comes into view, sometimes in infuriating glimpses.

In the yard, we join Piers and the other visitors. We're a half-hour late but still ahead of the honored guest, a traditional figure at Indian ceremonies, usually some kind of dignitary, though the farther you go from the palace, the lower the stature. At fifteen minutes out, you begin to get puff-chested minor officials.

Across from us, fifty kids, mostly boys, are lined up in rows. Their uniforms are cranberry and pink, an, uh, vivid combination, even for India. The effect is throbbing, though the rows are so neat, they look combed. Then just as a white fender becomes visible through the gate, a line gets tangled on an argument. Car doors can be heard opening. A teacher in his thirties sweeps down. Arm behind his back like a brigadier, he puts all errant parties on notice with his free hand. Then, turning, he signals a drummer to begin as the first sandaled foot comes through the gate.

Lulled by two beats, of the sun and the drum, I'm sleepy for the garlanding of the honored guest, in a trance as the students begin welcome drills, and then I'm snapped to, awake. A little girl in sneakers too big is moving out of time, marching right when she should step left, banging ahead as the lines pull back. I can't stop staring. It's the look on her face, concentration laced with misery. For here's the thing: I remember it.

As a kid, I had trouble hearing, a situation that, once it was resolved, wasn't much remarked on in my house beyond its curiosity value. "Kathy was deaf as a child," my mother liked to say for shock effect, a family story that became the one line. The full narrative, with its nuance, was boring.

Till I was six, I had a double set of adenoids that repeatedly grew infected, blocking my eustachian tubes and sound. The condition, chronic otitis, is fairly easily remedied now and may have been then, except my parents were Christian Scientists and didn't go to doctors. Untreated, I gave teachers fits. Sometimes I was visibly sullen, ignoring all entreaties, and other times I was compliant; nobody noticed that the first always coincided with an activity such as coloring that required my head to be down. If I had looked up, I might have read their lips, an ability I retained till high school.

"There were times that child wouldn't have heard a cannon go off," the doctor my mother brought me to after she broke with the First Church of Christ, Scientist, said, one of my few distinct memories of the experience. Absences don't imprint on the mind directly. I hadn't thought about this in years.

"They took out your tonsils and a second set of adenoids fell down, and after that you were fine," my mother concluded. And now, as the lines turn on the drum's vibrations, I reconsider this epilogue that has stood for so long. I have a hazy recollection of loathing the rude, bright, unyielding new sounds, of wanting to return to the cocoon. And another, sharper recollection of jeering kids around me, of fast-talking faces pressing in, shrieks each time I said "What?" Four years after I'd gained full hearing, I still compulsively said "What?" Automatic leftover repetition; old necessity become OCD. I hadn't noticed I did this, but the kids had. On the playground, they murmured sentences at me; each "What?" provoked was a score. They circled round. I kept a tense dog smile as the understanding came: this wasn't friendship. After years without friends, I'd misread the intent. I was a loner by default. I hated to talk, could not grasp forms of conversation. If there's a developmental brain stage for discourse, I'd missed it. At night, I remember now, out in the yard, I'd record exchanges from the day, try to figure out what the man had said to cause the woman to answer that way. I remember a college boyfriend who looked me up in my thirties saying he'd called it off "because you never said a word." The epilogue crumbles as it falls.

Multiplications click in my head. I became fluent in my twenties after taking writers to lunch for my job and imitating their rhythm and words. Connections rattle together, and there's no one to tell. You spend years growing up writing down conversations; that's the apprenticeship for becoming a writer, isn't it? You acquire language, aspects of it, late, you'd spend the rest of your life in repetition compulsion: a conjugant. Well wouldn't you?

In the yard, the drumming has stopped. The kids are catching their breath. I continue to stare, cross my arms against exposure. If, as Naipaul wrote, India brings out the concealed parts of us, this was a rapid unveiling.

"I was kind of deaf when I was a kid, and then I had an operation," I blurt out to Piers as the drills are ending. He regards me quizzically, then exclaims, "Oh! Let's tell the headmaster. You can make a speech." He rushes off before I can stop him.

In the inner courtyard, I have a long time to contemplate how completely I'll make a fool of myself. Under a canopy of bright fabrics, the students stage a play about the drought. A boy in a hat with a paper band that says DUSTBIN excels at air-trash comedy. A beautiful tribal kid, face already sculpted with the planes of adulthood, does a fine turn as a water pump going dry. The honored guest is up next. "*Jaanewale* technological developments," he intones, chest puffed out. *"Bindihindi* Osama Bin Laden." I whisper to Piers, "When you get to Osama Bin Laden, the speech is over," but it isn't. It rolls on and on, till the school's founder, a doctor, gives it a spin. He's full of suggestions, hygienic and otherwise. "Let us not dig ourselves into bad health with our tongues and our teeth," he tells the children through a translator. "Let us not be burdens to our families." Then the headmaster motions to me; there's no way out. A teacher stands by to sign. I take the proscenium, take a breath, see I've miscalculated. The answer to the question of how foolish turns out to be: Completely. My talk, which with grace is unintelligible in sign, starts with a mention of Hollywood actress Marlee Matlin, ace role model for impoverished Indian children there, then meanders through the promise of cochlear implants (promising here if you have the equivalent of enough to fund a space launch) and into my own story, which as soon as I begin it, is insipid beyond belief. These are kids, some with holes in their clothes, who've had to leave their families. I said "What?" on the playground.

Before shame can finish me, I'm off. On the floor, guests are chatting, tall islands in a choppy pink and cranberry sea. A man approaches, says, "Very, very good." Piers, from a distance, beams and waves. I hold up a finger—*Back soon*—and press on toward the yard. Out in the dusty courtyard, I'm clear, and then I'm surrounded, by the sensation of questions fanning my skin, by twenty gesturing boys. The Dustbin pulls me down to examine my ears. Someone else lifts a hand: *You're okay?* All I can think to do is to say *"Theek hoon. Theek hoon"*—"I'm fine. I'm fine"—hoping he can read my lips. A third signs a plane flying, shrugs: what? *When do you leave?* maybe. I try: *Not for a long time.* The boy shakes his head. He repeats the question, only now I see that his other hand has flown up to make a wall. No, a tower; all around, brown hands are crashing, followed by shrugs, and I'm smiling. Because this is the first time in all this time anyone's asked, even if I don't know what exactly they're asking.

The sensation of connection fresh on my arms, I locate the teacher from drills. "But what would you do?" he says when I say I'd like to work at the school.

"I don't know. Maybe help in the kitchen?"

"We have people to do that," the teacher, whose name is Anukul, says with Brahmin detachment.

"Chop? Clean?"

But they have people to do that, too. This is India.

"Come. See my class," he finally suggests. "Maybe you could think of something." He wears thin red glasses, precisely tailored trousers, has the self-possessed manner of an Italian architect. "Why not?" he says with a cool British accent. It's only later, when I visit his house—three plain concrete rooms in a dusty back division—that I realize, *Oh! He's a poor schoolteacher.*

At home, Alka wants to know about the kids. *"Badhir,"* I tell her: "Deaf," easiest vocabulary word of all time because of the way it's pronounced, "bad ear." Badhir/bad ear: they're practically identical if I say them, but here's a curious twist: they prompt entirely different images depending on which language I say them in. In English, what I get is zany, a tin horn, the kind a cartoon mouse would hold. A joke, but in Hindi, in a sentence with Alka, what comes is gleeful, a sense memory of talk fanning skin and, in my mind's eye, a wash of cranberry. It's extraordinary enough that when you learn a language, the new words, if you're lucky, quickly connect to emotions. In a little over a month here, the word for "peace," *shanti,* has acquired a sense of yearning, reminds me for some reason of the melancholy strains of a chant I heard one night on leaving the palace. But how can the same word, or nearly so acoustically, get the brain to produce entirely different emotions, different pictures, depending on its setting? The answer is probably related to an idea the Swiss linguist Ferdinand de Saussure suggested more than ninety years ago. The linguistic structure is a network, he proposed, and after nearly a century of contention among theoretical scholars, many neurolinguists are inclined to agree.

In the spreading activation network theory, as the contemporary hypothesis is called, every word you hear or read calls up every other word like it, rhymed cousins and distant cousins, "bell," "hell," "ball," linked *concepts:* belles-lettres. "You read a line in a newspaper story, 'Something is rotten in the state of Florida,' and from there, everything connected to Hamlet rises up because everything is connected in the network," Rice University professor emeritus of linguistics Sydney Lamb says. "Or you tell a friend, 'Are you ready to zoom to the camera store?' Why did you use the word 'zoom'? Because activation spread from one node to another and you were thinking of cameras." "Nodes" in this hypothesis refers to bundles of neurons arranged in cortical columns. Theoretically, they process information, an extrapolation from the discovery that cats' eyes depend on optical columns in the occipital lobe to do the same. Since that piece of information was arrived at by inserting microelectrodes into feline brains, it's unlikely that the spreading activation network theory will be conclusively proven anytime soon. "They don't do this on humans, and you can see why. I wish they wouldn't do it on cats," Lamb says.

Spreading activation, like all compelling theories, explains a lot. It explains, for example, the mechanism of puns, which, from this viewpoint, are managed network processing. "A talking duck goes into a bar, orders a drink, and says, 'Put it on my bill'" is what you might call willful activation of "bill" in both senses. It also explains malapropisms, why you might see the headline MUST-SEE TV LACKS MUST-HAVE BUZZ and read "Must-Have Bugs." And it explains, or comes close, why I was getting different images from the same phonological arrangement. "When you're speaking Hindi, then it's the Hindi nodes in your system that are getting activated,"

Lamb said when I phoned. "You're reinforcing the Hindi connections. When you're speaking English, the same thing happens.

"Connections are strengthened with use," he said, and as I string together wobbly nouns and nicked verbs to tell Alka about the kids, a strong connection is made: between the sound "bad ear" in a Hindi stream and this revelation that occurred in a small dirt yard, arriving through words that couldn't be spoken.

At dinner that night, it's just me and the grandmother. Usually she keeps up a steady stream of chat, posing questions and waiting fruitlessly for my answers. Until today, I've been a poor conversational partner, because to my ear, she's been sounding like a power motor— *Wrrrdiwap? Wrrrwrrrwrrrdiwap?*—but tonight, for the first time, I understand her. She's slamming down aluminum plates, darting in and out of the kitchen, when suddenly she begins to speak. She's been speaking all along, of course, in what I've thought was clattery Mewari. But now I hear, in a clear, raspy voice, "Where's the upstairs dweller?" The upstairs dweller? The Whisperer! I feel like Thomas Edison.

The grandmother cocks her head for a reply, as she's been doing since I moved in. *"She's at the doctor's,"* I say, and the grandmother doesn't look the least surprised to find me responding when till then, all I've done was repeat the word *"yes."* She nods. *"Oh,"* she says. *"The doctor's."*

THE NEXT MORNING, we assemble in the main room to reports of a disturbance. *"Ji,"* Swami-ji says slowly, tone of stark disbelief. *"Ji."* Venerable students. *"I am hearing that one of our students has e-mailed to Delhi, inquiring about the kidnapping of American citizens. Could this information possibly be true?"* All I'd said in my e-mail was that I'd heard rumors to this effect, simply wanted to know what they thought down there. But I've botched the nuanced Indian protocol I'm only starting to get, have made Swami-ji look bad by going over his head. Class is postponed till I get on the phone and straighten out the confusion.

"I am completely fine," I tell them in Delhi. "The students of Udaipur are concerned for the welfare of our families, but we are resting assured in Swami-ji's capable hands." Even so, he cancels my trip to Jaipur for the weekend.

By personal tutorial, two classes on, it appears I've been forgiven. We discuss forms of address. The talk turns to caste. *"Not like in America,"* he says so often I'm provoked into an explanation of de facto caste before I realize I don't have the chops. *"In America too is,"* I argue. *"Bankmen is not eating with janitors."* Swami-ji looks startled.

"But, Kathy-ji," he says in a rush, *"the students come here, they want Samta-ji and Vidhu-ji to sit down and eat with Raju,"* the cook; no *"ji." "I try to say in India that's not how it's done. They say in America, everyone eats together, servants and teachers."* In America, everyone would eat together once for show, then striations would reappear, I want to say, but we'll be here all day if I try. *"Ask the students how many times last year their parents dined out with black friends"* is morphologically possible, but tinged irony doesn't translate well into Hindi. Swami-ji would be handing out questionnaires on the subject tomorrow. I settle for *"We are having there a famous saying,* 'Class is America's dirty little secret.'" *"Claj ish,"* he repeats, rapidly feeling around for a pen. When he breaks into English, it's somewhat embarrassing, like a dad appearing at a slumber party.

In vocabulary, Vidhu leads with the sounds animals make. A *singh*, a lion, says *dahaarna*. Monkeys go *kitkitana* in the infinitive. I'm suspicious whether camels grumble *balbalaana*, don't think that donkeys say *renkhna*. Amazing, if they can manage the *kh* sound. The class is Hindi hip-hop. "'*Weak*' and '*man who doesn't work*' are linked," he says, building rhythm. *"Patience"* and *"slowly"* have the same root. "Antidote" is *tor*, from *torna*, "to break." "Indians just make up words like magicians," he says, cutting tempo for an aside. "They amaze me. They are uneducated, but they come up with these words. *Tor* is something that breaks the poison." *Ji-tor-kam:* "spirit-break-work." "*Jitorkam*'s when your heart is stretched to such limits, you don't give emotion to anything but the work," he says. "You don't give a second to your parents, your friends, or even to yourself." More felicitous than the English "workaholism." And *munhtor jawab,* "a mouth-breaking answer": you leave someone speechless.

Udaipur, increasingly, has become a mouth breaker. More and more, it leaves me speechless, even as words accumulate and by their weight pull me in. As words build to centrifugal force, Udaipur begins to seem so familiar, it takes exertion to see it's not. To notice that a street dentist sits on Station Road with used dentures for sale. That scooters speed past auto rickshaws, domed Ambassadors stall behind ambling sacred cows: Elsies with red bindi marks and humps. I don't register the rickshaws stirring up the yellow dust anymore, the low rows of open-air shops across from the cybercafe. My eye adjusts, I adjust to the sweetness of life here, sweet as Raju's morning lemon chai.

Late morning, I excuse myself from film discussion class, meet a visiting Australian journalist for lunch at her hotel, at its pretty rooftop restaurant. It's October, but we have to find a table in the shade. I splurge on spinach paneer and a peanut butter sandwich. "No thanks," she says. "I don't much fancy that." We stop by Biotech, an improbably elegant lotions shop, and drop way too much on saffron face creams and pistachio face packs and something called Bhringraj Therapeutic Oil. Afterward, I lie in a charpoy, a string bed, in the back, and a woman coaxes me out of my clothes, piece by piece, and as her sons scramble back and forth under the drawn curtain, gives me a long, full massage, even to my breasts. I doze and then wake with a particularly deep stroke, doze and wake.

The natural rhythms of life here begin to arrange my day. Afternoons, heated, are now largely indolent, evenings fantastically lush: rounds of raga concerts and poetry readings, dinner parties at Piers's. On his terrace, I listen to English ghost stories in the ruffly summer night air (except it's fall), debate whether ghosts exist in India. "Reincarnation probably puts them out of work," a dinner guest says. We eat perfect lasagna the Nepalese houseboys have made and watch the eerie diamond lights of the Monsoon Palace go on. I'm astounded, again, that I've stepped out of my old life and into this incense-laden one, at one month so fully formed. I hadn't known *Brigadoon* was a Hindu myth. "I've never been so happy," I e-mail a friend back home, leave it at that. My mouth is broken. I can't convey how I shine with happiness, roll in happiness, look again to see this extraordinary place I've come. Days, brilliant lime-colored birds swoop down from the palace to skim emerald green Lake Pichola; even an algae infestation here seems magical.

At the Jains', I've begun to chafe at the curfew they impose, 9 P.M., but otherwise I'm nestled in. It's steady state, companionable. In the mornings, we have thick oily fenugreek pancakes. Then Jain Dad 2 takes us out for a spin. After that, everything falls apart.

Part II

· 6 ·

"Let's leave now"

Afterward, you could have summarized it like this: One day, for reasons that were highly suspicious and quite likely extremely perverse, Rajesh, Dad 2, took the Whisperer and me downtown and dumped us by the side of the road. I wouldn't have put it that way, but apparently a report in that form reached Swami-ji, for we were scarcely back home when he was on the horn. There were official visits, pointed inquiries, strong denials. And even once the dust from the scooters had settled, there was trouble that lingered for a long time.

I'd have described events more like this: One Sunday when there was nothing to do but sit around and pretend to admire the neighbor's baby (whose butt was never covered, so made me extremely nervous when he was placed in my lap to coo over, which was frequently), I was crossing the driveway back to my room when Rajesh asked me to go for a ride. He extended the same invitation in animated Hindi to the Whisperer. I was surprised when my housemate, who had a dubious regard for Indian men in general and Jain Dad 2 in particular, agreed.

"But where do you want to go?" Rajesh asked as he and I waited in the car for the Whisperer to get her things.

"I don't know," I said. I was confused. His tone suggested I'd roped him into this outing, but his invitation had been quite enthusiastic. He'd stood by the Maruti and, waving his arms toward the interior, exclaimed, "Come on! Let's go sightseeing!"

"You don't know?" He shook his head like I was incorrigible. *"But where do you want to go?"* he repeated.

"I thought you said we were going sightseeing," I said in my crypto-Hindi, which, translated, went, "Touring . . . not?"

"You want to go for a beer?" he asked, switching to English. I blinked. First they all ate garlic, now this? When I said I wasn't much of a drinker, he backtracked. "That's good, that's good, that's good," he said.

The Whisperer climbed into the back seat beside me. I asked where she thought we were off to. "The bazaar," she said tightly. "That's what he told me." But bazaar plans appeared to have been scrapped. We drove down the highway, past the old army cantonment and the signs that said AVOID FORCIBLE SHOPPING, and occasionally Dad 2 would note a point of interest: a traffic roundabout, the place where he brought his office printing.

"I'm a tour guide," he said with a chuckle.

"How do we pay you?" the Whisperer snapped. She gave me a look.

"Not much," he said. "Just a beer." Eventually, we pulled up to Sukhadia Circle. "I need to go do business matter for five minutes," he said, pointing to the curb. "I'll be back at six, okay?" It was now 5:20.

"He'll show up at six-forty-five." I gave the Whisperer my best psychic estimate as we stood on the sidewalk brushing ourselves off.

"Yeah," she said, "and he'll probably plow into us." We sat on a bench by little Chetak Lake and watched the swan boats, then waited on a bench as a nearby Indian family watched us. At 6:30, the Whisperer couldn't hold out any longer. We flagged a rickshaw home.

Late that night, long about one, a car could be heard sliding up the drive. At breakfast, the Whisperer was regarding her plate with a look of strained forbearance. By afternoon, the Jains' phone was blaring. It had not been six months since Delhi had had to speak to Swami-ji about the carousing that had gone on under his nose the time the student ran off with the teacher. His response had been swift: calls to the Indian FBI to see if he could press trafficking charges against the guy, but all the same, the stain was not diminished. If one word of this situation—a host father cruising for beer with two charges—got back to Delhi, he could expect to be conjugating verbs at the elementary school down the street. For a while, I thought he was going to airlift us out of the Jains', but when no consequences attended the drive of infamy, I decided all parties had moved on. "Well, the swan boats were nice," I concluded, assuming the event was now behind us. The event, however, was only out of sight. It had not, whatsoever, been forgotten. Not in any quarter.

MID-OCTOBER NOW. The mornings are colder. The water in the bathroom is like a lake when I rise. *"We will be getting you a geezer soon,"* Jain Dad 1, Rajkumar, informs me, in the nasally local lockjaw that makes the men here sound like James Cagney on Hindi: *We're getting you a geezer, you dirty rat.* "What's a geezer?" I ask Helaena at school. "A water heater," she explains. Spelled "geyser."

Mornings are chilly, but midday is desert hot, ropy air through till three. The concentrated heat is like a scent, dust made muddy, which enters through the pores. When scientists announced they may have found olfactory receptors in the skin, no one who'd been to India could have been surprised. The heat slows the blood, thickens marrow, warps thought. A friend sends an e-mail about a fall bonfire she attended instead of a crisp orange-leafed setting, I imagine a scene out of Thomas Kinkade: pulsing, irreal glade with radiated foxgloves.

The e-mail's one of the few I've received that hasn't been about the attacks. From this side of the divide, the preoccupation appears feverish, relentless in a way that's self-absorbed. The event, from over here, seems to be spinning off into its own world, disconnected from the other longitudes. "How does it feel to be in a country without terrorism?" an acquaintance e-mails me the day after thirty-nine more were killed in Kashmir. I could write back and say, How does it feel not to know that seventy thousand, by some counts, have died from terrorism here in the past thirty years? Except then I'd be ranting.

On the shank end of an afternoon, when it's cooler and I can move, I phone Anukul, the teacher from the deaf school, the one with the red glasses. "Come visit," he says, and gives me directions. His house is way out, almost in the foothills of the Aravallis, the ancient mountain chain that encircles the town. "Yes, come." He has a plan for what I can do at the school.

"Simple life, high thoughts," he says, quoting Gandhi, when he shows me into the main room: flat white walls, one day bed, metal grates on the windows. On the floor, a sweet-faced girl is propped on her elbows above a book. "She has a sharp mind, but she does not want to read or learn," Anukul says, giving his daughter a scowl. She and her younger sister collapse into giggles.

Rita, his wife, beautiful in a green sari, nods somberly when we're introduced, takes a seat on the floor. Anukul pulls a book down from a shelf. It's called *The Indian Signing System,* a handbook of official Indian Sign Language. He and I practice the alphabet. Rita leans back and stares at me. Anukul pages ahead to words. "Address." He demonstrates how to sign it: palm stamped by fist. I try, giving mine a wide, merry flourish, smiling so Rita can see. *Oh, what fun! I am compelled to come here and learn deaf school signing in the spirit of friendship.* Her face assumes the expression mine would if a guest in my home had, uninvited, begun doing the merengue across the floor.

Anukul advises me to tone it down. Apparently I've just signed "AD-DA-DA-DRESS!" "My children do this," he says, repeating the more restrained version. "But in the book, you slap your palm with the back of your hand," he notes with interest, and I vaguely remark on the fact that the kids aren't using standard Indian sign.

After an hour, my concentration is shot. "How do you say 'love'?" I ask. "Already today I teach you," he says, but he shows me again: one hand petting the outstretched back of the other. He calls his oldest daughter over and strokes her hair. She lays her head in his lap. He and I knock off, and he outlines his plan: I can come to the deaf school each Friday and help him teach an art class, on two conditions. We discuss the main one: would I be willing to try to learn sign language?

How long, I wonder, would that take? "An hour," he says, and the prospect that something in India, finally, could be grasped in finite time makes me exclaim, "All right!" Later, when I'm more educated in sign, I'll realize he meant "per session."

Sign language isn't a kind of freewheeling pantomime that you make up as you go along, contrary to what many people assume — contrary to what most specialists believed up until the 1950s. Even in schools for the deaf, it was regarded as "a sort of broken English of the hands," as the neurologist Oliver Sacks says about the perception U.S. educators had, but in actuality, sign is a full and bona fide language, in every sense of the word. A sign language has its own proper syntax and complex morphologies, a precise grammar that jibes with what Noam Chomsky described as a generative grammar, meaning that an infinite number of correct sentence constructions can be produced (generated) once you know a small number. Sign is protean, the way all languages are: dialects develop; initially startling slang runs through communities and then sets as quotidian words and phrases. It is "the equal of speech," Sacks writes in *Seeing Voices,* "lending itself equally to the rigorous and the poetic—to philosophical analysis or to making love—indeed with an ease that is sometimes greater than speech."

Sign can be learned in an hour, in other words, if you're John Travolta with a supernatural brain disorder in the movie *Phenomenon;* the same rule of thumb applies here as with any spoken tongue: mastering one will take you a good five years, the e-mails that promise "Learn a Language in Your Car!" notwithstanding. At 60 miles per hour, consider, you'd have to drive around for 2,904,000 miles before you could pull over to the multiplex and skip the subtitles.

"Wow, but then you could communicate with deaf people everywhere," a friend said when, a couple of years on, I described my efforts to learn Udaipur sign. The idea is appealing—a visual code that transcends all languages, a workable Esperanto at last—but it's another common misconception. There is no universal sign language. At least as many sign languages exist as there are countries in the world. One article puts the figure at two hundred, but going on caseworker reports from India, I'd say there are that many on the subcontinent alone, hardly any of them mutually comprehensible. If you use one kind of sign, you'll be no more able to follow another than a French speaker will be to understand German. In Udaipur, an extended deaf family lived downtown. They'd learned their gesturing elsewhere, and whenever they paid a visit to the school, the kids were as stumped as I was.

From the corner of the room, Rita continues to regard me as the conversation wheels out to include general questions I have. Why aren't there more girls at the school? "We know thirty are waiting to come," Anukul says. "But the court has banned building in the area, so we are not getting permission for a hostel. We have limitations. We can't have big dreams. We have small."

And have I really seen only one hearing aid at the school? "We have hearing aids," he says. "The government provides them. But we cannot afford to replace the wires that are necessary to make them operate." He gives the figure for the cost of a new wire: the equivalent of thirty-seven cents.

So it's all set: I'll come then? No, he says. Better if I type up a formal proposal and present it to Mr. Paliwal, the headmaster. And maybe don't tell him that he, Anukul, knows about this. And maybe don't say that he thought of it. I'd forgotten: strictures of hierarchy.

I ask him about his marriage: was it arranged? Of course it was. "How can you fall in love that way?" I blurt, immediately regretting my rudeness, but the process still startles me. Without knowing I had one, I've maintained a lifelong position on arranged marriage: no one in the U.S. does that because it's a poor idea, that's why. "I don't know," Anukul says, face softening as he looks over at Rita. "But we are."

My driver raps at the door. We all stand. Anukul decides to try to broker an alliance. *"Do you want to ask her any questions?"* He asks his cool customer of a wife, nodding toward me. She shakes her head, smiles in a way that back home in the South would mean *Ah-gwine*.

"Do you want to ask her any questions?" He turns to me. I'm equally at a loss. An intensity appears on his face. "Ask her if she thinks her husband loves her," he says. I do, in Hindi, and she answers in kind, too rapidly for me to catch. Her cocked eyebrow suggests she's won this round.

"What did she say?" I ask. His face has lit up.

"She says she wouldn't be here if she didn't."

On the rickshaw ride home, I think about his second condition. Could I track down journals about deaf education and teaching materials for deaf students? Could I find him a book on American sign?

"I am helping you," he said, "because I am *laalchi*. I need to tell you this. I have a bad motive. I am *laalchi*. I want to teach the children literature." There were, he said, no extra funds, for anything. "I earn . . ." and he named a sum that was the equivalent of a hundred dollars a month. "I have not bought new clothes in two years. But I am not a poor man. I have my heart. And I have my hands."

He was, though, he repeated, *laalchi*.

"*Laalchi?*"

"*Laalchi*. Like, oh, *laalchi*. You don't know it?" I didn't but I said I'd get him the book.

At home, I found the dictionary, opened to the Ls. *Laayaq, laar*, there it was, *laalchi*. *Laalchi* meant "greedy." Anukul was greedy for his boys.

IN SCHOOL I'VE entered the long-haul trudge. Novelty's worn off. The catatonia that came from jet lag mixed with numbness—cultural, worldwide shock—has subsided. I pick my way along the path, keep my eyes on the ground, try to get to the next plateau. "Language learning is not a linear process," a brochure we received during orientation advised. "It works as a series of plateaus." Students would swear they weren't making any progress, then magically find they'd been bumped up the mountain. But the brochure didn't mention any complicating factors—the adrenalized sprints, for instance, that result when students conduct their studies with a guard posted at the door.

Our front door is now manned by a uniformed guard, a skinny guy who appears more nervous than even Swami-ji, a kid who looks as if he spends late nights figuring what he'd do if armed terrorists burst from the elevator without warning. Make a run for it, you can tell. But Swami-ji's hired him for that possibility exactly, and for once Swami-ji is not acting entirely out of hysteria. Tensions are rising around the world. People everywhere are bracing for more attacks. Until recently, there was an Al Qaeda operative living nearby. Muslims in other parts of the world have lately gone after Americans; we're among the few Americans here: the easily locatable, last remaining ones in town.

"The sign out front does not say American on it," he tells us, I think, to calm himself. *"It has the school's initials only."* But though the sign may not say that, the fact is I do. When I open my mouth, it's all shibboleths. People with high motivation to change their accents sometimes do, a sociolinguist named Dennis Preston told me; otherwise, the undertaking is dodgy. "You take Henry Kissinger and say, How does this man sound like he just got off the boat from Germany? No motivation," Preston said. "He has socioeconomic status, got beautiful women, held a key government position—why should he? But if you're a spy, it's pretty darned important, because they'll kill you. Or if you're a person who's tortured socially, you'll change."

Or if Maoist terrorists have just blown up a Coca-Cola plant to the north, precipitating a fast chutti to the south, you'll try. Maoist terrorists just have. I push myself to make the velar adjustments, to swallow sentences whole, although I know that no matter how agile I become, I won't fit in. The Tibetans outdistance me in the language, and they're still regarded as videshis, as foreigners. The Tibetans have come down from the Himalayas and set up a winter market. Their faces remind me of full fall moons, an image that comes to mind because in vocabulary Vidhu has just said, *"Chandremukhi,* 'moon face,' means 'beautiful.'"

At school, I'm still dead last, too self-conscious to push myself in front of the others, but outside, I ski Hindi, have long, gleeful conversations in shops (gleeful for me, long for my interlocutors). I kick off and really fly sometimes. "Your Hindi is very very good," rickshaw walas say, by which they mean it's intelligible. I talk till I drop, colonize my walls with Post-its that peel off in the night. I wake covered in complicated verb tenses, elaborate sentence fragments: *Jab kisiki chikhne mujhe jagaya,* when someone's scream woke me, from a comic book.

Determination makes me sanguine about some of the boggier aspects of the school—the way the language CDs in the workstation all stutter and freeze, how the two women teachers are under orders to lay off the hard-core Hindi. *"Swami-ji says you should not ask Samta-ji about grammar or vocabulary,"* small, studious Vanita tells me one day. *"He says you should not ask me either,"* she adds. When I ask Vidhu about this—fully half the Hindi teachers are requested to refrain from teaching full-out Hindi?—he cuts Samta a sharp look, changes the subject. Later, I'll remember the moment exactly. For now, I press on. *To acquire a language,* I flog myself, *you have to give up your accumulated assurances—this is how you say things, this is how it's done.* Pretty soon, I give up my American pretenses that things should be any way at all.

SAMTA IS PERMITTED to do light lifting. She's allowed to work on our pronunciation. *"Mat, math,"* she says during dictation, running a finger under type so small, it appears to be scurrying off the page. *"Mat, math,"* she says in a singsong, across a desk so large it takes up half the side room. I shake my head: can't get it, no. To an Indian, the sounds are as distinct as their meanings: "don't" and "monastery." To my ear, they're identical, *mat*.

"Bhatt, baat!" she sings, same chirpy tempo with which she says, "I am com-ple-te-ly fine!" each morning.

"Bhatt, baat?" she says, in a tone that asks, *Clear?* All I hear is a stutter: *bat-bat*. Speech is an illusion, the psychologist Steven Pinker writes, "a river of breath bent into hisses and hums by the soft flesh of the mouth and throat." The tiniest particles in the current are called phonemes, the smallest splices of sound: *aa, bu, cii*. In ordinary speech, we run through ten to fifteen phonemes per second, though souped-up, machine-pressed ads—"Tuesday! Tuesday! Atthepoconospeedway"—can pack in nearly fifty before the pitch goes from breathless to a buzz. Among the world's 6,500 or so languages, thousands of phonemes exist, all distinct to their speakers from

plain noise. You notice the ting of a fork on a glass, know it's not a semantically meaningful part of the toast. Given that everything you say is constructed of these bits, it's remarkable how few it takes to make a language. Pirahã, from Brazil, relies on just ten: seven consonants, three vowels. English, in the average range, has between thirty-five and forty-five.

"Bhaat, baat," Samta insists, but the aspirated Hindi *bh* is lost on me. Lost to me. There was a time, very early, when I'd have heard it at once. At birth, we have the potential to discern all the speech sounds used around the globe: the throaty Polish *dz*, like a slipped *j* to Americans, the high-*ba* and low-*ba* pitch phonemes of Mandarin. Phonologically, in infancy "we're citizens of the world," the neuroscientist Patricia Kuhl says, though even before we leave the womb, basic sound settings for our own language are in place. At birth, our brains are already tuned to the prosody, the characteristic lilt, of whatever our mother's tongue is. When tapes in French and Russian were played for four-day-old French newborns, the babies sucked harder on hearing the French, a sign that it was already familiar. For a brief period early in life, we can easily register anything anyone from anywhere says, then we can't. By six months, our ability to detect other cultures' vowels is waning, though other cultures' consonants remain clear for a while.

"Natnat." Again I say it, once more like the Three Stooges. Rhythms of speech are acquired before speech sounds, laid down like tracks. When a tape of babbling eight-month-olds of different nationalities was played for a group of French infants, they could tell the proto–French speakers from the Arabic or Chinese. But by the time we're a year old, through our mother's cooing and baby talk, our ears become set to our own small parcel of phonemes. Nature locks us into our tribes early.

"P-h-an, p-h-al, p-h-il, p-h-auj." But the grand finale bombs when my brain fails to grasp its similarity to Buddy Holly hiccups. *Paan-paal.* We try video clips instead. Faces of slack-jawed boys

appear on the screen. "The mentally retarded," Samta says. "They have wandered away from their homes." *"Laapataa hai?"* I ask, words from the newscast. *Laapataa hai* means "missing," she says: we are piecing together language from photographs of missing children. *"Chhota tha,"* the announcer says: "He was small."

The next one is stocky. He looks dazed by his fate, continues to stare bewildered from the screen after Helaena knocks and Samta presses Pause. Helaena is here for the neem sticks Samta's brought to soothe her nose, which is red as cooked shrimp on one side. Helaena takes a chair and eases out the gold stud. "Samta-ji," she says, once she's left off hooting. "When are we going to meet with your husband?" Samta's husband, Manesh, is an architect and astrologer, though presently without work in either capacity. There's been talk we'd go over, he'd cast our charts, but now Samta looks uncomfortable.

"Swami-ji has said we should not get together outside school," she says.

"Just to talk about architecture?" I ask.

She looks pained. "Maybe after," she says, won't say after what.

"He's a weird guy with dyed orange hair," says a woman who comes through on business. She was a student here several years ago. Slept through classes, was the black sheep of her year, she says, laughing, at dinner. Now she uses the language all the time, in the export business she started. The batiks her second host family made were a hit in the States. Her first host family, Samta's, lasted four weeks. She's quiet when I ask why she moved out, eventually allows: some trouble with Manesh. "He's a weird guy," she repeats when I press for details. Then she's eager to know: do I think I'll buy a scooter while I'm here?

UP AT PIERS'S, on his terrace, there was a tabletop disco ball you could hook up to music and make throb to the beat. Back home, it would have been embarrassing. Here it was arresting, as blatantly unusual as his collection of silver spoons behind glass downstairs. It wasn't Indian. One night at a dinner party, I tried it out on the Gayatri Mantra, a haunting chant I couldn't stop playing, both to see what it would do and because I wanted to hear the song some more. The music made the machine bleat light dyspeptically, then go black. It wasn't disco. Piers switched tapes. Soon "You're My Everything" was clashing with the muezzin calling from a mosque down the slope. The machine was growling light, making everyone at the table think of cologne and arms pumping dry ice. Everyone but the Indians, who that night included the jigri.

When I arrived, he approached in a nimbus of intensity. "You know me," he said. "We met at Sixteen Chefs. But your face is different."

"Her face is different?" Piers said with a laugh. He came over to examine me, mugging like he'd found something. "Her face isn't different!" he said.

"It's different," the jigri said. "Your eyes are red."

"They aren't," I told him. They weren't. Piers's mother, in a lounger that supported her braced leg, rapped sharply with a matchbox on a table.

"Mother, stop that banging," Piers said. After one of the houseboys helped her up to bed, he said, "A stroke is such a vicious thing."

On the terrace, the table was half-Indian, half-Western. The Indian contingent was better represented: cricket player, police chief, a woman who worked at an NGO. Over *chota*-pegs of whiskey, deviled eggs, and plates of Manchurian vegetables, we discussed the surveys Piers had been conducting at the tourist center. Someone had written in "Piers for mayor." "Nightmare," he said, grinning. He rose and went over to the table by the door to fiddle with the disco ball's connections. Light started to thump, flashed the evening ahead, so that when I checked my watch, it was already past nine, after the Jains' curfew. The jigri leapt to his feet when I did. He had his scooter. He'd give me a lift.

On our way out, he decided to pitch in with my Hindi. "You should say *meharbaani,* not *meharbani,*" he said: double *a.* I'd been trying for a flowery form of "thanks."

"*Haaan?*" I said, stretching the word the way I would have in English, to show polite, concentrated interest. *Yeees?*

"And don't say '*haaan,*'" the jigri said irritably. "It sounds like you think you're better than other people. The maharana says '*haaan.*' You should say it '*haan.*'" Crisp and to the point. On the scooter, we tacked past sleeping cows, sped around corners and down steep hills. I turned my head sideways to keep my hair from stinging, thought about a story I'd heard once.

A Canadian musicologist was doing research at a school for in-digenous kids when a number of the children in one class stopped coming. Their parents sent notes saying they were ill. But when a number of days went by and the students were still absent, the ad-ministrators held a meeting. The musicologist sat in. The adminis-trators couldn't think what was wrong. A mass attack of the flu or colds would have resolved itself by now. And the school year had started on such a high note. A very bright, really nice American teacher had come to the school. He was teaching the class. After-ward, the musicologist wondered about this detail. He wanted to test a hunch. Stopping by the classroom, he asked the new teacher's permission to try an experiment. The musicologist positioned him-self at the back; he took out a pencil and kept time as the teacher and the students remaining spoke. A smile soon crept onto his face. Exactly as he'd suspected—the American teacher spoke much more quickly than the kids. The teacher had, the musicologist concluded, been throwing the children off their rhythms, to the point they felt ill. Maybe, I considered, as the jigri and I careened around trash piles, I was making the man sick.

In tutorial several days after, Swami-ji was going on about local customs. *". . . and the color red is very important. For example"*—the English poked me awake—*"when a girl gets married, she wears a red sari. Do you know why? At a wedding, the center of attention is the girl. And in a prism, red is the straightest line. The red sari will scientifically draw the guests' eyes! Red also is the color of creation. Red is the color of anger, or love. The Indians,"* he said, *"believe that when a person falls in love, red threads appear in the eyes, the eyes turn red."* India reprising word after word. But the jigri was wrong. It was only dust, or mostly.

"WE HAVE SOCIAL PROBLEMS, equipment problems," Mr. Paliwal says in English after I hand him the proposal, addressing his remarks to the paper. Mr. Paliwal, Anukul's boss, has neatly oiled hair, brightly shined shoes, the tense arms of the second language learner suddenly aware of his shortcomings. His spring-loaded arms announce, *Anyone can hear me talking like this, even that woman there.* A tiny woman with a whiskbroom has drifted in through a curtain that's the same faded blue as the walls. She doesn't so much as glance over as he says, "The boys are rural. Some are tribals"—the original inhabitants of India; aboriginal. "They are coming sometimes fifteen, sixteen. What can we do with them?"

We join together in regarding the battered ledgers on his desk. "Some teachers won't like it," he says after a while, in the direction of the woman's departing back.

"Indians aren't generous," he tells a wall calendar.

"Ask Anukul what he thinks," he finally says, and when he looks at me and smiles, the effect is jolting, like metal crashing by my head.

When I stop by Anukul's classroom to tell him we're on, he decides to get a jump on my signing lessons. "Ask that boy what his mother's name is," he says, nodding at a thin kid who glances nervously right and left. The boy's about eleven. The ages in the classroom range from nine to a gawky fifteen. "How?" I ask. Anukul shows me. "You," he says, and points to the boy, who appears to be forcing himself through nerves of steel not to bolt for the door.

"Mother," Anukul says, and brushes the side of his nose.

"'Nose?'" I interrupt. "A mother is a nose?"

"Nose ring," he says. "For daughter you do like this," and we go off on a digression, with me attempting "daughter" (nose brush, swing fingertips to the shoulder) and Anukul correcting my hand positioning.

By the time we return to the boy, he looks as if he's stopped breathing: *Youmotherdaughter,* Anukul has just signed, gibberish, and this is a test.

We try foods. *"What do you like?"* Anukul asks the class. *"Mango?"* He peels one. *"Apple?"* He takes a bite. *Potato* is a tap on the cheek, because, he explains, a potato's peel is the same color as skin. *Chicken* is a hand-on-hand finger flap, fun to do but gets no takers, the majority of the class being vegetarian and Hindu. The one Muslim, the only girl, doesn't eat poultry either. A few hands shoot up on *goat:* forefingers pointed skyward against temples. Several Rajput boys, one tribal, and as Anukul counts the goat eaters, a thought occurs: *This is the one place I've been in India where the castes and religions come together.*

The signing word order seems to follow Hindi's exactly: *To me . . . potato . . . pleasing . . . is,* verb at the end. Some of the boys keep on track precisely, a little stiffly. Others get to midword, *potato,* look befuddled, drop off. It helps to know what I figure is the template language to remember this gestured one. "Learning Rajasthani sign was like learning kinetic Hindi!" I'll excitedly report to friends when I'm back in the States, but when I told the linguist Deborah Tannen this, she sounded puzzled. "It's my understanding that signed grammar doesn't follow spoken grammar," she said, and she was right, of course, when I checked.

Turns out, there was a reason for all this. But I wouldn't come to discover it for a couple more years.

Do I eat meat, a boy, looking slightly green, wants to know. When I see how you sign that one—head decapitation—I do the sensible thing. I lie and say no.

We fly through meal possibilities, express gustatory preferences, and by the end of the hour, gawkers are lined up four deep outside the door. They discuss the proceedings. They sign what I recognize is my name: vertical right hand speeding into the raised left palm. Name signs, like spoken nicknames, evolve from some association about a person that immediately springs to mind. Anukul's name sign is squared hands to face: "Glasses." A rangy reporter who wrote about a Nicaraguan deaf school he visited came to be known by the sign for "tall." The whole year, I'll be startled again whenever someone excitedly greets me by my name here: "Plane Crashing into Tower." On the outskirts of Udaipur, I am the World Trade Center.

ALL THESE SIDE excursions conferred benefits beyond revved language. They meant I didn't have to hang out with Harold, who was becoming more of a live wire each time I looked. At a temple, he got choked up at the sight of Shiva's lingam, Shiva's iconographic penis statue. Near the school, I ran into him wandering the streets, shaking his fist at passersby. "That's right, bud," he was saying with a sneer. "That's right. I'm speaking English—what do you want to make of it?" Harold had had a little too much Hindi.

At school, when the day ended and we'd sometimes stay on, he was itchy, at loose ends after more than a month of no recognizable Saturday nights, no Friday nights, no goddamn, for that matter, Wednesdays. He'd been in the same day too long. "You've found the deaf school. Helaena's found a prince. I'm going to find a bar," he complained. He'd resumed a drinking habit the previous summer.

The Whisperer, too, was showing signs of strain. Some mornings, she was spotted being led, trembling, from the back office, overcome, she said, by incessant pestering by men. A yoga instructor was sexually harassing her, and an art shop owner, then gangs on the street, but after she left a letter lying around in which she apologized to the art shop guy for going over and taking her shirt off, concern lessened.

At school, that is. At home, she was making me jumpy. She'd developed an odd tic: whatever I had, she had to have, too. "I'm going to go in early and read the paper," I'd say at breakfast, then arrive fifteen minutes later to find her gripping the *Times of India,* a triumphant expression on her face. I mentioned a camel safari I had planned for Christmas. She hopped a train and journeyed to the Great Thar for the dromedary action that weekend. I got on the school's computer. She needed it immediately. ("Oh, right, make the Indian go," she said darkly when I suggested she use the cybercafe down the street.) The Whisperer, it was becoming clear, spoke softly but was a flaming ball of competition. She called people she'd never met, with whom I was lunching, to say she'd be joining us, slid in between when I was with a Jain and fuel-injected the conversation to levels I couldn't follow, stole a study date with Harold out from under me.

That should have been the least of it, but for some reason, it was the last straw. "Final answer?" Vanita asked when I said I was moving out. "Final answer," I said sadly, but when I went home to tell the Jains, a remarkable thing occurred. In Alka's room, on the bed where we'd all assembled, the wives and kids began wailing. Alka grabbed my leg. Various family members flung themselves on top of me.

"You can't leave us alone with her!" one girl wailed through her sister's hair. "We cry to have her in the house."

"She calls Swami-ji to complain about us."

"She said my father asked her for a beer."

"She will not speak to us, or even *namaste* us."

"And we do not like her clothes," Meenal, the youngest, said.

"It's us. Tell the truth," Alka said, crying. The weeping and fling-ing continued for an hour. Finally, I was no match for the com-mando Jains. I left to visit Renee, and in my absence, the upstairs dweller and her questionable clothing were shown the door.

On my return, the mood in the kitchen was exclamatory. "Tension-free!" Alka cried when I walked in.

"Yay! We got our room back!" one of the girls shouted. The ar-rival of the Whisperer had forced the kids to bunk down with their parents.

"I hear her new family is very mean. Sometimes they don't give food," Meenal, the youngest, said hopefully.

"Karma," I said, but she just looked perplexed.

· 7 ·

"My car is stuck (in the mud/in the ditch)"

 When it started to become clear that Harold was losing his mind, it was around the time I lost my face, not long after the Whisperer had to go live with the family that did, in fact, forget to feed her. Dissolution by language was taking us all down, though in Harold's case, he appeared to have help.

Harold had developed an extended back problem, one that required a number of visits to the pharmacy. "If you're a videshi, they'll give you anything, so long as you don't send your servant," a friend of a friend in Delhi had e-mailed when I wrote from the States to ask about drugstore supplies in India. I thought about Harold's back when he glowered at lunch, threw bread at a chair. He hadn't agreed with the opinion I'd just expressed, that Raju used too much salt. When my mispronunciation of a long Hindi *a* nearly made him choke, I ate Raju's weepy spinach and watched him. "Oh, he's just like that," the Whisperer said after. This was before he revealed plans to kill her.

"That's just the way he is" was the covering line the other two used for a long time. "Oh, that's just the way he is," they'd say, as if he were a puckish coot in overalls instead of a guy in tight shorts who'd go off his rocker at the sight of Indians speaking Hindi. Mine was "Well, he and I are different." That one worked as long as it did because it was so roundly applicable. When Harold and I encountered wedding fireworks on leaving the palace, for example, I didn't stand glint-eyed on the balcony, making hallucinatory comments about how Helaena must have arranged these for us. This was one instance in which our differences put me ahead, but there were others, particularly in language learning styles, for which I envied him.

There are two kinds of language learners, Gabriela, my New York teacher, had said when I'd complained that I couldn't absorb Hindi by ear, was compelled to write everything down. The i-dotters, the ones who don't take the reflexive lightly ("Why do they say *se fue* in Spanish? Doesn't that mean 'he left himself'?"), linguistic Felix Ungers—these were one type, though Gabriela didn't describe them this way. "The analyticals," she'd said, using the correct term for the category into which I fell, "want to figure everything out. Even if they understand an expression, they want to know what's going on in it. What is that verb doing there? Is it always singular? They're more meticulous in note taking, in deducing the rules." The other type, called globals, can listen and learn. They are intuitive, visually oriented, approach problems spatially. When asked to take embedded-figure tests, they detect patterns, don't—as is the analyticals' tendency—key in on the figures and miss the overall picture.

I was unhappy in my division, even after the neurolinguist Michel Paradis told me that in adulthood, my kind did better with languages. In one experiment he mentioned, globals had excelled only when instructed with global methods—that is, any that emphasized conversation. Analyticals scored well with either conversational or rule-bound techniques. In Unger style, however, some of the analyticals went too far and invented grammar rules that didn't exist. And of course, Paradis added, "there was nothing to have prevented them from sneaking off and buying grammar books on the sly," in between tests, an action that did sound like one we'd take.

We were fussbudgets, and I knew it, and so I longed to be my opposite: the rakish, expansive global. I could learn from the globals, Gabriela said; their strengths were my weaknesses. Harold, for instance, was a textbook global: more interested in knowing when to use an expression than in diagramming it; undaunted by the prospect of failed verb constructions; uninhibited, willing to plunge into discussions. So even though I was instrumental in getting him kicked out of India, he and I made a good study pair, and from time to time, I'd faintly miss him.

AN INNER VOICE RETURNS in late October—a chorus, in fact, most of these voices belonging to someone else. Hindi fragments I've picked up set and blend. *"Gayab ho-gaya,"* I mutter, feeling under a shelf for my shoes. *"Gayab ho-gaya,"* what the cybercafe wala said when the computer screen went black and he fluttered bird fingers: disappeared. *"Ke saamne,"* "in front of," comes back, a snippet from the directions a tea vendor gave me. *"Is my pleasure"*—that one dates to a visit with a restaurant owner's polite, veiled wife. With Hindi acting like a stain on my thoughts, I can see the astonishing number of people, or bits of them, I've incorporated in such a short time. I'm taking the town into my head. But if words this banal could root unnoticed, couldn't more charged ones settle in as well, in a second or first language? Could half a remark the sour office gossip made—"only out for himself"—take hold and whisper to us later, make us view the man in question with newly cautious eyes? We are, through language, a lot more permeable to each other than we'd like to know.

Stray Mewari appears without warning. *Shakkar,* the Mewari word a waiter uses for "sugar," drives out the Hindi one I know: *chini.* My brain absorbs *shakkar* so quickly, you'd think it was Eng-

lish, and you'd be nearly right. It's a distant cousin, though I don't
realize that as I congratulate myself on being such a language
sponge—*you name it, it just comes to me.* The word is descended
from the Persian *shakkar,* which in turn looped down from the Sanskrit *sharkaraa:* "candied gravel." Reports of sugar's existence first
appeared in Europe in the first century, when cohorts of Alexander
the Great returned from the subcontinent with stories about an Indian cane that could produce "honey without bees." The word itself, in its Sanskrit form, surfaced soon after in the Latin and Greek
texts that lauded this exotic new medicinal tonic. In the Middle
Ages, Arab traders carried the Persian derivation along with the
sweet stuff to Italy and Spain, where the word became *zuccero* and
azucar, respectively, then proliferated, evolving into *sucre* (France),
Zucker (Germany), *sakhar* (Russia), and sugar (England and points
west). "Oh, you can use *shakkar* in Hindi, too," Helaena says when
I tell her I'm advancing in Mewari as well, whereupon it becomes
clear: I've been learning Hindi on the circular plan.

Creaky Briticisms startle me midthought. Indian English hijacks
my reflections. "I have been on this posting too long," I sigh to myself one night, weary with India. "I am merging with Udaipur," I
find myself writing in a journal, have to stop to figure out what this
character channeled from the soap opera *The Flower of Delhi* is saying. All I mean is that I'm more used to it. To the commuter goats:
at sundown, whenever I take a rickshaw into town, I pass a herd
scuffing dust along the artery from the Lake Palace hotel, being
driven home by tiny women in billowing skirts. To the post office:
at the open-air stall across from the school, the postmaster waves me
to the head of the line, preferential videshi treatment I either accept
now uneasily or decline and, in the process, confuse everyone. Caste
and social hierarchy shape everything here, post office lines, verbs.
There are seven ways to say "Don't touch that plant," depending on
whom you're addressing. At the beginning, when my American impulses still triumphed, I'd insist that rickshaw walas use verb forms

of equality with me. They'd smile oddly or lower their heads. When I caught a flash of fear on a driver's face, I understood that I was forcing him to be cheeky. I'm supposed to be imperial; that's how it is. At the head of the line, I give the postmaster my envelope. He delivers two stamps, which I bring to a glue pot and dab with a glue-encrusted pen. That's what you do.

ALONG WITH THE language, common knowledge appears unexpectedly in my thoughts. I am now mysteriously possessed of random gossip, national and local, that I know with the same utter certainty that everyone else does. I know which Bollywood star is one hundred percent, absolutely having an affair with which costar, though I can't recollect ever having had the conversation. On the local front, I know that every year, the maharana installs a new Western girl as his assistant in the palace; that every year, after about three months, he suggests they think about expanding her responsibilities. Helaena, though, close to two months along, has missed this piece of floating wisdom.

"Oh, I don't think so," she counters when I pass it along at dinner. She contemplates the chicken sizzler we're sharing. In the Rose Garden restaurant, down the slope from the palace, I'm hiding out from the vegetarian Jains.

"Uh-uh. I don't think so. He's pretty old for . . . that," she says, sentence going into a Parkinsonian freeze as she's overcome by a southern accent. *How could he?* But the Indian rulers are famous for their ability to surmount amatory obstacles. Unsightly frailties of the flesh such as sweat? Of no consequence. "Concubines were wheeled to their beds," Ann Morrow writes in *The Maharajas of India,* "so that their silken skin would not be sullied with perspiration." Personal challenges of physique? A trifling. When concern grew that the 270-pound maharaja of Kapurthala might be too corpulent to perform wedding-night duties, a contraption was built, like the one used to aid elephants, so that he could practice in advance with a courtesan. Given the collective track record, I'd think advanced age, in this case fifty-eight, is unlikely to be a hurdle.

"KA-TY," MEENA CALLS from the other side of my door. It's 9 P.M., and I've just removed my shirt, am dropping from exhaustion. But the walls are iced by loneliness tonight, and so I'm glad for the interruption, even if, precedence suggests, it means I'm about to get scolded.

Early on, Meena confined her commentary on my unsocialized behavior to smirking at Alka as it occurred. *Who was it said that's how they'd act?* her eyebrows would note as I placed my sandals on the children's backpack shelf, again. But formality has eased to a familial accord. Now she's apparently shuffled through the 153 kinship terms they tried to make us learn at school and which I'll be damned if I will, and not finding one that describes me — not *"husband's younger sister cousin"* or *"sister's husband's aunt's sister"* — come up with a 154th of her own: *distant relative with the faculties of a street cow who needs constant watching.*

"What's that?" she'll ask, strolling into my room. *That* is always something wrong. The damp evidence of an ink stain freshly scrubbed from the sheet. New pistachio throw pillows I'm wildly happy with but have gotten wildly taken on, in Meena's scoffing view. I'll shoot back an answer in chilly body language: crossed arms, pressed lips. *Three hundred fifty rupees for pillows doesn't prove the guy thinks I'm a chump,* my posture will inform her, or try to. My body is as inarticulate as the rest of me. *"You came in what time last night?"* she'll ask, switching inquiries, poking at the bottle of hydroxy acid that defies explanation. *"Beauty for skin from above is going. Death skin,"* I'd tried; now she eyes it warily.

At the center of full-time scrutiny and invisible, both, I'm wilting under Meena's blind gaze. For it intensifies a notion that's becoming conviction: this plunge into language, this devouring of new words, is not having the effect of doubling my world, but is making me disappear.

Recently, while combing my hair, I'd glanced in the mirror and froze: a face I didn't know was staring back. Apprehension had not been preparation. This face was unfortunate. Skin that, even tanned, was sallow; contours so flat they looked dispirited; a nose that refused to rise, magnificently or otherwise; an overall flaccid form. The eyes, the brackish green of an old well, squinted back, then looked away.

I willed my old features to reappear. They did, then before I could relax into relief, they flickered out again, and that was the last time all year I'd see my face.

A preposterous debate followed in my head. *Hadn't I been attractive? Or not? Or more than this? I was.* But this face was as clear as anything else that was visible to me then: the white pig snuffling out the window, the man pumping water across the street at the well. By the next day, I'd acceded to the plain and all-too-visible truth: this is how I looked, was how I looked when I came and forever before that. Who changes that drastically? To try to believe otherwise was to engage in the luxury of pumped-up memory, to make more of yourself than you were. So far from home, you could tell yourself anything.

In this world without end, I didn't consider other possibilities, one being that going into another language may, indeed, reshape you physically. "Your face gets very much changed," A. L. Becker says. "Most language sound systems have one central vowel. It's the *schwa* sound in English. In French, it's *Uu*. It's that central place that shapes your face at rest. When you're speaking, it's the recurrent place. If it's far back, it changes your cheeks, changes the way your mouth looks." I didn't consider that perhaps I'd adjusted to the fierce desert features around me, had lost some ability to register my own, was seeing myself through native eyes. Or that, more dangerously, having yanked myself out of context with no thought to how

context shapes self, I was paying a penalty, one that could be ex-
tracted again.

Context is inextricable from self—the smaller self that the Hindus say exists within us and which they call atman. In the Hindu
belief, we're all connected to an infinite self as well, this one known
as Brahman. Brahman is ultimate reality. Atman is "the reference
point from which all experience takes its meaning," theology professor Paul Younger writes, and in coming upon that observation later,
I'd think, *Yes, of course.* The self is mutable, open to experience.
That's what had enabled me to go to India in the first place, I'd reflected, what had allowed me to lose sight of myself there. But in the
misery of trying to avoid the brackish eyes, I couldn't comprehend
that then. Instead, I mourned my missing face with the same sharp
regret I felt for the missing words.

"Ka-ty," Meena calls again. Slipping my shirt on, I open the
door. *"Lock, Ka-ty, lock,"* she says dreamily from the step.

"Lock, Ka-ty," she repeats. She's been to her parents' for the festival
of Navratri, we establish. Her loose cannon of a husband stayed behind, I learn. In her dress-up green salwar kameez with two stains on
the chest, she looks Chinese and pretty, even in the room's hard neon
light. Her face has been changed as well. *She feels more loved by her
father,* I think, as in the thrum of light, we have the same conversation as always. *"Aap kaise hain? Aap kaise hain?"* "How are you? How
are you?" We are, as usual, *theek hai:* "fine." But now, after *"fine,"* we
press on. Her mother was there; her sister was there; her father, grandfather, all of them. They talked, and they ate. And if I move out, as
I'm starting to think I might, this will be the one time I haven't seen
Meena submerged, slowed, like she's turning underwater.

"OSAMA BIN LADEN on tape has said, 'When we buy American
goods, we participate in Palestinians' massacre. American companies earn wealth from Arab countries and their government
given'—fuck. Taxing place?"

"Taxes," Vidhu tells Harold.

"American companies earn wealth from their government given taxes. With this taxes three thousand million dollars per year Israel is taking. With this wealth Israel is massacring Palestinians. By means of America, bin Laden draws our attention to fanaticism. Oh, God." Harold sighs, frowns at the newspaper clipping—homework for current events hour, when, in pairs, we examine issues of the day. Last week we did "The New Saris." "Man," he groans, "I want a cigarette."

Vidhu sniggers. Him, too. I stare at the black-and-white photos of the institute's academic advisers behind his head, don't say anything for a number of reasons, the least being that when it's Harold and I together, the male teachers conduct all exchanges with him.

"On the other hand," he continues, *"fanaticism is that which—who?"*

Vidhu shakes his head. Wrong pronoun, Harold-ji.

". . . which each Muslim to nonbeliever upon declaring on him wants attack in."

Harold-ji has found a pencil, is drumming in time to his homework. *"Islam's invasion on India complete different reason is—*is for a completely different reason. *According to Islam, idol worship is prohibited and so is discrimination on the basis of caste. As a matter of fact, Hindu idol worshiper isn't."* He flips the pencil with a flourish: ta-da!

"Protestant problem is complicated. With the personal experience that believes in consuming, God's entity becomes of lesser importance. Therefore, American Protestant disbelievers have been made . . ." He recaptures the pencil, elaborately rotates his head, the way bodybuilders do: cricked neck. On the foreheads of the academic advisers, I notice, someone has dabbed respectful tilaks, the sandalwood paste marks that on women, are called bindis.

"Both sides weakness afflicted by," he proceeds in a monotone. *"One side American exploitation is whose democracy's cloak came dressed in, Protestant individualism is, other side, fanaticism is,"* he says,

drumming faster to get to the end. *"Thus situation in struggle to solution to come. War is inevitable."*

I don't say anything because Vidhu wouldn't understand why I'd take exception. But we are teaching Hindi only. I don't say anything because the voice I had is leaving me; because the new one is shaky; because I remain in the tense-armed slump, in that language stage where comprehension outstrips the ability to speak, to say much more than *"wrong talk is."*

I became acquainted with this stage during a study-abroad semester in France (became reacquainted, to be precise; everyone goes through it with a first tongue). But when you're nineteen, the prolonged agonies of what linguists call "foreigner talk"—your own and the dumbed-down responses it pulls—aren't that dissimilar to the prolonged agonies of teenage life. *Je pense . . . rien.* In both cases, you're resigned to sounding stupid while comprehending more than anyone knows.

Speaking garbled Hindi now is, in a way, easier. With Hindi, I have the surprise element. "The first time I saw a Westerner speaking Hindi, it was like seeing a chicken barking," Vidhu recently remarked. "Until then, I thought they were just coming here walking on their toes, looking at us like animals. But when a foreigner came to my house and started speaking Hindi, I was like, *va!* My whole world changed." In France, the simple fact that I was saying it in their language elicited eye rolling and contempt. In India, I can mangle words till they squeak, but the fact that I'm saying anything at all provokes astonishment. "Oh, very good! Very good!" someone will invariably say after a sentence such as *"Your shoes are nice."* I set up the cheap ego trick, fall for it constantly, don't care that it's merely proof that there aren't a lot of other leghorns talking.

But the thrills to be had now by asking for more bread only go so far. There's still the daily schism to contend with, of having the mind of a woman who's worked to have one and a voice that's the Indian equivalent of a U.S. sitcom character named Babu. At nineteen, I'd been monosyllabic anyway. At forty-five, I have something to say on reading in class, *"Our political leadership is the culprit of compromise with Islam, but there is also an invisible enemy: our liberal public opinion"*—nationalist right-wing *Hindutva* talk—but when I try to, once again I can't.

The split can be nearly unbearable, but it's only an extreme instance of what's commonplace with language. "Even in English, comprehension can exceed your production abilities," Sydney Lamb pointed out when we got on this subject. "We can understand the writing of William Shakespeare but cannot begin to reproduce it. We admire the saxophone riffs of John Coltrane, can't wail like him."

With a second language, speech lags until you're fluent, one reason this stage is so exasperating. Because it's not truly a stage, it's a marathon, an irrational undertaking: the minute you're in it, you're unbalanced and can expect to stay that way for some time.

Recently, a cognitive neurolinguist at the University of Washington made an extraordinary discovery about the extent to which our brains understand more than we can say. Lee Osterhout scanned neophyte French students, kids in a 101 class, using an ERP (event-related potential) machine, a device that measures electrical activity in the brain. At two weeks in, after test participants had received only eight hours of instruction, Osterhout attached electrodes to their scalps and showed them lists of words. Some were French, some were made-up. When the students were asked to say which were which, they did as expected: scored, on average, 50 percent. They guessed, in other words. Nothing surprising there, but here's the part that, if a scientist hadn't been relating it to me, would have been a little eerie: the scans showed that their brains were getting the answers right. The students couldn't consciously tell which were the French words and which were gobbledygook, but their brains could, and the findings get weirder still, at least to the layperson and, judging by Osterhout's hushed tone when he conveyed them, perhaps even to him. At nine months along, when he quizzed the students on vocabulary and syntax, "their brains were doing it like native speakers," even though the students were still blowing the answers, and often. "They were wrong," he said. "A. Lot."

As with so many neural discoveries in the field of second language acquisition, Osterhout could only say what he'd found, not what the findings ultimately mean. Neurolinguistic exploration is still in its infancy, at a point where it's short on explanations but long on tantalizing speculation. If a foreign language, even just elements of one, exists within us so deeply that we aren't even aware of it, does it affect us? Is there a way to pierce the barrier? Does that language exist in the stratum of dreams and puns, in the layer of metaphors and visions? Was Noam Chomsky right: is there a language acquisition device in our heads, part of the innate mechanism that automatically generates grammar? Those in the Chomsky camp will find Osterhout's discoveries appealing, and French teachers, he said, "are going to want to hear this. In learning a second language, the learners' brains evidently know how to do this really well."

HAROLD'S RESTLESSNESS seems to seep into me. The narrowness of the Jain women's lives is always apparent to me now. The white room once again closes in. In the mornings with Vidhu, I plot my escape. Afternoons, I return long enough to drop off books, then bolt again for anywhere: for tea with the travel agent's daughter, Tui, who'll answer any question I have about India. To pretty Dudh Talai park, where I go to study and, bored, pay twenty-five cents to ride a camel. For a tour of hospitals with the deaf school founder, which started as a polite invitation to come to tea and ended up rattling me to my core.

When I'd approached Dr. Aggrawal at the school, it was to ask if he could recommend an oncologist. He couldn't, for good reason. There wasn't one for hundreds of miles, which put me in a bit of a bind. Mine had allowed me to come only after extracting the promise that I'd get checked regularly. My blood tests, called tumor markers, were in the normal range but could, my doctor had reminded me, spike at any time. "Remember," he'd said, "you need monitoring."

Dr. Aggrawal invited me to his home. Let us talk, he said. He was a gnome of a man, with a gray plume of hair and a fondness for aphorisms. "Cakes, creams, curries clog coronary arteries," he said in his living room when the subject turned to the recent spike in obesity here. "C, c, c, c, c," he added, apparently commenting on the wordplay. "The greatest battle of life is the battle of the body bulge," he continued. "B, b, b," he said, and paused to gauge my reaction. I had no idea what he was getting at.

"That style of speech is from the *kalas*," an old gent told me later when an opportunity arose to ask about Dr. Aggrawal's alphabetic peculiarities. The kalas, that man explained, were what the cultivated studied in Sanskrit times, arts that ran the gamut from forehead adorning and creating music with water to mynah bird training and the use of alliteration. Dr. Aggrawal, I deduced, had been displaying erudition.

"Oh, no one talks like that anymore," a third old gent scoffed when I reported what the second one had said. As soon as I learned anything here, someone else harrumphed it down.

In the living room, a daughter-in-law brought spiced tea. The doctor had just come from an appendix operation during which he'd found tuberculosis. "A surgeon is married to a wife, knife, and camera," he said. I was unsure how the camera figured into the union till he produced a collection of photographs. We flipped past a colonoscopy, a tubercular chest. "I've never seen a guinea worm before," I said, automatically adopting the tone for family albums. In one photo, a woman craned her head away from a breast festering with small bubbles. "What do they think of cancer here?" I asked, exhaling. "That it is a cancellation," he said.

The doctor's driver knocked on the door. Dr. Aggrawal had late-afternoon rounds still to go. He asked if I'd come. In the car, he outlined the plan that would have to be set into motion if I wanted to have tumor markers done. What we would do would be like a water-bucket relay: He'd phone a pathologist, who'd draw my blood and have it airlifted four hundred miles south to a lab in Bombay. There, a technician would candle the vials and mail a report back, whereupon the pathologist would phone with the news. The monthly cost would be 1,000 rupees, only $25, but easily half a month's rent locally. *How could anyone here afford to get cancer?* I thought, then shifted uneasily when the answer came.

The conversation turned to the subject of the new India. Udaipur had become an aspirational town, Dr. Aggrawal said: lots of cell phones and MBAs. "These days, everyone wants a top position," he said. "They go by hook and crook. They live in tension." He shook his head. "Aspire less. Perspire more," he said, smiling benignly.

At a nursing home, our first stop, a man in a robe was helped onto the veranda. His eyes were still jaundiced from the gallstones that had been removed. His nurse leaned down and brushed the air above Dr. Aggrawal's toes. Gallbladder operations cost between five rupees and ten thousand, he was explaining. "What he has spent, he has spent. These people are not insured," he said, waving the uncollectable sums away with his hand. The consultation took place on the front steps, as scooters and jeeps whizzed by. Dr. Aggrawal and two men from the nursing home held x-rays up to the setting sun. The patient peered over their shoulders. I tried to breathe shallowly against a stench that rose from somewhere beneath the veranda.

Dusk was gathering when we entered the gate at Saraswati Hospital. In the grassy courtyard, a family surrounded a man asleep on a blanket. Already they were receding into darkness. I was flying on new adventure till we got to the operating room, where a small dark man with an amputated leg lay naked from the waist down. At one time he would have been a laborer. I felt dread to know my vicarious interest would mount, that I wouldn't look away. I tried to make a face that conveyed I was sorry for intruding. The man stared back, incurious. Dr. Aggrawal lifted the man's penis. He motioned me over. "Opening too small," he said in comradely tones. The stump kicked reflexively. "Learn something new every day and be wiser today than what you were yesterday," he said, laying out a tube of Xylocaine jelly and three dilators of increasingly large size. As the first dilator slid in, the man clenched his hands. The third rod made him groan and arch his back.

Downstairs, in an office, we found a man dazed and fiery with tuberculosis. The two brothers with him were twitchy as caged cats. A nurse arrived with x-rays that shone incandescent around a blur. A tumor, Dr. Aggrawal suspected. The man left with the scans. Parents brought in a deaf boy with a neatly slicked cowlick. "Mildly retarded," Dr. Aggrawal said, though the boy was bright-eyed and working multiplication tables. The parents looked like country people. They murmured appreciatively when Dr. Aggrawal interrupted the consultation to pass around photos of cases he'd had in Lucknow: A man with one terrified eye peering out from the elephantiasis folds of his face. A speculum propped between a woman's legs. "Big smell," Dr. Aggrawal observed. The boy hummed. RESTING IS RUSTING, an office sign read.

His driver reappeared. On our way to the exit, we stopped outside a room. "Uterine cancer," he said at the door. "How is she?" I asked. "Miracles are not very common here," the inspiration-happy Dr. Aggrawal said flatly, twice, because I made him answer twice, unable to believe he didn't have a peppy reply.

"Don't look so glum," he commanded the woman when we entered. She was curled up on a bed, about my age, I learned, though I'd have said twenty years older. Thin wisps of hair looked tickly on brown scalp. "Don't lie around frowning," he said. "Look at her." He meant me. "She has had cancer, and she is not crying. She is happy and hale." I cringed. The woman's eyes widened. She struggled out of bed. "Thank you," she whispered, bowing gratitude on shaky legs, beaming at our connection, at this solid proof of hope, and in that moment, it was as if I'd been socked. All this time, I'd thought what I'd had was miraculous luck, but in this plain white room, the knowledge came, inescapable: miracles are limited by place. What I had was a pharmacopoeia of treatments. She didn't. To stand here and present it any other way was to be the lowest kind of fraud.

"If you smile, you heal faster," Dr. Aggrawal told the uterine cancer patient, but away from her room, in the dim scruffy hall, he said simply, "If you get cancer here, you die." And her? Too advanced, he said matter-of-factly. He brightened. "If you make a patient smile, you make them healthy," he chimed. *So cruel,* I thought, breathless with anger, then I saw. That's all he had. All he had were words.

"I am leaving by the early train"

The language twists; it burrows and soars. It pulls an inverse maneuver. The more Hindi I understand, I find, the more perplexing my life becomes.

One morning, a week before the midsemester break, the sink in my bathroom sputters air. I press the handles, stamped KRISHNA, a plumbing supplies brand. No water. No reason. The *dhobi,* the washerwoman, has not been in this week, could not have siphoned off the reserves. The Whisperer, who twice left her taps open and drained the tank, has been relocated, unhappily, it's turning out. The breathy calls about the family have begun. "They've taken me somewhere, and I don't know where I am," she phoned Swami-ji to say, alarmed when they tried to include her in an outing. "Harold, I only feel safe with you," she said the next day from the floor by his feet.

Though Harold is no closer to being what might, with any true certainty, be described as a safety zone. "All right, all right. Cut it," he explodes on the street whenever a driver honks the horn. Many drivers do, which might explain the topic he selected for conversation class. "Weaponry," he said gruffly from beneath the turban he's begun turning up in.

We outvoted him and went with Divali, the festival of lights, ended up learning synonyms for "meddlesome" instead. Helaena, annoyed, was having problems with gossipy palace staff. *"To put your leg in the matter* (nosy)," *"personal, mentality, talky* (nosy)," *"bad mannered," "foul mouthed,"* my notes from that class read. Lately, Helaena has been jittery. She confessed all regarding his nephew to the maharana, who is now not returning her calls. "Tell me again. He's busy," she says hastily to Jen, a new palace arrival, who's here for a month studying traditional dance and whose room gives out on an expansive view of the lake. Helaena's offers a thin peek of courtyard. "I may talk to him about that," she said after a visit to the luxe other digs. Equally distressing, the marriage charts the nephew's parents sent out for comparison in October have never come back. The month's now November. It should have taken the pandit ten minutes to scan the astrological layouts and say if it's a match. "I'm submitting a new birth time," Helaena declared at the end of class, having located several more propitious ones in *Linda Goodman's Love Signs.* American can-do will trump Indian mysticism, at least in this room.

"Closed chapter," Swami-ji had said when the Whisperer moved out of the Jains', meaning on all this student hubbub, but that's not what it's looking like. No, it's looking like things were just getting started—that that was just the prologue.

Across the drive, I report the problem with the sink, provoke a rondelet of speculation. *Water is not working? Is not working in her room? That is because you are evacuating it by means of your washing. No, no, we have water here. She is not having it there?* (This last from a latecomer.) *Yes, this is a true report. A true report. Water is not working.* The Jains go into medley slide, which sounds like a legal summation and where I have to supply half the meaning in my head: *Yes, sometimes the water does not come to her room,* for arcane reasons that will be divulged, but only in the fullness of time.

When the situation isn't resolved after breakfast, I bring my toothbrush to the kitchen. *"Water is still not coming?"* Alka asks. She and Rajkumar are deputized to investigate. They lead everyone into my bathroom, where Rajkumar tests the sink, squeezes the wall faucets, straightens and delivers a verdict. With my Hindi improved, it's a lot more confusing than it might have been.

"Ah, Kathy, in the evening, you are creating an air lock.*"*

"Air lock?"

"Haan." He points to the ceiling. *"You have been creating an air lock upstairs,"* he says, followed by fast, cupping hand gestures and the judgment, *"isliye* vacuum of your making." ("Vacuum?" "Vacuum, vacuum.") This is a problem, I determine, that can be averted if I pound on the wall tap with my foot. Rajkumar, in flip-flops, demonstrates.

"Only five minutes," he says, and the dangling clause adds complication. Hard to say if he means five minutes of stomping required or five before the water returns, but no matter; it's only five either way. We gather round the sink and wait expectantly, till he nods and pushes on the handle. The water comes roaring back.

"THE MUSSULMANS CUT off cows' heads," Vanita says in flat-lined tones as we edge on into the break. In English, her usual means of communication with me. Some days I coax Vanita into Hindi. Then there's fuzziness to pay. "Vanita-ji, I have to make a phone call," I say. "This person does not know English. How do I ask when her husband will return?" But this person cannot understand when I repeat what she said. *What?* this person will frequently exclaim; *Whaaat?* then fix the sentence for me.

"I was living in Calcutta only then," Vanita continues. In 1992, the topic of today's tutorial, a time when communal riots swept the country. In December of that year, Hindu extremists demolished a 450-year-old mosque in the temple town of Ayodhya. They'd been whipped into a frenzy of outrage by the BJP, which was claiming that the mosque had been built on the birthplace of the Hindu god Rama and was therefore an abomination to Hindus. Never mind that Rama is a mythical figure with no carbon-datable place of birth, or that, by a strict reading of the texts, he was not a god but a man. He was a legendary king, certainly, the hero of the epic Ramayana, and over the past decade and with the help of a popular TV miniseries, the BJP had worked to elevate him into a triumphant deity, one who, in his revised nationalist version, symbolized the rightful dominance of Hindus. Just as Rama, aided by his devotee Hanuman, had vanquished the rakshasa demons, so, too, would good Hindus one day rout the internal threat the country now faced — that is, the Mussulmans, the Muslims. To further this end, right-thinking Hindus could raze the blasphemous Babri Mosque, and they did, touching off furious riots that left three thousand dead, most of them Muslims.

"My parents were coming for my wedding," Vanita says. "Their train was stopped for several days. They were having to sleep on the train," she says and swallows. In India, a stalled train has grisly associations. These date to 1947 and Partition, when the British, having agreed to end their long colonizing reign, helped engineer a plan to divide the country along religious lines. At the stroke of midnight, on August 15, India became two nations: Pakistan, a new Muslim homeland, and the Union of India (later the Republic of India), which, though not expressly given to Hindus, now existed in comparison to a Muslim state and so was associated with Hinduism.

Gandhi expressed strong reservations about creating this kind of communal divide. "My whole soul rebels against the idea that Hinduism and Islam represent two antagonistic cultures and doctrines. To assent to such a doctrine is for me a denial of God," he wrote. In the months after Partition, his fears were realized. Up till then in India, Hindus and Muslims had, by and large, lived together in outwardly peaceful coexistence, but now a division had been laid down, made official. Between fifteen million and twenty million people found themselves on the wrong side of the divide as sub-merged tensions exploded. Muslims turned on Hindus who'd been their neighbors for years; Hindus killed Muslims they'd welcomed into their homes. People rushed to board trains for the imagined safety of the new homelands, but at points along the track, mobs lay in wait. When the trains pulled in, they were ghost trains, many of them. Family members who'd come to meet their relatives found them grotesquely slumped in their seats, the floor slick with blood. When the carnage ended, at least half a million were dead, and a retaliatory cycle of violence began that continues to this day, that's resulted in the destruction of the Babri Mosque, the yearly murders in Kashmir, all the market explosions in Bombay or Delhi or the state of Assam.

"The Mussulmans at that time were killing many people," Vanita says in the same spare trance voice of forbearance Vidhu uses when the subject of the Mussulmans comes up. (Swami-ji presses his lips and stares blankly into middle distance. He dislikes Muslims more than either of them.) The subject comes up a lot less since Helaena suggested, sweetly, that Vidhu knock off the rhetoric in current events class. "Helaena-ji does not understand," he'd stopped our tu-torial two days later to say. "Muslims *do* act as one." He'd sounded wounded.

"In Udaipur, they cut off cows' heads," Vanita continues, and I exhale loudly. *We both know,* I am hoping by means of breath to convey, *that this is not the full story.*

By means of breath, I do. "But these people were killing cows," she protests, drawing up against her dupatta. Her voice has gone shrill. "That is how they are," she says, and sets her jaw against them.

"And what were the Hindus in Udaipur doing at that time?" I ask, sweet as Helaena, since I already have a good idea.

"Ohhh, the Hindus? Oh, maybe the Hindus burned some Mussulmans' houses," she says pleasantly. "Maybe some Mussulmans were killed."

I'm not learning in this place, I fume in the week before the break, sick of this talk, of its firewall logic, of the flaring impulses it produces in me: self-righteous, reflexively oppositional, ignorant in their own way. Reactionary. In this rift so vast it's been echoing for years, I can't see where I'm standing. All that's immediately visible to me are the fetid streets of the Muslim neighborhood down by Delhi Gate. The inhabitants there are poor and small, with hard bright eyes, the men dressed in shabby polyester pants. They look worn and dark, like dalits, like outcastes. Because that's what they were, Helaena says one night when we're hanging out in her room.

"When the Mughals came through, the lower classes jumped at the opportunity to become Muslim, to try and escape caste," she explains. She's reclining on her side, in white *churidar* pants, polishing off French fries. "Although some of them," she says, "were converted at sword-point." The muted skirls of the palace bagpipers, remnants of the Raj, sound from outside somewhere. "But most of them? They stayed where they were. Nothing changed. That's why they tend to be uneducated, except in places like Hyderabad and Delhi, where many of them are descended from princes and the courtly Mughals."

These, then, are who Vidhu and Vanita are railing against: poor people collectively despised once for their caste, once again for their religion, pushed to the margins throughout all of history, consigned to subsistence jobs and decaying quarters, with no escape possible, not even karmically. Oh, the teachers' talk! It's heartless.

Telescoped down, attached to India only cerebrally really — tethered by dry facts and a meager collection of words: *"probably," "important," "not possible,"* today's vocabulary assortment — I'm unable to see that Vidhu and Vanita are reacting viscerally, are keeping their voices flat against the ghosts of Partition that still whisper through the country. Their jaws are squared not against the men with eyes like black centroids down by Delhi Gate, but against the stories everyone raised here knows: of how the corpses were piled so high, tank drivers had to get out and nudge them to the side; of how people were pulled off bicycles by mobs and hacked to death; about the stains black as midnight on the steps of the ghost trains.

Their jaws are set against all of that, but then mine hardens, too: not just against their rhetoric, but the way it catches in me. *Maybe Vidhu does know,* I'll think, before the firewall flares. *Maybe they do act as one.* In the unbearable intimacy that comes from building a second language with someone, you feel fully alive, at a price. You leave yourself open, to something like love, but also to hatreds that are no less powerful for being engineered. All the snippets can take root and not just some, if you don't look to see what's there.

"LOOK, KATHY," Anukul cries, hand tracing an orbit through the sky, over a moon so electrically bright you can practically hear it crackle. Everywhere else in the world, it's dawn that breaks. Here in Rajasthan, it's evening, when the planed black night comes on with such force it snaps the sun from the sky, when the heat cracks into a thousand rivulets (earlier now that it's November). "Look," he calls from several rows down in the bleachers where we've all gathered. There's a book open on his lap. "What they do for moon is this," and he makes the sweep, "but what we do is this," and he forms a viewfinder with his fingers. The American Sign Language book has arrived just in time, just before I'm due to take off for the break. I squint then smile to mimic concentration and enjoyment, but the day has now gone into its fourth language—English, Hindi, Rajasthani sign, American sign—and a landslide is threatening in my brain.

The bleachers are the only ethnographically incorrect detail in the anthropologically exact tourist village where we've been since noon, a Williamsburg with wattle and daub. Mostly Indian tourists come here now, but today there are no shambling groups up from the neighboring state of Gujarat, no women in veils leaning forward with cameras, looking like Victorian photographers. Today the village is reserved for a handicapped conference, a rendezvous of every specialized school from here to the Rann of Kutch. At lunch, blind boys in blue leaned together as they talked, each facing a slightly different direction. Posters on the walls declared SEE OUR ABILITIES NOT OUR DISABILITIES, in the universal language of social workers. Udaipur is an epicenter of NGOs—five thousand of them here, a reporter told me, 90 percent corrupt.

It was after lunch, during a postcard-drawing competition, that any polyglottal abilities I had began to go south. All around us, on rugs, children were crayoning happy scenes from the festival of light: clay Divali lamps gamboling merrily through the air, the beauteous goddess Lakshmi raining golden coins from her hands. My boys were sketching collapsing towers, a topic of persistent interest. I'd been absorbed in a perfectly pleasant conversation with several teachers, when one from Goa took sudden offense at the rate I was going with Hindi.

"You have arrived when?" he asked. "You are still speaking like this? You should be ashamed. Your school should be ashamed." A woman with English so broken it clattered piped up, "You Hindi like my English." I didn't think so, but soon after, I stopped capping sentences with verbs, became communicatively incompetent all-around.

"Look," Anukul calls to me in the bleachers as we wait for a show to begin. He claps his hands, and the American sign for "school" knocks the book from his lap. He bends, which is why, when the gang of thuggee Bikaner deaf school boys try to shake me down, he's oblivious. In fact, so am I, in my stuporous state. I nod eagerly when the tall boys surround me, all adolescent elbows and intent, pretending interest in getting acquainted. *Do I have parents?* Yes I do. *Brothers?* Oh, yes, one. *Sisters?* One there, too. *Ten rupees?* But they've picked someone too sludged for communication. I don't get it. The Bikaner visitors grow more forceful in their questioning, hands vigorously dotting mouths, 10-rupee note jabbing the air, till Hemant Patel, the Dustbin from the play, gets a load of what they're up to. Hemant Patel, all five feet of him, hurries over and signs stern suggestions to the Bikaner guests about what they can do with their 10-rupee note, then turns and taps my forearm, points to Anukul: *"And you might consider changing seats."* His gallantry offsets my deep embarrassment at having been so dim.

On my resettlement, Anukul glances up from the book long enough to give the Bikaner boys a glare. He's busy figuring out the logistics of the word "cooking." "In America they do this," he says, then stops midway through turning his hand, "like a pancake," the book directs, which would be like a paratha. Down below, a man with a suspiciously puffed chest is ambling toward the bleachers.

Then the evening goes into drag time, then the evening soars, bobs high like the lantern fixed to a kite that's straining to escape into the night. For an hour, I don't care that I'm daft in three languages, that a loneliness comes on me now with such suffocating swiftness I can't move, as the boys in blue line up and sing a low, mournful song about what happened in my country in September (*No one there*, I think, *will ever know they have*), as a young guy gets up and dances a dance that's pure exuberance, on his hands. He has no legs. As kids with polio convene in the bleachers, then move fluidly down the stairs in a crab crawl—all but one, with braces, who makes his way haltingly. In the sidelight of the stage, where the group gathers nervously, the red ribbons in the girls' braids are revealed. An announcer's voice squawks, and they're bounding toward center, loping and swinging toward applause. I see their disabilities and abilities both. The kids are singing themselves into center light, into view and into being, weaving harmonies so agilely that even once the lantern's bobbed high and small and has disappeared, the lives they've made there will still glimmer.

"WE ARE HAVING A CHUTTI," Swami-ji says on a day just before. Not a moment too soon either. Commotion is riling all the ranks, new chapters starting up unexpectedly in the staff room, in the classrooms, sometimes by the minute. Staff side, the hubbub goes unexplained. Vocabulary is delayed when Vidhu shoots, black-faced, from the back and past us out the door. A few minutes later, he returns and clears his throat. "The ergative is required with compulsion verbs," he begins in collected tones. No one says a word. Dictation is postponed on account of tears. "Swami-ji has said I butter students," Samta says, lip trembling, and I know to add the preposition "up," not what she means.

On the student side, the troubles are too clear. The Whisperer is not speaking to me on suspicions that I masterminded her departure from the Jains'. "She's insanely jealous of my Hindi skills," she tells Helaena by way of explanation. Harold is in a turban. Helaena is in high dudgeon: Sri-ji, the maharana, has not called.

Only the Swamster, Helaena's new name for him, which has caught on only with her, appears chipper, though he's merry like a cat tripping to the kitchen before it's time for a can: insistently. *"Give them more! Give them more! Give them more!"* he sings to Raju when Helaena says she likes the new cookies. In tutorials, he piles on the English. "Under the surface, Udaipur *bahut* traditional *hai,*" he says in *kicheree*—literally, "rice and lentils," but slang for "mixed Hindi-English." At first I'm amazed that he's coughing up the English, but then a curious thing happens. I no longer notice that he is. When he speaks to me, I hear it as pure Hindi. Without my conscious knowledge, my mind has automatically sifted out the rice, and to such a degree, I find myself thinking, *So funny, but I can understand that guy like nobody else here.*

Because he's practically speaking English half the time, hello?

During the other half, when he keeps it to just a sprinkling, biological forces kick in, the ones that allow you to conjure someone's full face on a side glimpse, that fill in the blanks when your sister says "Did . . . store . . . up . . . Mom's birth . . . ?" while running the blender. "Narrative imagining is our fundamental form of predicting," the cognitive scientist Mark Turner writes. It's not just speakers who make up a story as it goes along, but listeners to some extent do, too, by determining the gist, the central patterns, then filling in the meaning of the words that streaked by. Storytelling is a collaboration between listener and teller.

Even in a relatively quiet room, you can miss 20 percent of what someone is saying. In the din of a restaurant, half the words might be static. But even if you were to chat with someone in a vault, their words wouldn't come at you clipped and distinct. In the flow of speech, there are no boundaries. Your brain imposes them.

The ability to detect and predict patterns, to wing it, is crucial to conversation, so much so that the capacity for it seems to be wired into the language regions of the brain. In one experiment, when subjects were shown patterned symbols, the visual sites in their brains lit up: no big surprise. What was unexpected, though, was that the subjects also showed activity in Wernicke's area, one of the main language sites of the brain, thought to govern speech comprehension. It didn't matter whether the volunteers consciously recognized that they were looking at patterns or if they thought the scenes were random lines; the same results were obtained. The researchers were nonplused: they proceeded to ask, Why would a brain site responsible for language comprehension be so exquisitely attuned to visual sequences that it would detect them in nanoseconds, even before the cognitive regions weighed in? Because, they concluded, language is composed of patterns—in other words, grammar. What is proper syntax, after all, but the predictable ordering of words, words combined in patterns? Given the "stunning automaticity of speech," the linguist Derek Bickerton's phrase—words come at us at the rate of a fifth of a second each—Wernicke's area needs to sort out the patterns at flash speed.

This stunning automaticity, moreover, has led to our brains being configured so that we reflexively deduce what's going on in conversations in terms of probabilities. It's a tendency that can misfire in the early days of language study.

By now, however, when I snap awake to hear Swami-ji saying, *"In that place, the festival of Holi* was very rude. They threw mud and also *gobar,"* and also cow patties, my brain automatically fills in the correct location. We're back on the mean streets of Benares. Of all the possible conversational destinations, that's the one that is most probable.

We tend to think in probabilities rather than possibilities, according to a widely accepted theory called the exemplar theory, for the same reason New Yorkers consolidate their worldly goods under their beds: space is limited. "With memory, speech, and voice, a debate's raged for years: how big is the brain's hard drive?" Michael Vitevitch, a psychology professor, told me. "Does it have enough memory to store every single detail?" Not nearly, according to the exemplar theory, and so memories have to be compacted. Specific details disappear, and in their place what you have is an amalgam of images, an exemplar. "It's as if you took a bunch of film negatives—well, if we still used film negatives—and laid them on top of each other," Vitevitch said. "You have all these details available to you, but your mind extracts the gist of it." He gave an example: Suppose someone says the word "bird." What will likely come to mind is the image of a common bird—a robin, let's say, and not an ostrich.

Or suppose someone says, *"For three days during Holi,* no one there went out!" In the instance above, what may come to mind are the apparently ceaselessly rampaging hooligans of Benares. In the guidebooks, the City of Light is described as one of the most sacred places on earth, where Hindus, if they can, arrange to come to die so their ashes can be placed in the nearby Ganges. But after enough personal tutorials with Swami-ji, I've got it fixed in my head as an Indian Newark-during-the-sixties.

"*When we moved to Udaipur,*" Swami-ji says, "we thought it would be like this. *But there was no* Eve teasing!" No pestering of women. "*There was no gobar* throwing! We were very very surprised."

By the end of the hour, all this talk has him wistful. "*There people are carefree!*" I learn. "*Boatmen are drinking chai next to scholars!*" I find. "*And there are four universities. No, five! One for Sanskrit alone,*" I discover, and what's more, the festival of Navratri there leaves the one here in the dust. With five minutes to go, he chuckles. He tells me again about his favorite Benares guesthouse. "*They had* a sign *outside,*" he says, and we both brace for the guffaw. "*This sign, what it said was,* STAY HERE AND DIE! Stay here and die," he says, shaking his head, and I'm careful not to move my lips in time.

ON THE EVE OF the break, Alka and I high-fived for the last time. Harold thinks he is in love, I reported as we stood in the driveway, after ten, late for the Jains. She'd come down to restrain the vicious Pomeranian Taffy so I could slip through the gate.

"*He's forgotten his wife?*" she asked.

"*Haan,*" I said, and gave a half head wobble, the one that means *This is life.*

"Wow!" she said, and pressed for details about this love that had flared, for the Whisperer. With each one, she high-fived me, puzzling me as much as I must have perplexed her the first time I'd slapped her palm. Did she mean *You called it?* Of course not. *Way to go Harold?* Uh-uh. I think it was just an expression of conviviality, a physical connection to a laugh. We laughed and slapped in the soft hold of evening, then just before we went inside, I bid her *shubh rati:* "good night."

· 9 ·

"Birds of the same feather fly together"

 After friendly, small-town Udaipur, magisterial Jaipur was disconcerting. In the state capital, where I'd come to start the break, the roads were wide and dusty, not lanes so tight shopkeepers could lean out and examine your clothes as your rickshaw rolled past. The roads here were boulevards, lined with tarp shacks and, farther back, estates with clipped lawns, where small, brilliant birds were like scattering marbles beside the peacocks' sweeping trains.

In Jaipur, I saw how geography shapes the psyche, that three months in Udaipur had made me a yokel. Without the protective circle of the Aravalli Hills, I'd lost a sense of being in place. The buildings here were grand, the grimy air biting, the people both: *uunchi naak,* "high-nosed."

"You're beautiful," the women beside me in the hotel beauty parlor said when I cried "Beautiful!" to the pedicurist. Weeks of road dirt filtered through sandals had taken the pedicurist thirty minutes to scrub off. "But that's because you're white and we're black," the woman said coolly, before I could get out "thank you."

The shop girls in Jaipur were disaffected, as unwelcoming as any on Rodeo Drive. The street outside the hotel was rubble. The hotel bathroom became a disco whenever I opened the door. Just a crack, lights would flash, music swell, and this was before the trip turned hallucinatory. That occurred on the train to Bikaner, after I'd stayed up late talking with Vikram, a Brahmin physicist whose father knew a man who knew a man who knew my uncle. On the basis of those slim lines, the father, an economist, had placed his family at my disposal, had invited me to come up on my vacation, go travel into the desert with his son and see the educational institute they ran in Bikaner. Indian hospitality proceeds on connections as complicated as the gods', is every bit as divine.

Vikram, in his thirties, was slim with an aquiline face and a brooding air that was contagious. Between stretches of train silence, we talked about the water-management software he was producing for the villages, about Indian writers, philosophy. "Always judge someone by the best thing they've done, not the worst," he said, quoting a physicist, and I thought indignantly: *But this is the trip I thought I was going to have.* Lots of convivial chat with erudite individuals. Contrasting remarks from the school flashed to mind. *"Pesh aab"* means to present water. "A leak!" Vidhu had tittered yesterday in vocabulary. "Yes, but 'leak' is also something that comes from the ceiling," said Swami-ji, who had to make chugging sounds when he was unable to keep a straight face at this bit of fancy wordplay. For the next mile of the journey, the two of them hovered above me in the carriage, bad relations who wouldn't stop yammering.

The train rumbled into another patch of silence, into the night and the Great Thar Desert. "My Hindi is so bad it's embarrassing," Vikram said when, after a while, I pulled out a copy of *Teach Yourself Hindi.* His language was a dialect, Marwari, similar to, but not to be confused with, Mewari. The remark started the conversation

up again. Above the creak of train wheels, we talked about the institute, named the Ajit Foundation for a brother who'd died, about
how dalit kids came there to peer through its telescope. We talked
about the mobile library they sent out into the town, about the lecture series they held. We talked till the train rocked us to sleep, and
when I woke at first light to a lunar landscape—flat-topped trees
that appeared to be strutting, ocherous land rushing back to the
sky—the effect was to make me think I'd slipped the world.

It was 6 A.M. and chilly when the train pulled in. "Look at that
trash," Vikram said on the platform. "Indians don't have a sense of
communal space." Four years away, in Utah, teaching physics, appeared to have left him with a double vision of homeland that could
be irritating. Like one of those corrugated cards that blink different
scenes depending on how it's turned. Here was the country, intact
from before: the mirrored disks on girls' skirts; the shoemakers' tools
spread on blankets over yellow dust; the lush blue shutters and pistachio doors. Here it was again: littered with waste and ignorance.

"If the station were private, they would keep it clean," he said.
"But it's not theirs, it's the government's, and what is the government? Some big thing."

On the car ride in, a shimmering emerald mirage appeared up
ahead, a rippled mound by the side of the road. Watermelons, I saw
as we came closer. *Water*melons: for the first time ever, I thought
about the name. Water melons, melons with water—but the name
was descriptive. Before it had only ever been diffusely ruby. *This is
why you go away,* I thought sleepily: *to see what you left behind.*

The walled city of Bikaner formed in inches through the haze.
Past the gate, goats on lanes as thin as kerfs slowed the progress of
the car. The buildings, some of which dated to the year Columbus
sailed, were ocher, with high balconies and pretty latticework windows. "When I was little," Vikram said, "we went to Verona, in Italy, and I thought, *It's just like Bikaner!*" An hour or so later, when
we climbed, bleary-eyed, to the top of the institute, I thought of

another Italian city. This high up, Bikaner looked like Pompeii. From here you could see where roofs had worn away, revealing staircases to nowhere.

Even intact, houses here were surprising. An uncle's house, where we went for dinner, was nothing much to look at on the outside. Inside, each room was a different carnival color. The silver ceilings appeared embroidered. Rooms unfolded unexpectedly off others. We sat in a crimson front room, then a jade-colored middle room, then a kitchen with roses on the tiles, then a persimmon back room that looked out over a courtyard. "When I was a child, they used to live there," Vikram said, pointing to a shuttered expanse of house. "But then they moved here."

A niece was conscripted into speaking Hindi with me. The effort made her shy. Everyone else took polite passes then switched off into Marwari. I tried to follow, but the language was like Hindi bent or rolled, all wrong. In three months, my ear had locked in on an exact set of Indian phonemes: the bouncing James Cagney Udaipur sound.

The dusty smell of garam masala drifted in and made me groggy. I was struggling to keep awake when a ripple like black mercury shot through the shadows, bolting me upright. On our walk over, dozens of rats had shot past us into drains, spillover from a nearby temple where hundreds lived and were worshiped as the reincarnations of holy men.

Between the heat and the comfort of Vikram's intelligence, I slept two, three times a day. Midmornings, toward dinner, I'd make my way back to a hot-pink room, where the cabinet contained a tube of Brylcreem. After months of being braced—for fleeting meaning, against danger—what a luxury it was not to have to parse all nuance and coding on my own, to have someone who could just say why my attempts to buy water all ended in failure ("It's your accent *and* your grammar"), why there were ads for "courses" plastered everywhere (because Indian teachers were ditching school, then charging students for makeup), that not all Hindus reviled Muslims en masse.

"That's why people don't want to learn Hindi," Vikram said with a moan when I mentioned the Mussulman talk. "The right wing has hijacked the language."

What a relief to have someone who'd also made himself an outsider, who'd had to circle into another country, mine, and so knew when to offer interpretation with his. Swami-ji et al. had never traveled farther from home than Udaipur, hadn't watched one world form word by word while they were only halfway gone from their own. They'd never been changelings and so couldn't act as intermediaries.

"Language intermediaries aren't that uncommon," the linguist John Schumann had told me before I'd left the States, when I'd mentioned that my Hindi teacher was Bulgarian. "People often talk about being in France and learning French from North Africans."

The neuroscientist Arturo Hernandez also remarked on the phenomenon. "When someone's had to go through the same process," he'd said, "they've had to go through the same brain remapping. When you're used to doing something one way, then try it differently, the second way's a lot harder than if you were learning it fresh. You get neural interference from the first." The principle can apply to language, but Hernandez used a sports analogy. "When I was swimming a lot, I wouldn't play tennis," he said. "If I was used to doing the crawl and went on a court, my tennis serve would have suffered." An intermediary, someone who's gone through the same wiring jams as you, will understand why your lob, or your verb, is off like that.

In Bikaner, the first morning, I slept through breakfast. The second, a man brought pink teacups and a dish of millet to my room. The third, when I was still vertical by noon, Vikram suggested that we get in the car.

On the drive, in the desert, small revelations appeared, though the first ones were more like warm-up appearances. At a camel farm on the edge of town, the fields were like sight gags. From above, all the bobbing, disgruntled, long-lashed faces resembled a convention of annoyed housewives; below, the spindly legs under barrel bodies made me think of accountants hiding with their knees exposed. In the high sun, I had to pull my dupatta over my head, take small stubbing steps as we went along. The sweat trickling down my back was pooling in my sandals, making me slide into the thong. A thunderous sound, like booming rifle shots stopped us. A stampede had started in a far paddock. Camels run like girls; that was the revelation then. Forelegs stiffly flying, heads strained for balance, they had the same look of resigned misery I'd seen in ninth-grade gym.

At the next stop, a complex of pillared domes, called chhatris, looked like a collection of pavilion tops, bizarrely festive for what they were: monuments to the dead. *"Sati ma,"* Vikram said when we came to one carved with small figures of a couple. Sati, ma: "virtuous woman," "saint." The woman had been burned alive on her husband's funeral pyre. She'd committed sati, an act outlawed by the British in 1827, had climbed on his pyre to demonstrate her devotion. Or had been forced on; not all satis were voluntary. Sometimes villagers broke the woman's legs with shovels to keep her from crawling off. A sati, people believed, would confer boons on a village. People believed that, demonstrably, as recently as 1987, when one took place not far from here. *"Glory to the* sati ma,*"* the crowds reportedly chanted, above the girl's dying screams.

In front of us, offerings were piled on the weathered marble: marigolds whose scent fuzzed the back of my throat; a wall clock still wrapped in plastic. A glint behind the clumped flowers caught my eye. When I leaned in to see what it was, I felt sharp fear: a copper brazier, frosted white with live embers, left to the glory of the sati ma. The clarity that came then was searing, for it forced me to admit what I hadn't wanted to: I could not handle the knowledge that kept expanding, of how grotesquely women's lives could end here.

We continued through the field, past other chhatris that, the longer I stayed in the sun, looked more like tipsy umbrellas, till we found our driver by the gate, a film of sweat on his face. In the steamy back of the car, I turned and felt a sting. My hair, tangled and damp, had caught on the ornamentation of my head covering. On the drive back, we slowed for goats, stalled at a blockade of cows. Before dinner, Vikram showed me the library. The long, cool room was lined with stacks of *Scientific Americans* and newspapers written by kids, filled with the bright cries of the reporters themselves. Children ran over. Vikram disappeared. Boys crowded around, chattering in a cappella Hindi. I scanned the room. Vikram, dignified somehow, bent into a small child's table, was watching intently from by the door.

The girls held back, shy, then two approached. What did they want to be? I asked. "A teacher," one answered. "An economist," the other said softly, and I started, then remembered: Vikram's father, a beloved figure here. And that was the final revelation of the day: it's through your devotions that your future begins to come in.

On the last afternoon, we stopped by the house of a family friend, a writer named Nand Kishore Acharya, well regarded, Vikram said, throughout India. Mr. Acharya's tiny front door was set three feet off the ground. We had to fold ourselves in half to get inside, then wait for a servant to come find us. Upstairs, a gray-haired man in his fifties rose to greet us from a day bed. He appeared the way I'd imagined a venerable Indian writer would: loose white pants and glasses thick and black as drafting tools. A ceiling fan stirred air that smelled brackish, like years of concentration was rising from fabric.

"Growing up, I spoke Gujarati with my family and Marwari with friends, but I think in Hindi or I couldn't write in Hindi," Mr. Acharya said in English when I tried to establish what language he was speaking out of. I grew excited when I saw he was willing to indulge my obsession with India's panoply of tongues, still unaware that everyone else here shared it. In a country where language had redrawn the lines of geography—when state boundaries were reestablished in the middle of the last century, the decisions were made according to linguistic groupings—the multiplicity of tongues was an all-round wonder.

"When we interact in Jodhpur, we speak in Hindi," he said, referring to one of the meetings attended by the most illustrious poets—by speakers of Marathi, Punjabi, Bengali, all the official tongues, and any number of the nearly inestimable unofficial ones. No one without God on their side has ever had the courage to calculate how many languages are found in India, but when the U.S. missionary Bible translators tried, they came up with a mind-blowing count: 415 living, 13 extinct, putting the country behind only Papua New Guinea (820 live), Indonesia (737), and Nigeria (510) in numbers. "Though Hindi is not the mother tongue—of anyone. Very few use it in their households," Mr. Acharya added somewhat darkly, edging back into the discussion he'd started to have earlier when he'd said his parents forbade him to use it at home. Any talk about India's language tangles quickly gets you into the subject of English, which gets you into linguistic imperialism and the countervailing legislative attempts that have gone into trying to make Hindi the official tongue, which gets you into bloody riots.

People died in the south of India when, in 1963, Congress, in acknowledgment that the country needed a unifying language, voted to make it Hindi. English, and before that the courtly Urdu of the Mughals, had been serving as the bridge, but when the government decided to elect a more homegrown language, violence erupted. Men burned themselves in protest. People worried they'd be cut off from the state jobs, that they'd be severed from any national discourse. This was in the states where what they speak—Kannada, Malyalam—is as alien to Hindi as English is to Mandarin. Hindi never exactly took, but its appearance in the south can still be rancorous. An Indian friend reports that recently when she traveled through Kerala, a man threatened to harm her when she asked a question in Hindi. "If you speak that to me again, I will abuse you," he said.

"Every Indian boy hates Hindi," Mr. Acharya said from the day bed catercorner to the one where I sat. The fan was causing a literary journal to make small slapping sounds. "They teach it pedantically in school, like badly taught math," he said in a disparaging tone I'd heard before. Once in the States, when I'd brought *Teach Yourself Hindi* to the doctor's, an Indian nurse asked curtly, "What do you want to study that for?" Overlooking the edge in her voice, I tried out a pleasantry. She straightened, gave attention to something outside the window, glanced to see if the other nurses had heard. They hadn't, and I got the message: neither would she.

I told the men about the nurse. A shadow crossed Vikram's face. "Oh, the same thing happens here all the time," I said. "I can barely get anyone to speak Hindi with me," I added, not stopping to consider all the possible causative reasons: that my Hindi was still so blundering, some found it too trying; that others looked at my white face and heard what they thought they would, English. The brain naturally supplies the expected, as demonstrated by a story a university professor in Manhattan told me. The professor, who is half second-generation Indian, half African American, teaches Mandarin to American-born Chinese kids. One day, as he was leaving the class, he spied one of his girl students playfully shove a boy and say something in a sweet, high voice he was sure was an ancient Chinese aphorism. Disbelieving, excited, he rushed over and asked her to repeat it. She did. He frowned. "Say it again." She obliged. What she'd been saying, in a perfect homegirl accent, was "Mooooove, nigger"—a line from a rap video the kids all knew.

On the day bed, I recounted how the previous week, I'd tried to use Hindi to buy a notebook. The elderly shopkeeper had stopped the transaction and demanded, "You speak in English." But I need to practice, I'd insisted. "Okay, then, you speak Hindi, but I speak English," he said, and we proceeded haltingly. Vikram's face went black.

"We don't want our own language!" he cried, sounding as if he'd barked a shin. "We are living in a postcolonial hangover! We do not want our own languages!"

"English is the status language," Mr. Acharya agreed, and the ads for fast-track classes plastering Sector Eleven came to mind—ARENA MULTIMEDIA: CREATING WINNING CAREERS, ACE COMPUTER EDUCATION: FIRST STEP FOR A SUCCESSFUL CAREER—all in English. The meaning was clear: if you knew only Hindi or, worse, Mewari, you could forget about a beautiful career.

"Companies use Hindi as a line of demarcation," Vikram said. "Civil servants look down on people who speak it, but that's all they have, their ability to speak English." By exercising it, he said, people were trying to show they were as good as Americans. Mr. Acharya nodded.

"We can say, 'We're better than the Chinese. Look, we can speak it, they can't,'" Mr. Acharya said, and for the first time, I began to understand I'd been plowing ahead naively. When I forced people into Hindi, I was signaling, in some minds, *You're not as good as me.*

"In Hollywood movies, Indians never speak properly," Vikram said heatedly. "The BBC puts subtitles on our politicians! That's why you're getting the response you are. Those people you're meeting are saying 'Don't make me like that.'"

Don't make me like that—a plea impervious to the argument "But your language is so beautiful." I'd tried. And for a while, it seemed the Indians and I were operating at cross-purposes: they were speaking English to separate themselves from themselves, and I was doing the same using Hindi. The real configurations, though, were more complicated. Among other reasons, the Indians, like everyone else, were using English because it was the global market language. But there was some truth to the equation, too, foremost the fact that I was speaking their language to divide myself from myself, though it'd be months before I'd understand exactly what I was keeping myself from.

In Jaipur, on the return, I spent several days at Vikram's family's home, a blinding-white cubist marvel, with a plashing fountain in the living room and exquisite Rajasthani miniatures on the walls. At dinner, the talk was soft and restrained. All conversation was subdued and orderly.

"KA-TY! THE GEEZER IS HERE!" Meena shouts when I come dragging into the Jains' late morning from the train. Meena and Alka are cleaning furiously—someone, I swear, has just finished hosing the living room down through the window—but everyone takes time out to show me the new geezer, purchased, Alka says, not in some backwater Sector Eleven shop, but in a fancy store downtown. At this allusion to cost, the grandmother makes a face.

"See?" Meena says as we all crowd into my bathroom. A gigantic coiled contraption is now bulging from the wall.

"See?" Meena, in her nightgown still at noon, shows me how to work the switches. "This is hot. This is cold. This is hot. This is cold," as if I've never encountered the hot-cold principle before. Ten minutes hot: does this strike me as good? Ten minutes' hot, it does.

"See, Ka-ty? The geezer is here. Are you still going to move out?" she teases. The gleaming new appliance is making her bubbleheaded.

"Just to the Lake Palace," I say with an absolute straight face. The Lake Palace hotel is five stars. "I'm moving there. You come."

The women return to their cleaning, leave me to my ten minutes hot. I fire up the tank, step under the water. My inaugural geezer shower shuts off all the electricity in my half of the house. Snatching a towel, I dash out my door and through the floral grotto to try to locate the circuit breakers.

At lunch, I think I'll miss the hushed talk at Vikram's, the mannerly exchanges ("Ravi says he knows a scientist who was interviewed by Naipaul. Wasn't too bad." "Oh?"), but I'm too distracted by commotion. A small, dazed man keeps wandering into the kitchen, wearing an unlikely FISHERMAN FROM HELL T-shirt. "I'll ask the *nauker*" — the "servant" — "to bring a bike up for you," the oldest girl says, and I guess that's who that was. There was no servant that I knew of when I left, and now we have a nauker and a geezer.

On the train down from Jaipur, I'd loaded up on Hindi, inhaled half the textbook, and I'm hoping they'll all be impressed, but everyone is talking so fast, no one can tell I'm speaking double time. The dwarf at the phone shop across the street can, though. "Wow, your Hindi is good," he says, after listening in on my conversation.

"You've certainly improved," Vidhu says when I stop by the institute and find all the teachers in the back room working during the break.

"You guys are really toiling," I say.

"Swami-ji has put in the most time of all," Vidhu says in the deeply admiring tone he uses to refer to his boss when his boss is around.

I have improved; the signs are there. When reading, I can crest now, can hear rhythms that will boost me till the verb kicks in. "The verb carries the meaning," Gabriela had said, and since in Hindi the verb comes at the end of the sentence, the meaning often isn't revealed till you've sat through clause after clause. But overnight, I can make the pieces hold. This development and the others I'm discovering are slightly odd. I went away and, except for one train blitz, blew off my Hindi, and have returned vastly improved. I know instinctively now that if I imagine Meena saying the sentence I want to read — imitate in my head her verbal pauses for commas, the way she runs a clause up the scale then lets it drop — I can keep the long assembly in my mind. I know how to tell the candy shop owner, *"I was touring"* — easily, offhandedly, in the past tense. I no longer have

to speak in one strange, singular dimension. I know how to skim a paragraph for just one word, the way I can with English. Before, the snakes would writhe into one ball.

Shabaz: I've made great strides, but it's all slightly spooky, for this all happened when I gave up the struggle. I'd worked feverishly, and as soon as I stopped trying, I made enormous progress. This kind of experience feels bizarre, though it's a frequent occurrence with creative undertakings. You struggle fruitlessly at your desk to come up with a presentation, are seized by inspiration listening to *The Amazing 80s* on the drive home. You take the dog out and turn a corner, literally: suddenly you know what that letter should say. Cognitive psychologists have known for years that knocking off leads to creative breakthroughs, but they couldn't say why. Lately, brain scientists have gotten a handle on the mechanisms.

"In creativity research, we refer to the three Bs—for the bathtub, the bed and the bus—places where ideas have famously and suddenly emerged," Washington University psychologist R. Keith Sawyer told a reporter from *Time.* "When we take time off from working on a problem, we change what we're doing and our context, and that can activate different areas of our brain. . . . If we're lucky, in the next context we may hear or see something that relates—distantly—to the problem that we had temporarily put aside."

With language study and all the challenges of the mind, breaks lead to breakthroughs. Swami-ji, with all his chuttis, turned out, had been a linguistic visionary all along.

BACK IN THE KITCHEN, I hear a thwacking. Meena is in the next room cleaning. *"You are happy with the geezer?"* Dad 1 asks, after telling me that Pakistan is collapsing from internal complications. I'm not about to say that the geezer has the unusual ability to cause light switches to shut off spontaneously. I'm a little worried about all this light and air locking I'm able to provoke, but the

family didn't notice me dashing from my room in a towel, and I think we'll just keep it that way. *"I am liking the geezer very much,"* I tell him.

Dad 2 is delighted to see me. DELIGHTED. *"You're back!"* he says. *"Back! You were away! And now you're back. You didn't like Jaipur? No, you don't like Udaipur. You do? You like Udaipur? Truly? The* mithai *you brought us was bad."*

I think he says the sweets, the mithai, I brought them from a fancy Jaipur store have given somebody food poisoning. *Who?* I ask, horrified.

"The mithai could *have given someone food poisoning,"* he repeats: multipart verb; still a bit beyond my grasp. *"It had fungus all over it."*

"But it didn't yesterday," I say.

"Yes," he says sadly. *"The mithai was bad."*

"That Jaipur," I say. *"Not nice, like Udaipur."* But he's already on to American misbehavior in Afghanistan, how I paid too much for curtains in Jaipur, and I'm pleased to note we haven't said *one word* in English. Except "fungus."

· 10 ·

"The matter is not one for laughing"

 Harold was the first to go down, and soon after, others followed. Because these events occurred in a cluster, they would always later on seem connected, like an implosion that had happened in segments. The episodes weren't really linked, however, except perhaps by centrifugal force. If they had been, I might have been better prepared for all that happened, but Harold's was the only fall I saw coming.

That wasn't hard, though, of course.

"IN THE JUNGLE, a greedy lion was living. This lion was eating all the animals." Swami-ji is telling me a story from the *Panchatantra,* a collection of fables compiled in the fourth century to educate the sons of a king. I'm worrying about how I've ruined the school's one copy, having secreted it out in my backpack for practice, then dodged my own good intentions for so long, the book looks like it's been chewed. This is one of several school publications I've shredded through long-term ferrying, along with a Jain true-confessions magazine Meena hasn't guessed yet is missing. A pile of dead reading material is growing in my room, evidence of the troubles I'm having with Hindi script. After so many defeats and masticated hopes, just the sight of Devanagari makes me nervous.

"In time, all the animals met," Swami-ji says in the rosy tones of storytelling. *"They came up with a plan for the lion. Each day, one animal from a species would volunteer to be eaten. When it was the rabbits' turn, they chose a rabbit who lived for many, many years and was very wise."* A cry drifts up from the street, a man collecting old newspapers. *"This rabbit took his time in going to the lion's lair. When he arrived, the lion was angry. 'Venerable lord!' the rabbit said. 'A thousand apologies, but the delay could not be helped. Another lion has attacked all the rabbits and eaten the others. Only I have escaped.' The lion roared in fury to hear this. But the clever rabbit was remaining calm."* Swami-ji, then, is the picture of calm himself, his face set in easy concentration. Helaena and I have not yet gone to his apartment to tell him about the letter. *"'Where is this lion?' the lion cried. 'Not far from here,' the rabbit said. 'I will show you,' and led him to a well. 'That is his cave,' the rabbit said, pointing, and the lion, seeing his own reflection, attacked it and drowned."* The letter is to the governing advisers, the ones with the forehead marks in the photographs. One of the students has been making death threats, it reports.

Harold had, in, of all places, his Hindi journal. *"There is a young girl,"* he'd begun one rambling story after the Whisperer had balked at sealing the deed and turned him down. *"I am watching her broken body. She is going to die."* On a train the two of them had taken from Jaipur, he'd apparently screamed, "You're getting what you want in India. Why can't I?" The Whisperer was so startled, it took her three days to squeak out the words "sexual harassment."

"Harold-ji, in this sentence, the word 'body' does not take the oblique case," Vidhu said in journal class the day Harold read his opus. He was not quite grasping the story line.

This student must be sent home immediately, the letter urged, citing this example of his conduct, though truly, the rest of us weren't taking his blather all that seriously by then. What ultimately did Harold in weren't the death threats. No, his real fatal error had been to shout an Anglo-Saxon epithet at Helaena while she was getting a manicure, one they didn't toss around freely back in Tennessee. Or in the posh Trident Hotel, where she'd been counseling him to lighten up with the Whisperer after he'd tagged along. "Why, that wasn't very nice," she'd said slowly, and from then on, he was headed for the well.

Poor Harold. He'd skipped the orientation seminar on sexual harassment, so had no sense of the terror those words struck here. But Helaena and me, we'd gone.

"Maybe he will get better," Swami-ji says weakly when he answers the door that evening and we tell him about the letter, the one we composed and e-mailed to the supervisors of his supervisor some time earlier. Not possible, we say, and in low voices explain: "Harold has committed sexual harassment."

"Sexual harassment?" Swami-ji swallows, then, shaking his head, acquires the bemused look of a man accepting his fate. Within a day, another one of his charges will be ingloriously packing it in.

Just the sight of Devanagari makes me nervous, I.

That profound, stubbing freeze that written Hindi brought on — puzzling betrayal, briefly, each time: *But always before, books were such comfort* — continued so long, troubled me so, that after my return to the States, I investigated. One group of researchers I found, also wondering whether second writing systems bollixed reading abilities, had rounded up Chinese students fluent in English and tested them on passages in Roman, the script used for English. The results could not have been startling to the students, who probably had tattered copies of *Aesop's Fables* in their dorm rooms: they came in "four standard deviations" below their American counterparts, notably lower. People are slower in foreign scripts, many studies report, partly for obvious reasons—because they're reading in a foreign language, with all the bumpiness that entails. But also, partly, for reasons having to do with the effects of the writing itself on the brain.

For years, hardly anyone (Western) was much concerned with second scripts, with the neural ramifications of them, or any aspect, when you got right down to it. The feeling was that unless you were a Bible translation missionary, who really cared? even though, as missionary translators could have reported, a multitude of scripts exist in the world: alphabets, syllabaries, *abjads* (alphabets that are mostly consonants), complex writing systems composed of ideograms. How many, even a rough figure, is impossible to say.

"It depends on how you count," UCLA professor emeritus of linguistics William Bright wrote to me. "Is the French writing system, which uses â à ê è é etc., different from English? Probably most people would say no. Then what about Icelandic, which uses the two additional symbols 'thorn' and 'edh' in addition to accented vowels? Or the uncial script of Irish, or the blackletter 'fraktur' script* used for German until the end of World War Two?

"The short answer is," Bright wrote, "there are a couple of hundred."

And yet 90 percent of what specialists know about reading is based on studies involving one alphabet, guess which one. Although that's changing. With scores of immigrants arriving in the West, with shop signs in West Yorkshire and Rome and Oakland written in forms like waves or snakes or squares, with the all-around boom in second language studies, it was inevitable that an offshoot field would emerge: second script studies. Just as surely, it has, in no time, acquired its own jargon—the metallic-sounding term L2WS, for second language writing system—and a rally is on (with luck, short-

---

* Fraktur is still kept alive in the gift shops of Pennsylvania Dutch restaurants.

lived) to refer to someone who knows a second script as "biscriptal." Gabriela, with five, would be "polyscriptal."

At a reading symposium I attended in Toronto several years ago, three panels out of sixteen were devoted to second scripts. At "Cross-Linguistic Perspectives on Reading Fluency in Second Language Learners," it was seats down front only, the talks roiled with news. A research team had discovered what it was calling a "Chinese region" in the brain, an area in the left middle frontal gyrus that lights up when people read Chinese but not English—and gets lit even when someone's grasp of Chinese is limited to a few weeks' lessons. No one could say for sure what the area did, only that it was part of a larger pattern being observed: Chinese writing fires the brain differently, in certain key respects. On scans, it activates both brain hemispheres, whereas English engages mostly just the left, the half where language functions generally reside.

"Something about the visual properties of Chinese requires recruitment of the right hemisphere," Jessica Nelson, a grad student who'd worked on the studies mused, then added the refrain of the day: "But we don't know why that is."

Although the focus of the symposium was on children and reading, there was a reason the participants, mainly educators, were flocking to these side discussions. Between 1998 and 2000, the number of U.S. kids who spoke "a language other than English at home" more than doubled, according to one study. By 2015, the same study predicted, they'd constitute 30 percent of the American school population. When you consider that increasingly, the other languages spoken around the house aren't written in Roman, it's easy to see why the auditorium was filling up. As more and more kids go through school with knowledge of two scripts, educators are going to need to know whether there are peculiarities to that kind of wiring that convolute reading.

So far, where they're most up to speed is in understanding the universals, the common ways all writing scripts affect the brain. Be it in Manchu script, Cyrillic, or Hebrew, within five hundred milliseconds after your eye has swept over a word—any word, let's say "fleece"—three main neural areas act to produce a brief and woolly image. So quickly that you have no sense of it, one area of the brain, the left inferior frontal gyrus, gauges contextual meaning: the fact that in the sentence you just flew past, the author was referring to a lamb's coat. Another area, the left parietal-temporal region, is busy calculating the phonemes, the sounds, encoded in the print; it also analyzes the lines of print—ascertaining that they amount to letters and aren't random squiggles. A third area, the left occipital-temporal region, has gone to work to automate recognition, to speed things up. Through some as-yet-unidentified mechanism, all three areas fire in coordination, symphonically, whether the lettering reads 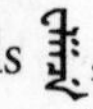, овечья шерсмь, or חזג—Manchu, Cyrillic, or Hebrew for "fleece," respectively—so long as it's familiar to you.

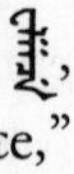

The process sounds both miraculous and exhausting—if you had to enact it using will, you'd end up running screaming from the chair. And things get more flabbergasting when it comes to the differences in the way the brain processes 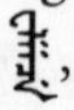, овечья шерсмь, and חזג, or they do as far as anyone can surmise. The guys who have the most-worked-out theories on this are the ones who make deductions from observing the aftermath of neural trauma. They were at this before the advent of machines and technological advances. They've had longer to formulate their beliefs. Michel Paradis, for instance, through his studies of bilinguals with brain damage, is convinced that in people with two, three, or four scripts, what you have are two, three, or four subsystems at work. If you're talking broad overview, he agrees with the neuroimaging specialists—all lettering flows through the same three brain sites. But at the most microscopic, theoretical levels—so minute, no scanner invented has the facility to explore them—he believes that each script, each written language, is processed separately.

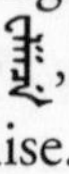

"You can be dyslexic in one language and not another," he points out, and elaborates: you can get reading glitches in Chinese but not English if you have facility in both, in French but not in Italian. That would indicate, Paradis surmises, that the brain is running the Chinese and English words, the French and Italian, on separate tracks: same highway, different lanes, he believes. Up in Toronto, they were arguing entire other blue routes for Chinese.

Chinese script comes up a lot in these discussions, attracts numerous studies, being so starkly different from Roman — it's through contrasts that information is revealed. Chinese-English bilinguals are popular with scanning teams because they're fluent in two of the world's three major writing systems: morphemic and phonemic. (If the testers wanted to go for all three, they'd include syllabic, and get someone also versed in Blackfoot, Iberian, or hiragana Japanese, systems where the symbols represent syllables: *to-yo-ta,* spelled with three characters.)

With Chinese, which is morphemic, each symbol stands for one thing or action or concept. Each arrangement of brushstrokes has its own meaning, is, in other words, a morpheme. The system seems staggeringly inefficient if you're used to a phonemic one, the Roman alphabet, say, with its letters that can be perpetually reassembled to spell out thousands of words. With Roman, all you need to know are those twenty-six sound-based symbols. With Chinese, nothing about the brushstrokes tells you how to pronounce them. You need to be able to recognize each character, or ideogram, and since there are five thousand to six thousand of them, that's a hell of a memorization effort at the start. This might seem like a lumbering approach, but actually it's streamlined to fit the character of the language. Should the Chinese vote, as the Turks did, to convert to the Roman alphabet, they would no doubt immediately elect to switch back, because Chinese, unlike Turkish, is tonal. It'd do them no good to transliterate words into alphabetic form; *mao,* for instance, can mean one of eleven things, including "mother" and "horse," depending on which tone is used. Chinese is full of homophones like that. Each one needs its own character.

Chinese-English speakers are popular on the MRI table for another reason, because they can cross a basic reading divide. In the overall scheme of things, some people, monolingual Chinese being among them, read mainly by sight; some, the alphabetically inclined, us, read mainly by sound. You can sound out words in English, c-a-t, although English is notorious for how often it confounds this rule. Italian and Finnish, Spanish too, are straight-up phonemic, not booby-trapped like English, which springs irregularly spelled words on the poor, increasingly suspecting learner every time they think they're moving. Just when they've gotten the hang of "through," the language throws in "tough." It's so loosey-goosey that the word "fish" could be spelled "ghoti," as George Bernard Shaw pointed out, using the *f* sound from "rough," the *i* sound as it appears in "women," and the *ti* from "nation."

On the whole, written English and Chinese are apples and oranges, 蘋果 and 橘子, so drastically different that all you have to do is see them laid out side by side—Chinese rippling top to bottom, English tumbling left to right—to suspect what Paradis contends: the brain handles them differently. And though you might not arrive at the same conclusion comparing French and Italian, same alphabets, he believes that the same argument holds. As evidence, he cites the numerous cases of bilinguals who have suffered a stroke, or advanced syphilis, or a bad car crash, or some other event disastrous to the brain, and subsequently lost reading ability in one language but not the other.

Looking over the cases in Paradis's textbook—Patient M., half-Georgian, half-Assyrian, after a blow to the head could recognize one letter only in Georgian, nearly all in Assyrian—I wondered whether the afflicted lost, along with their lettering, the larger perceptual effects that apparently go with it. Recently, arguments have been advanced that the alphabet you use shapes the way you see the world. You can, if you want to, test the proposition at home. Take a copy of Picasso's frenetic *Guernica* and hold it to the mirror, and you'll find, guaranteed, it looks flatter. The reason is, it's been composed so the elements—the trampling bull, the knifed horse, the howling woman—rush right to left, against the direction you're used to reading in. The result is abrading, gives a sense of imminent pileup. Though presumably, if the painting were to tour right-to-left-reading Saudi Arabia, museumgoers there might wonder what the fuss was about.

In the L2WS camp, lately there's been a lot of testing of perceptual effects. Some of the studies have been boondoggles: someone got the big funding bucks to document that with laundry detergent ads in right-to-left Hebrew, the "after" shot, the sparkling-clean clothes, runs on the left, while in English it appears on the right. Some have been mildly provocative: Japanese students, one investigation determined, have better visual memories than the English do, for the reason the Japanese are schooled in Chinese ideograms and so get a prodigious workout in the corresponding brain areas. Bilingual Arabic readers, another found, accustomed to an alphabet in which vowel sounds aren't indicated, complain on reading English of a sensation they're being given "too much information."

And one was chilling—or it was to me, given the sectarian divisions I'd come to witness in India. In this study, the researcher showed Indian subjects who spoke either Hindi or Urdu a straight line and asked them to say where the middle was. (Spoken Hindi and Urdu are very nearly the same, but are written using different scripts: Devanagari and Arabic.) Repeatedly, the Hindi speakers insisted on a spot that was, in reality, closer to the right. That group were left-to-right readers, and mostly Hindus. The Urdu speakers, right-to-left, Muslims, consistently skewed to the left. "Even though they thought they were bisecting [the line] in the middle, there was an error," Jyotsna Vaid, the researcher, observed, and as she did, I was needled by a thought: if something as slight as lettering can slant the way we see the world, what does that imply about our ability to transcend the stone gray barrier of words?

DUE TO HIS SUDDEN change in plans, Harold is not in attendance at a local symposium on terrorism that's being held, though just about everyone else I've met is. The event takes place in a plain oblong building, like a Kingdom Hall, I think, having mentally converted the Ganesh statue onstage into background molecules. Renee and I are shown to seats in the front. To the right of the elephant god, Udaipur's graybeards are taking chairs for a discussion of "chaos and creation," the euphemism the organizer came up with for recent events, more grandiloquent than another we'd just recently heard: "9/11."

A live American, I'm asked to go first, get up and say a few words. At a loss for any, I read a poem a friend, the poet Dennis Nurkse, sent by e-mail, which hit like a smack when I opened it. He wrote about lines of stockbrokers shuffling north, about the odor that lingered for days, and the dimension of smell, filling in so suddenly, arriving so late, blasted me there in the cybercafe, was expiation for escape.

Next, a kindly faced—what? poet? artist?—gets up and speaks in Hindi. English surfaces, glistening, slippery: "republic of thought"; "we wait for final reality"; "in India, we are immune to temporary situations"—then he's lost to me across the gulf of understanding, and I'm keening, cursing my traveler's Hindi (*as far as you'll ever get, admit it*), and he holds his palms out, his intelligent face up to the light. I'd give all my first language to know what he said. The man has a high forehead, wide black glasses, shocking white mantle of hair. His upturned palms are a plea—*This is the way;* his tone, too. He smiles. The audience chuckles. I just want to know.

"*So, our . . . wins, but when*"—two sentences sunk—"*other desire that other world is built.*" Then the relief of English: "I do not know any kind of liberty except artistic creation." Then I'm plunging again: *"Jhanjhaton ke beech hi hota hai lekin jhanjhaton se mukta hone ke liye."* I think of the deaf boys: how do they ever stand the weight, the layers on layers of incomprehension? *"Har baar hum likh kar ek choti si duniyaa se mukta ho jate hain. Saara lekhan swadeenta hai."* Outside, a cow lows. I'm grateful for pure sound.

Afterward, when everyone's milling around, the man comes over. I ask him his name. It sounds familiar, which seems eerie, till I remember, but it is. Nand Chaturvedi, a respected Rajasthani poet — the Bikaner writer had mentioned him. This same sense of *kal,* of yesterday winding ahead, continues to loop through the rest of our conversation, so that by the time he asks if I'll visit at his home, each rise of his voice has already become a reminder of something else he said.

WHEN SWAMI-JI WAS the next to be kneecapped, Helaena and I were briefly lanced with guilt, sure we'd somehow scuttled his career when we'd facilitated Harold's exit with the letter. Then we reviewed the events. What the bulldog-faced Indian head of operations had told us, specifically, when he'd appeared one day in the flesh from Delhi, was that he'd received "hundreds of complaints" about Swami-ji. Hundreds. It was a puzzling figure, since at the school, we'd only ever numbered four at our greatest, and since, furthermore, you had to request official permission to contact the man, which would have slowed the complaint process. But perhaps he meant he thought he'd get that many once he hauled us into a back room one by one and grilled us for dirt. Which is what he did, immediately.

When I'd seen movies in which forcibly detained men ratted out their leaders, I'd jeered. They were curs. Now I was yapping within minutes. Classes were starting late or not at all, I complained. Homework was coming back ungraded. Cooking class? Waste of time. The weekly guests were lame. The Whisperer and Helaena barked, too, then everyone was reunited in the main room. When Swami-ji joined us from down the hall, he strolled in casually, but pieces of his hair were pointing straight up.

In movies, the troops pay for their treachery down the line, but this was India, where they invented karma. At the source, it comes instant. That night, the supervisor took Helaena and me to the Trident, for dinner and to hint at the sweeping changes we'd see. Like what? I asked. He thought about it, glared. "That's for you to figure out," he said cryptically, then relaxed into chummy confessions. "When I asked them to talk to me about Swami-ji, the women teachers cried," he said, alluding to whatever ruckuses had been going on behind closed doors. The sudden confidence inspired me to respond in kind when he asked about my plans down the line.

". . . and possibly write a few newspaper stories while I'm here." I was up to the part about how I thought I'd maybe look for a dalit to interview, when a low vibration in the room seemed to make the potted ferns sway.

"A dalit?" he began. "Did you say a dalit?" "Da-leet," two traveling syllables, the second stretched so wide, it was halfway to Jaipur. Slow to catch on, I smiled. I had!

"And can you define what you mean by that?" he said. "Do you mean a street sweeper? No? Are you discussing this in a political sense? Ha! You can't even say what a dalit is." He leaned back; that's what he'd thought.

"People believe they can talk to tribals. They believe they can talk to dalits," he said. "They do not know what they're talking about. Have you applied for my permission for this? No, you have not. I'm afraid if you do decide to go ahead with this plan, if you do decide to talk to a dalit, then you will be blacklisted."

My head continued nodding as I tried to fathom: from what? Further educational pursuits on the subcontinent? The next semester at the school? The blacklist possibility was confusing, but I was gaining clarity on why, when the phone rang from Delhi. Swami-ji answered. *"Kab tak?"* How high?

"You will be blacklisted by the Indian government," he said. "You will never be able to return to India." I imagined a functionary in the New York visa office snapping as he pushed my passport back, "It is known you have spoken to a dalit." It wasn't terrifically hard.

We paused to give me a moment for contrition. The evening picked up again as he regaled us with stories about the time terrorists had shot half the passengers on a plane he was on, then the next morning, he was on the first flight out. For a week after, Swami-ji and Vidhu had to teach standing side by side, to demonstrate that Swami-ji had been demoted. That requirement was soon dropped, and no other changes ever became evident. The visit had not been fruitless, however. The curriculum did improve, beginning with the quality of the weekly guest. No housewives he'd encountered on his way to check what the deal was with the mail, Swami-ji had evidently been told. For the debut upgrade, he announced he'd arranged for a special visitor, an activist from the community, a firebrand, an intellectual.

"You will ask five questions." His tone was sure as he crisply passed out the prep sheets. *"This woman who is coming to the school is a crusader,"* he said with a smile of achievement. *"She is the author of many books, the woman you will meet today,"* he said, looking nothing like a man who was begging to be sent to Guyana to teach Hindi. *"This woman, she is a* dalit.*"*

WHEN THE NOSEDIVE that followed turned out to be Helaena's, I wasn't surprised to find that hurtle being analyzed all over town. By then, her face had often appeared in the papers, smiling demurely at various candle-hoisting events. She'd frequently been visible through the curtains of the maharana's car, or emerging from the snooty Mansai Plaza boutique calling to the sales force in the door, "Just send them to me at the palace." Her local renown had grown so, you'd have to have been blind and confined to a wheelchair to miss it.

Once, when I was walking down the street, my thoughts were interrupted by the sound of a small stampede. Turning, I found five pimply Hindu guys huffing.

"Madam," the tallest, about nineteen, said. "Excuse me. Do you know," and he lowered his voice, "Helaena?"

Sure did, I said.

A shorter friend inhaled sharply. "Where is she?" he asked.

"Here," I said, meaning Udaipur. She'd been traveling. Their eyes widened, the boys went speechless, two gasped. Clearly, they thought I was saying, Right here, about to materialize in front of you.

"Oh, I love being me!" Helaena said annoyingly when I related this.

So when she had to flee the palace, the din of discussion that followed was no surprise. Dhanesh, the young goat who ran the Rose Garden restaurant, had the following meta-analysis: "Maybe she was proudy," he theorized. "She was getting free mobile phone. Free car. Maybe she was saying, 'Oh, I got all these things.' That is proudy." He was taking the long view, the karmic one.

But any proudiness—and certainly, there'd been some—had not, even indirectly, led to her departure, which had occurred in mid-November, about a week before. I was not about to tell Dhanesh what had, however, even though I knew, for Helaena had phoned me the night the maharana decided the bill had come due for the cable connection and all the French fries.

Two weeks before, I don't think she'd have called, but we'd recently gone on a weekend to Jaipur, and in the course of the trip, a friendship had set. Until then, what we'd had was, more exactly, an alliance. In the first weeks, I had not, truth be told, any intention of taking someone half my age seriously. Helaena had the same misgivings in the other direction, as evidenced by the time she grabbed my passport off a pile and, reading out the date of birth, exclaimed, "Why, I don't even *know* how old that would make someone." But that was early, before we'd both looked around and calculated what the friendship pickings were.

The occasion of the Jaipur trip was my birthday, which I'd been planning to spend hunkered down and oblivious. "Uh-uh," Helaena had said. "You've been sick half your adult life," something I'd recently melodramatically declared while confiding to her my medical history. "Do you want to be unhappy on your birthday? Or any day? I'm going to remind you of that periodically." She also, I knew, regarded Jaipur as a shopping mecca, but all the same, I was touched.

For the big day, we hit a Pizza Hut. Months of curry were making me desperate. We tried to go to McDonald's first, in fact, took a rickshaw a half-hour out, then discovered all they sold were Mc-Aloos, potato burgers. There was Ronald, and there were the arches and the children's play area, and there they were trying to palm off fake McDonald's, Helaena said, put out. Like *The Martian Chronicles,* I agreed. We took a rickshaw back, and the next day for lunch reverted to real life, the one we'd come into.

From the veranda of a palace hotel, we watched a peacock fan the air. The weight of his tail made him stagger like a drunk. Over *aloo gobi* yellow with cumin, we told each other stories about our lives, adjusting for decades the way I'd learned to with Renee. We did twenty minutes on whom we'd liked in eighth grade to buoy Helaena's spirits, twenty on careers to lever mine, and she contributed with good cheer, though she didn't yet have one.

The stories entered the family realm. I said I'd been a stepmother. She mentioned having one. Her father, an academic like her mother, had moved out when she was eight, had been asked to, it sounded like. For a while afterward, she told me, he'd dogged them.

"He wouldn't stop showing up," she said. "Even when we moved.

A shrink told me that didn't necessarily mean he wanted me. It seemed like that, but it didn't mean that." The father had gone on to have two girls in another marriage, not the two, I supposed, that were in a photograph on her wall, alongside the maharana's. I pegged them as the two more her mother had had, for she then told a story about how once, when she'd gotten an internship in her father's town, her stepmother had barred her from the condo.

"I could stay two nights," she said, and paused. The peacock, down the lawn, was making racketing prehistoric sounds. "Two nights," she submitted. "That was it," and she laughed. "She just didn't want me there."

Jaipur was the first time I heard her voice go flat, no lilt, no slow amused roll. The second was the mid-November night my cell phone went off in my room, a stuttering, close to midnight, that made me quickly sit up. "You're going to have to hear this. You're my only friend here," Helaena said, starting off on a drawl. The next sentence, she was uncurled, all business.

At a reception that night, she said, she'd worn her finest sari, a Banarsi silk thick as cream. This was the first palace affair she'd been summoned to in weeks, but Sri-ji, what relief, was himself again, teasing her under his breath when she circled past, casting appraising glances while nodding to a diplomat. Before the meal was laid out, he cocked his head. When she stopped beside him, she mimed surprise, as if she'd just now found him. She smiled conspiratorially: *The palace wags had nothing on them.* A project had come up, he said. He needed her support. They were going to have to move on this thing fast. He could tell her more when they met after dinner, and he named a room she didn't know, one that sounded dim and far away.

When she crept in after searching the halls, she discovered no servants holding trays that sparkled with diamonds, the way the books said the preliminaries went. No naked girls frolicking in a bubble-bath pool, beckoning her to join them. All she found was that up-close, the maharana's beard was more *paan* stained than she'd thought. When he smiled and described the project he was imagining, she saw how blackened the betel nut juice had left his teeth.

To this day, the central mystery of India for me remains how Helaena could have been shocked by the encounter, but I could hear, at that moment, she was. Her voice caught, lost its high scalloping, till she sounded small and unadorned, till she sounded how she must have back when she'd taught Sunday school in Pulaski, Tennessee. Another puzzlement is why, to fend him off, she thought a foolproof dodge would be to claim she was frigid. "All he said was we'd have to take care of that," she said sadly on the phone.

The line did buy her time, though, and that Friday, when the maharana left to visit his wife in Bombay, I corralled two rickshaws and pulled up at a side entrance to the palace around dinnertime. If fleeing implies haste, Helaena didn't do that, but she was gone by the time he got back.

A few days later, I ran into her at Renee's hotel, where she'd moved in her self-deposed exile. How was she? I asked.

"Why, I am so mad," she said. I waited for her vowels to stop elongating.

But why? I asked.

"Well," she began, "last year, you know, someone took naked photos of me?"

"They took naked photos," I said flatly. I hadn't.

"Yes," she said. "And, you know, they sent them to me at the palace."

To the palace?

"Yes, and before I moved out, I tore them up." This said primly. "And I made sure to throw them away." This, ruefully. "But the houseboys found them and pasted them back together, and now they're circulating all over the palace."

She brushed a speck off her knee, as it was taking me longer than

Meena to get the gist. Then I did, and my eyes bugged out. *Here you go,* she'd in essence told the maharana. *Here you go, bud; take a look at what you're missing.*

And the photos weren't all that Helaena had left behind, I discovered several weeks after when Piers asked me to the royal birthday party, a lavish annual event. Everyone in town knew that fat nawabs and princes so handsome they robbed the court artists of their abilities would arrive glittering with jewels. Court musicians would compose ragas for the occasion that were denser and more narcotizing than opium. The palace bards, the *charans,* would write verses as perfumed as sandalwood paste. There'd be fragrant platters of mutton and fowl, melons carved with images of geese and swirling fish, though the thirty-six Mr. World contestants I found when I arrived were a complete surprise. Beauty pageants were all the rage then in India, to such a degree, the governor of Gujarat had just outlawed them in his state. The country had gone pageant mad since India had taken the Miss Universe title a few years running, but it was hard to get people to let their sisters and daughters work it onstage, so what you ended up with were a lot of pec show extravaganzas.

The evening got off to a labored start. I had to spend a good part of it in the bathroom, tugging on my sari. Not having put one on before, I didn't know that unless the fit was plumb, any movement, walking or breathing, would cause the fabric to start to bunch at the middle. Some algorithm of sari silk would take over, the drift would gather force, till you'd find you were bulbous about the waist, like you had on a giant diaper. Every half-hour, I had to mince into the ladies' room in what, except for the clutching, might have been mistaken for a stately slide, till I waylaid a partygoer who was washing her hands and got her to rewrap me.

The slow strolls were very nearly worth it, though, for the chance they afforded to admire the courtyard of the zenana, the old harem quarters, site of the festivities. The quadrangle was dazzling that night, transformed by candlelight and the guests. Delicate women in gold-lined saris were wearing gems the size of fruit. Men in fitted white britches and with diamond buttons on their jackets had postures as straight as their swords. The zenana glittered even at the foreigners' end, where the Mr. Worlds were seated across five tables, hair coiffed and gleaming.

Piers, who'd made a beeline there, dragged Mr. Germany back. Mr. Germany settled in at our table and detailed the rules of competition, repeatedly winking as if he'd been interviewed too often. Several of his companions joined him: Mr. Smile, Mr. Photogenic, Mr. Physique. Mr. Argentina, who had Fabio hair. Mr. Swaziland explained that when he wasn't in beauty competitions, he was employed as a financial adviser. "Best believe I'm handing over all my rupees pronto," I said sotto voce to Piers.

"What, no Mr. America?" I inquired of the table, after a glance around.

"There was someone in Mr. Manhattan Manhunt, but that was as far as it went," a skinny Mr. Landmass said in a clearly pitying tone.

"That's outrageous! I'm contacting the embassy!" I mugged. Mr. L. M. nodded — good idea. An official hurried over. The misters were collected and taken to be presented to the maharana. On the way back, they broke into a spontaneous chest-to-chest catwalk strut, reflexively, without being told.

"What, you've never met him? Come on," Piers said. He stopped to greet the nawab of Gujarat, a portly young man in a white Nehru tunic, then escorted me to where the Divine Mr. M. was standing, somber-faced, by a cannon. "Divine" here is a literal, not figurative, description. The rulers of Mewar are descended, it's believed, from the god Shiva. At introductory range, this one wasn't intimidating in appearance — about five foot four, with sprouting werewolf hair on his ears and the wide, clear glasses AV crew members wore in the 1970s—but I was terrified all the same. For this was when I discovered what else Helaena left behind.

"One minute," he said after performing Braille calculations on my face with his scowl. "You are an American here?" he asked.

Sort of, I said. I had some idea where this was going.

"Do you know Helaena?" he repeated.

I'd possibly seen her at my school, I replied.

And that's when I learned what else she'd left: one rankled potentate. The maharana's surname, like all Rajputs', was Singh—"Lion," and this one now roared.

"She is crazy. Helaena is crazy. This girl is very very crazy," my host thundered, then calming himself, invited me to spend Christmas Eve at his quarters. He had concerns he wanted to air. "We are in our office at nine-thirty in the morning," he said, directing me to phone that day.

As Piers steered me back to the table, my hair looked spiked, the way Swami-ji's had. But later, I reflected that while the maharana's growl had caught me off-guard, that wasn't what was really startling about the night. Helaena had, after all, just turned a 1,200-year-old tradition of royal rampaging on its head. A bellow was only in order.

No, what was truly surprising was that he'd appeared as hurt and disbelieving as she had. In those seconds when their voices had been unguarded, there'd been no mistaking: they'd both got their feelings bruised. Yet he'd known about the nephew for a while. She'd been aware of the in-house palace assistant countdown. Surely, anyone would have had to agree: the writing was on the wall.

Just the sight of Devanagari makes me nervous, 2.

One gray December afternoon, in the middle of judging yet another beauty competition (that theme having begun to haunt my days), I came to the blinding insight that I'd been reading Hindi the wrong, drawn-out way. Now, smile-and-flash shows aren't ordinarily a catalyst for orthographic understanding, but first of all, what is? and secondly, that was just the drift my life had taken. By now there was nothing unusual about my sitting at a long table, holding a number up, and thinking about other matters as a Miss Rena Menara did a perky folk dance in purdah, with a scarf over her head. I'd given her an extra point for not falling off the stage. In the postcolonial hangover that existed here, being Western meant you were in demand as a judge, for anything. By the end of the year, I'd have presided at a terrorism symposium, an envelope-making competition, a kindergarten opening, a poetry meet, and at this, the local university's beauty and talent exhibition, which was rapidly turning into a Michael Jackson impersonation contest.

"You can practice your Hindi," the university's blow-dried, strutting student union president had said in persuading Helaena and me to sign on. But so far all we'd practiced was flashing rating cards, through three moonwalkers dressed as "Beat It"–era Michael; a girl in a sky blue costume who gave an homage to Krishna her all; and one Miss Jahi Janee, who wiped the stage with her previous competitors, a dispirited group of girl singers. Miss Janee had stormed on to whoops and paper airplanes and delivered an enthusiastic MTV-inspired performance.

"There are no gay people in India," the teachers at the school periodically insisted, but someone had neglected to tell the next contestant, who was astonishingly slinky in all-black. He'd put in a lot of time practicing in front of his bedroom mirror, you could see, and I was giving him a 9 for swivel, when a chant went up from the stadium: "We want a song, yes! We want a song!" I heard it distantly, assumed they were asking the guy for a reprise.

"What Hindi songs do you know?" Helaena whispered beneath a stage smile, and then I keyed in. They meant from us.

"None," I said. "Well, kind of one," I said, and gave the name of a song whose lyrics contained a lot of English, one I recalled from film class.

"Huh?" She frowned. I scrawled the title on a judging card, in transliterated Roman. I assumed she'd appreciate the conversion, that she automatically did what I did: skipped the Devanagari and wrote the words the way they sounded in Roman, if no teachers were looking.

"I'm sorry," she said. "It's so weird, but I have to see Hindi words in Hindi writing to get them," and it was like a bolt of clarity had struck. Helaena, I suddenly perceived, was reading organically, not regarding the Indian print as nuisance stand-ins for substantive letters, not translating one script into another before doing the same with the words. She was not, in other words, proceeding in the most cumbersome, book-shredding way possible. She'd rigged it mentally for herself so that Devanagari letters produced sound directly; hadn't built in extra, time-delay steps; wasn't detouring back through the U.S. to get to every sentence. Small wonder, I saw, my homework took days, while she had time to laze around with the nephew. A flurry of questions distracted me: Why would anyone settle on the hardest, most convoluting method of reading, a veritable bench press each time, when common sense should have led straight to Helaena's approach? Why didn't I just read Hindi right? I wondered if our orthographic differences had to do with a difference in age —whether learning a second script gets harder, the way, majority opinion holds, learning a second language does?

But there wasn't exactly anyone to put the questions to then, and besides, the blow-dried student union president was hustling us toward the stage.

"WRITTEN LANGUAGE IS a cultural invention," Ken Pugh, Yale University researcher and senior scientist at Haskins Laboratories said at the start of his presentation in Toronto. This was several years after my Bollywood possibilities had been eclipsed by the fellowship's end. "Spoken language is a biological specialization. Speech is mastered naturally. But there is no natural reading zone in the brain," he said. "It's a challenge of brain plasticity to learn to read." All around, people were adjusting their handouts, rummaging in pockets for pens. What Pugh was saying was warm-up, old news to them. But I straightened, leaned forward, as it became clear he was indirectly addressing the central question I'd had about second script: is there a window of opportunity for learning one?

The brain is configured differently for spoken language than it is for written, Pugh continued, alluding to the well-known observation that humans are built to speak, the point at which this discussion begins. A number of biologically based arguments support the idea. Our larynxes, for instance, are lower than the early hominids', having descended into this position for the reason that, though it puts us at greater risk of choking while eating, it also allows us to produce a wide range of speech sounds. (Though this particular theory was briefly called into question when it was recently discovered that dropped larynxes aren't unique to humans, as everyone had been thinking, but can be found in red deer and koalas as well — presumably to allow males of the species to bellow more ferociously. At the end of the analysis, however, a general conclusion was reached that the mating-roar belief did not cancel out the better-speech hypothesis.)

For years now, to give another example, the argument's been made that the capacity for speech is encoded in our genes, passed down through the DNA. Certainly, many speech disorders appear to be genetic. The best-known example of this is the so-called KE family, which lives in England. Sixteen of the thirty members studied display an identical, genetically programmed constellation of language problems, including serious difficulty with verb tense. The ones with the gene disorder are missing the natural ability to use the past tense of regular verbs. (With irregular verbs — "swim," "swam" — they're generally fine.) Even after the *-ed* principle is explained, they won't automatically generalize. "Tell me about your weekend," the teacher will say, and they might answer, as one man did,

"On Saturday I watch TV and I watch *Plastic Man* and I watch football." "No, you watch*ed* TV," the teacher will say, and the correction will stick, but only for "watch." When asked the next time, the man in question replied, "On Saturday I got up and I wash myself and I get dressed and I eat my breakfast and I watched TV all day and I went to bed."

Speech, the ability for it, is preordained. In his book *The Language Instinct,* about the potent, innate quality of the drive, Steven Pinker remarks on how difficult it would be to *prevent* a child from learning to speak. Under ordinary circumstances, the ability just comes—in the form of babbling at about six months, in two-word exclamations at around two years—predictably, so long as children are exposed to words. It's through the instances when children aren't—sometimes as a result of deafness with no exposure to sign; rarely through some terrible isolation—that scientists have been able to determine there's a cutoff point for acquiring full language. Beyond a certain point, a child who's been blocked can't. In the case of Genie, a girl whose disturbed father kept her alone in a dark room, frequently strapped to a toilet seat, for her first thirteen years, she was always, after her rescue, stymied by tense markers. Pronouns eluded her. "Momma love you," she'd say, pointing to herself. "In all, Genie inhabited a prison not unlike a stroke victim's, with more to say than she was able to say, and aware of her inability," journalist Russ Rymer writes in his extraordinary book *Genie.*

With reading, however, there's no biological cutoff. People can learn to do it at eighty. That's because we're not hardwired to read: there are no crucial print centers in the brain, no Broca's or Wernicke's area for written words, no innate mechanism that propels us toward books by a certain age. Take a child and raise him in a family, surrounded by words, and he'll be babbling his head off by the time he's toddling. Raise him in a library, surrounded by books, and unless someone shows him how to decipher the print, all they'll be are blocks of paper to him.

You have to be taught to read, an activity humans have engaged in for only five thousand years. It's not, as Pugh observed, a biological specialty like spoken language, which has been around for hundreds of thousands of years. We're built to speak, the theory goes, because speech is a survival skill. Reading, by and large, isn't. Sure, if you're a Wall Street mergers and acquisitions specialist, you could get steamrollered if you couldn't check the business pages. But if you belonged to a warring Amazonian tribe, you'd have as much need for frontal gyrus semantics action as New Yorkers have for poison darts: possibly, from time to time, but not often. That's what Pugh meant when he called reading "a challenge of brain plasticity." The brain, with its finite resources, co-opts space for it if needed —gray matter that could be put to other uses. When I asked a neurologist named Ragnar Steingrimsson *what* uses, he observed that one of the areas that lights up during reading also sparks when a birder has a prized sighting or when a car fanatic flips through an Aston Martin catalog. "Some people argue the region has to do with expertise," he said, adding the standard qualifier: "But it's not a done deal."

These regions used for reading aren't ones synchronized to any internal timing. Check the demographic composition of the local birding club: there's no cutoff for acquiring the skill to spot a semi-palmated plover, except maybe dementia.

That, then, is the answer to the question of whether there's a biologically decreed window of opportunity for picking up a second script: highly unlikely. But here's the catch: this isn't the same as saying, however, that it's as easy later on.

If you wanted to start a flap among the L2WS crowd—which might be impossible, as they seem to constitute one of the more mild-tempered assemblies I've met—you could try to by asking why it's tougher, if it is. Everyone has a theory. Pugh's is that reading in a foreign alphabet initially replicates a reading disorder. "When you're learning a language, each word in another script can take an eternity. What happened to you with Hindi," he said, for I'd described my travails, "is what happens with dyslexics. A bottleneck occurs. By the end of the sentence, you've forgotten what the beginning was." This pileup can seem like more of a block when you're older.

Psychologist Charles Perfetti casts a dissenting vote. He simply doesn't think it's more challenging later. "Acquiring the visual forms isn't hard as an adult," he said. "You show Mandarin 101 students made-up Chinese characters, and after only two, three months, they can figure out the ringers."

Paradis believes it is. All skills, he argues, get harder to learn as you get older, and that includes this one. First off, you have interference from any similar pursuits you've already mastered. If you're a pinochle player and take up bridge, you can expect scrambled plays due to old impulses kicking in. Second, it just is. "If you tried to learn to ride a bicycle at fifty, it'd be very, very difficult," he said. "If you tried learning to drive at sixty, it'd take a long time," and I was glad when we stopped the examples there. Had I known that a second script in my forties might be classified hieroglyphic, I'd have closed the book at *namaste* and missed the decoder thrills that come even with lettering that makes you jump. I didn't want to know what else I couldn't do.

ONE SKILL SET that doesn't get rusty: social skills, or not in Udaipur, where I get chances to exercise them daily. "That's really something," I say when Piers takes me to dinner at the home of a Gujarati princess named Lucky Singh. Lucky has a tender heart. At the family estate, down in Sudarshana, she and her daughter Sweetie take in injured street cows, camels with broken legs, dogs that have been abandoned. They pay a man to give the animals Ayurvedic treatments. A Pomeranian's tumor disappeared. A Samoyed is in very good health now. "The security factor is so important in animals and humans, Kathy," Lucky says, and in her indolent voice, my name sounds full of regret. "It makes you feel calm." She's an animal rights activist, she's been telling us, when her husband appears with a small lacquered box. Mr. Singh is barefoot, in a military jacket. His head is shaved, which, combined with the regalia, gives the impression he's expecting an overthrow after dinner. He brings the box to me, opens it. A leopard's head, glares through cold glass eyes. "Really something," I tell him.

Lucky Singh on that first night: loose wavy hair spilling down her back, lime green sari, in a small modern home with numerous heavy frames, a sign of decaying aristocracy I recognize from having grown up on the Main Line. An improbable Playboy ashtray on the living room table, English novels from the fifties, one by the writer Dennis Wheatley, who'd been an admirer of Mussolini. Blown-up cardboard cutouts, pasted with black-and-white shots of various ancestors, propped on tables. Paintings of forebears everywhere, unsmiling rajas: "The men who came to paint them were not their equals, Kathy," she says to explain their flat expressions; several startling tiger skins: "I shot that one," the husband says.

In my memories after, their voices break through. Memory is primarily phonological, Ragnar Steingrimsson said when we met. It's preserved more in sound than in visual detail.

"'Oh, mummy,' that girl said, 'he is very nice, and I would like to marry him,'" Lucky tells a friend once more in the ozone of old thought, one of many woeful stories I remember them telling one night about Rajput women marrying out of caste. "At first the man was very kind," Lucky tsks again in memory. "But then there were problems. When they had a birthday party for the child, we—"the Rajput collective"—would have had everyone come, but his family just wanted a cake." The friend, forever out of my earshot now, might be nodding. "Eventually, he was taken out of his job, for a reason I don't know," Lucky Singh informs her. "Then he just sat there and drank all day. After ten years, she divorced him," I hear her say again, and remember the sideways cock of her head, the preserved tiger in the entry hall behind her. "Guests keep plucking out his teeth," she complains when Piers and I are saying our goodbyes. There are holes, either moth or bullet, in the skin. Piers pats its back. Dust clouds his hand. "Oh, the guy next door is building," Lucky says, embarrassed. "The cement is getting all *over* him. I'm going to vacuum him tomorrow," she resolves, as we prepare to leave. He's really something, I assure her again in memory, barely audibly: *sreallysomething,* but imprinted forever.

When you read, you subvocalize as well. When you read, are able to, in two languages, you hear, half-muted, a scattering like Esperanto. New MRI studies out of the Netherlands, the Nijmegen Institute of Cognition and Information, reveal the somewhat startling news that when a bilingual sits down with a book, every word in it conjures every word like it they know, in every one of their languages. Every time, in a third of a second. A Dutch-English speaker sees *lief,* "nice," thinks of "leaf," can't turn off the associations. "Word" will cause its own brief chorus: "work" and *vork,* Dutch for "fork," the spreading activation network, but with print. "It's a really kind of stupid system," the researcher in charge of the study, Ton Dijkstra, said fondly when we discussed it. "It's stimulated like a coffeemaker—it simply activates all the working systems you have." Though not at first with an alien alphabet, he adds. To the beginning aspirant, the Hindi word होटल won't conjure "hotel," even though the word sounds out *ho-tal.* The Hindi *h,* ह, is still too different. Once the connection between the new symbols and their sounds have solidified, however, the same chain reaction will begin, *hotalhotelhopeful,* as the midlevel student scans the paper. Similar ripples occur with monolinguals—"word"/"work"—but don't raise as many intriguing and still-unanswered questions. Such as: If a babel lights up when you're able to read in two or three languages, how does any multilingual keep comprehension linear? How is it the book doesn't turn into babble?

Reading propels sound, and sound in turn triggers the imagination: So strongly, anecdotes from a book can linger like your own vague memories. So forcefully that when you come to an action verb in print—"pick," "kick," "lick"—blood rushes to the motor cortex strip in your brain, the part that, were you to enact the movement, would orchestrate it. In the mind, in the physical body, language and movement are linked.

You misplace your car keys, Harvard professor of psychiatry John Ratey notes, you scratch your head, stiffen in frustration, move your lips as you talk yourself through the routes around the house you wandered, smile as you feel the keys in your pocket. "Gesturing and speech are closely bound; they are acquired together in childhood and break down together in aphasia," he writes. It's the sequencing that the motor strip oversees that physically allows you to talk. The complicated movements of the tongue, face, and larynx necessary to produce words are orchestrated in that area.

When sections of the motor cortex were magnetically blocked in a group of epileptic patients, the patients were suddenly rendered incapable of speaking. When children, first graders, were given instruction in folk songs, were taught the melodies and rhythms (a form of sequencing), they scored higher on reading scores than control groups that weren't. Gabriela sometimes had me walk the room when I recited my homework; occasionally I set my written assignments to song. I can report, then, that pacing to the tune of the old R & B number "Oh Girl," relyricized with learner vocabulary —*Ohhh girl, Vimal does not eat meat*—will sure-fire, positively do the trick.

Unless you've had to move to an unheated hotel room so small that when you pace, you smack into the bed, where there's a cold-water shower down the hall and a wedding field out back with off-key bands playing the "Brazil" song till 4 A.M. when not tattooing Bollywood lyrics onto your brain. Then, all the kinetic approach to homework is going to do is jangle your nerves. I know, having tried.

Because I was the next to go down.

"I do not like that"

 For a long time, the chickens of Sukhadia Circle did not come home to roost. For months following the ill-fated drive with the Whisperer, Jain Dad 2's own clucking had been steady and, all things considered (his personality), good-natured. *Kathy, you have paid three hundred and fifty rupees for curtains; too much. Kathy, you have invaded Afghanistan.* Then one day, there were problems.

Around this time, early December, the first semester was drawing to a close. It was now Adhikmas, a sniveling, bad-tempered stretch when "the god is sleeping," as an Indian friend explained, a kind of horological bin for filler days. In the Hindu lunar calendar, the months don't add up neatly to solar years. When too many fall short, the pandits called for a leap time, usually lasting a fortnight. Adhikmas, "half month," was highly inauspicious. With no god on the case, you could not get married, purchase housewares, start a business. Whatever you bought now would jam, crack, or smoke.

An all-night chanting began, a low tumbling hum, impossible to locate, that quickened my pulse in the dead of night, when I'd pause on the way to the bathroom and forget why I'd left the bed. By day, the distracting echoes sounded in everyone's head. Later, I'd wonder whether this hadn't perhaps explained the lawlessness that mid-month slithered into Antriksh Flats.

It was on one of these afternoons without steerage that Rajesh, the Art Carney one, Dad number 2, started up in the kitchen. Alka had been reporting a pleasant remark the candy shop owner had made about me when he interrupted. "He said you were sincere because you pay whatever he asks you," he said. "You know, Kathy, he asks you three hundred, you pay three hundred. People in India think you are a . . . child. Somebody asks you two hundred rupees" — he demonstrated me gladly peeling off two bills — "you give them two hundred rupees." The subject of the Jaipur curtain extravaganza was placed back on the table. *"You paid three hundred fifty. You could have gotten them here for fifty,"* he said, raspy voice rising in wonder. *"For fifty!"* he said. Alka nodded.

I would never live down the infamy of the nine-dollar curtains, I conceded then. The purchase would be remarked on long after I'd packed up my overcharged possessions and boarded the flight I'd paid too much for home. *I did,* I thought. *I forked over three-fifty, because the curtains were pretty and came from an elegant store and you, you marble head, wouldn't recognize good taste if it came sliding up the drive and bit you on your cherry-shorted butt. If you put one more plastic bouquet in the stairway-to-heaven room* — the unnaturally pink and yellow flowers having come to mind — *you're going to start getting mausoleum inquiries.*

"Haan, three-fifty,*"* I began, but he'd moved on. Having established that the man across the street did not, contrary to what Alka had indicated, like me, that he in fact regarded me as an easy trick and a chump, Dad 2 needed to know why, if I was so fond of the neighbor's baby, didn't I have one? You don't have a baby? Why? I'd

been warned they'd do this in India, grill you on your plans for parturition, but actually "they" hadn't, only this smooth conversationalist had. But before I could get through my prepared dodge, Jain Dad 2 was on to my looks. Did I know I was a ringer for J. K. Rowling? He flipped to her picture in a magazine, poked it. She's your older sister. Normally, Rowling's appearance struck me as unremarkable either way, but just then, she snarled up at me, gorgonian.

When a lull arrived, I cut out and across the drive. In a flash, Meena and Alka were at my door, their arms in windmills. Some kind of plan had to be enacted right now, they conveyed. I had to go somewhere immediately, and with Dad 2.

Once I'd been pried, sobbing, from my room and placed in the car (I realized as we backed down the drive that three days of *Meena mata-ji* talk had meant that Meena's mata-ji, her mother, was having me over for dinner), I found he'd been thinking even more about my life and had a few more observations to air. There was one, I believe, about my being husbandless, to which I countered, "I have a good life!"

"Yes, you have a good life!" he agreed. I relaxed. "You are free!" Yes I was. *"But in five years,"* he said—somewhere in there we'd switched to Hindi—*"you will be old and have no husband and no child and somethingsomething in akelaapan,"* in loneliness.

"Haan, but sometime then all the other husbands will start to be dead, and the women will also be in akelaapan because the men will dead," I parried. It was the best I could do. He didn't get it. "You're right. Some men are not honest with their wives," he said. "Some men are not good. You're right."

By the time we'd reached the neighborhood of Muslim shacks, along the stretch by the stacked poultry cages, he wanted to know what I thought of him. "The negative," he challenged. "Give me percentages." I kept my gaze fixed on the dashboard. "You think I am a bad husband. All right. Maybe there are times I am," he said, in a conciliatory tone that showed he was a soul-searching man. We pulled over beside a fruit stand. "You think I drink alcohol," he said when he returned with two clearly innocent OJs, and the whole picture clicked into focus. The beer offer that had been made and rescinded! All these months, Dad 2 had been stewing over the anonymous call to Swami-ji that had followed—had never been convinced, in any airtight way, that the Whisperer was the lodger who'd snitched.

Oh, poor Meena, I thought as we sped toward her mata-ji's: poor Meena, irreversibly wed to this jabbing lug. Although Meena was not, come to think of it, a blazing IQ source. Then poor Alka! How could she live life in the same house saddled with him? By the time the car was overtaking the Horoscope Analysis and Remedy shop, I'd revised my position on arranged marriage once more. Because what if they fixed you up with someone like Art Carney Dad? The only piece of you anyone would see again would be your bubbles, rising up from under the water.

IN ADHIKMAS, WHEN THE karmic laws of transgression and debt were suspended; when the god, snuffling deeper into dreams, could not be roused by prayers or chants; when bad luck could arrive in a wheeling free-for-all, people kept their heads down and felt a little like they'd fallen off the map. That sensation was nothing new for me; I'd been living that way for months. Now, though, I entered a more extreme state of dislocation, like homesickness, but more viral. The sharp dog teeth of depression shook me awake at night. I missed blueberries to the point of torment. In my room, I'd play the white noise machine to hear noises from home; that's how low it got. The "Crickets" setting was like insects roasting on a video fire, but it didn't matter. You couldn't get sounds anything like that here. "Oh! It's raining in America," Meenal gasped when I played "Thunderstorm" for her. Having only ever known drought, she was startled to hear what one sounded like.

This misery coincided with another leap in my Hindi comprehension. At four months in, it was as if some part of my brain, having realized I was serious—we were doing this; we'd cleared out and left home—had calculated that we were gone for good and had sensibly decided to make space for new words. These leaps, I should quickly add, were by no means pole vaults. My daily mantra continued to be *"What?"* I listened a lot more than I spoke. The silent period still lingered about me like a gas, though more oxygen was starting to get in.

Helaena, curiously, was in the same loquacious bad way: her Hindi was rocketing, she could barely get out of bed. It was as if our brain synapses were being tuned in sync by language acquisition, so much that at one point, we entered psychic mind meld. *I can see why they call donkeys beasts of burden,* I'd think in the rickshaw to school, passing a line weighted down by rocks. "You can see why they call donkeys beasts of burden," Helaena would note that evening on the way to dinner. "This is so weird," she announced one morning "All last night all I wanted was blueberry pie, and I don't even like blueberries. They didn't even have them where I grew up." (The Whisperer might have been in the same slough, though that would have been hard to tell. Since Harold's departure, she'd holed up in a side office and was insisting on private lessons.)

Up at Piers's, a mood of subdued unhappiness hung in the air as well. Often, when I went there now, I was the only guest. No parties flowing down the stairs from the roof, no jigris out on the front lawn chatting. We'd spend evenings, Piers and I, slumped down watching the swirling Ganesh show, till the revolving elephant heads on ovals (that was the programming in its entirety) made us one with the sofa. Or we'd pop in a Julie Andrews movie to try to soothe his mother's longing for England, but the appearance of tidy Julie in this florid, unbound place would at some point unhinge her, and she'd bang the table with her glass and caw, miserable in her illness. When Piers and the boys would take her up to bed, I'd stroll the edges of the room, examining the photographs from his unimaginable world—the honest-faced brother, the fleshy sister, black-and-white grandparents—and in my own layered misery, feel black-and-white. It seemed that all my certainties from before had been long, drawn-out spectacles.

Only years later, in a conversation with A. L. Becker, did I begin to understand what had happened to me. "People who study languages think of them as codes, but they aren't really," he said. "A language is a whole map of reality." It was Wittgenstein who first compared language to a map. A language should mirror the world the way a map does, he said, but what Becker was talking about was more profound. "Most of the distinctions we make about ourselves—what time it is, where we are—we learn through the map of language," Becker said. He described how in Burma, he'd learned firsthand that languages aren't, at base, codes with essentially the same fundamental components. His "attunement to the world," he said, had to be changed in order to speak to people. "In Indonesia, you say, 'How is everything here?' and by 'here' you mean not where the speaker is, but where the hearer is. More than two sentences would give a foreigner away. If I'm talking with someone and using 'here' and 'there' in ways that are strange, I won't be understood even if I know the words of their language. I'll be treated as nutty or as a child."

"Here" and "there" fall into a linguistic category called deictics—words that rely on context for meaning. "Here" and "there" are meaningless unless used in a sentence, unlike, for example, "bottle" or "chair." The way deictics are conceived change from language to language. In English, we have just two positioning signifiers: "this" and "that," "here" and "there"—the first in each pair indicating a location near the speaker, the other near the listener. But a number of tongues—Korean, Thai, several Romance languages—employ a third signifier that refers to a place that's far from both.

"This array [of deictics] lies at the center of a language," Becker said, "That's what makes it like a map, only a map that involves time. Each language tells you what 'now' is, where 'I' am, orients you differently in space and time." He'd been speaking quickly, and now he paused. "You can see," he said, "why the shift into another language is so disorienting—you don't know where 'here' is, literally."

MORNING IN UDAIPUR, in the dense rolling present, preserved now forever in my head. A scrofulous street dog, legs hobbled by rubber bands, yelps at the demons the traffic sounds raise. The cur is an outcaste. Pomeranians are Jain. The wolfhounds in the yards of the havelis are Rajput. Dogs have castes now, not breeds. In the tide without ebb, boys towel off at a street pump. The distant Aravallis are dark green with shadows. Winter's coming on; the Tibetan market displays cheap sweaters. I sleep in one the rickshaw drivers all wear, in loose olive pants brought over from the States that once had a descriptive name. (Parachute? I think.) "Too much rain is bad. Too much sun is bad. Too much speech is bad. Too much silence is bad," Vidhu says in overlay, on the same flowing morning, riffing and quoting the poet Kabir. Vidhu can circle all India before he gets down to the vocabulary lesson. Today, though, he zeros in. "*Lokendra:* 'the god among the folk,'" he says crisply. "*Mahashakti:* 'superpower.'" "*Threshold.*" "*Application.*" Words, decanted, hang in the air. "*Real,*" "*in reality,*" "*as a matter of fact,*" then he stops, lights out for a ramble. "Sacred cows can tell if you're foreign," he says with a crooked grin. "If you go to the villages, you will startle them." It's not true, I think, somewhere in that morning, that I ever had a house or life back there. Too much memory is bad when it's jagged or sublime, but then it fades, and with it the life you're not convinced you had anyway.

FOR ALL ITS disruptive ways, Adhikmas doesn't mess with mail delivery. Just the opposite, it seems, judging by how quickly I receive a package a friend's sent. "I'm teaching drawing, and I don't know how to draw," I'd e-mailed him one week; the next one, this,

Swami-ji is handing me an envelope containing a book with a smiling duck on the cover. Inside are instructions for how to sketch anything using geometrical means. You can make a rhomboid, you've got a cow.

At the deaf school, Anukul raises an eyebrow in cool admiration when I show him what I've brought. He positions the beautiful tribal boy Banshi Lal at the board beside his desk. *"Now draw an oval,"* he signs. He checks the steps in the book. *"All right, a circle. No, no—on top. Now, two lines there. No, there."* Banshi Lal frowns, uncertain where this is heading, but tries it anyway. Lines, waves, a curl, and presto. A turtle! The class shrieks. Without even knowing he was, Banshi Lal has drawn a turtle. *Samudri:* Anukul underscores this development by writing the Hindi word on the board.

Banshi Lal was the test case. Now the floor is open for turtles on paper. In the same mysterious assembly, lines become dogs. We're all enthralled. The paper supply is running low, though. Anukul calls for a break and razors a stack of sheets into eighths.

Cylinders turn into cats, into cows, into long smoking trains, but then the thrill starts to wane. After a while, we all know the trick. Anukul decides to up the ante. From now on, we'll be working with a limitation: only colored pencils can be used; no erasing possible. "I see," I say. "So they have to pay attention."

"No, for their fine skills," he says.

Circle, square, smaller circle, and ten teddy bears, in a fiesta of colors, start to take shape. Banshi Lal is stuck with light yellow. His bear's all but invisible. We're finished with the feet when a problem becomes evident: one of the directions is calling for the artist to erase the line he's just drawn. We're stalled. We all stare at our emerging bears. "I know," Anukul says, and with a razor, lightly scrapes off the mark that's supposed to disappear. "Necessity is the mother of invention," he says, and smirks in flagrant self-appreciation.

The exercises grow tiresome, too complicated or too predictable. Anyway, the paper's almost gone. Anukul hands me the razor to use on the last two sheets. My eighths are a regular shame: ragged edges like teeth, deep Vs. He smiles. "*You* don't have fine skills," he teases. This last round is a bonus round. Anyone can draw whatever they want.

With the paper gone, the art portion of the afternoon is concluded. *Kya karun?* What to do? We do what you do in India most of the time. We talk, which means a sign lesson for me.

"Ask that boy what his father does," Anukul suggests, and shows me how. The boy answers with a fast ripple of his hand. Anukul stares.

"The father is . . . He is saying the father works in marble I think." He asks the boy to repeat himself. "He makes disposable cups," Anukul says hesitantly, checks with the class. *Cups?* The boys all shake their heads. Noooo. One runs up to the front. He translates the answer.

"Oh! The father makes butter," Anukul says, sounding relieved. "You know, that other boy is smarter. Because the first one, he is poor. Nobody shows him anything. The second is poor, too, but the first lives in the hostel. The other lives in a family." Then he says something that will stick in my mind for years: "The children have so many words even we don't know."

Words they don't know? The idea is slightly jarring; I think of Anukul as the authority on sign. The boys come, he teaches them. Whoever names something has power over it, and I'm curious to know where the children's power lies. "What kind of words?" I ask.

"Like they have one we think means 'plow,'" he says. "All of them, when they come here, they have their own words. The first thing we do is try and learn what they are."

The way deaf kids do in poor areas around the world, children come here for the first time at all different ages. At ten, twelve, even older; up till then, many of them have never been in a classroom. Most of the kids find themselves here through the same enrollment process that's typical in Nigeria or Nicaragua. Word reaches the school that way out of town, there's a child who's deaf. Someone then goes out and tries to persuade the parents it's in their best interest to give up the labor he's been providing and allow him to come. If the school trains him, he'll get a paying job and be able to send money home. I say "he" because in India, in many impoverished areas, education for deaf girls is a lost cause. Why bother? They're just going to get married. Here deaf girls frequently become indentured servants through arranged marriages, sometimes as young as eight or nine.

But even when the parents agree, educational possibilities are often minimal for the kids who are brought in too late. At the deaf school, one of the things that struck me was how radically staggered the ages of the newcomers were, along with their cognitive abilities. In a normal school, students would be grouped by age, but here that doesn't make sense. Here you have younger kids who are sharp and perceptive, whose parents enrolled them in the school not long after a fever took their hearing, for whom the sight of moving lips still triggers "phantasmal voices," the novelist David Wright's phrase. You have children who've been deaf from birth but who sign easily because their parents, too, are deaf and taught them to. Those kids' talent for learning is robust, unlike some of the teenagers seated beside them, who arrived only a year or two before, by which point their abilities had ossified. These were the ones Mr. Paliwal had been referring to when he'd told me despairingly, "They come here fifteen, sixteen." Those boys will remain forever without language and all the attendant cognitive expansion that language sparks.

With all children, deaf or hearing, language develops in predetermined stages. All babies babble, the deaf ones with their hands. All two-year-olds begin to speak in what are referred to as two-word strings—"Mommy eats"—though in the case of deaf kids, these might be called, more accurately, two-sign strings. By the time a child, deaf or hearing, reaches age three, these word strings are blossoming, expanding, gaining complexity, inflection, word endings.

They turn into sentences: "Mommy eats cat food," a friend's son's first joke, which he found as riotous on the thousandth telling as he did on the first. From then on, words take shape in greater and greater complexity, except when the brain is malformed or when children are severely isolated.

The case of Genie, barred from human contact by her disturbed father, demonstrates what happens to the hearing in these circumstances—how the concept of word order must be acquired by a certain age, before the window of opportunity squeaks shut. When it does in the hearing, any prayer of grasping the full complexity of language is extinguished, and the same occurs with the deaf. Chelsea, a woman who in deaf educational circles is as well-known as Genie, was diagnosed as retarded at a young age, though, in fact the trouble was blocked hearing. The mistake went unrecognized till she was thirty-one, and by then, she was caught in twilight—if the full light of understanding depends on the ability to make fully ordered linguistic sense of the world, as many experts believe. She was fitted with a hearing aid and started on intensive instruction in English, but though she's managed to acquire many words, syntax remains elusive. Her speech is forever shuffled: "The woman is bus the going."

"What can we do?" Mr. Paliwal had said. The answer, unfortunately, is not a lot, and what's more, the problem becomes systematic. How are the teachers supposed to contend with a classroom of kids with a vast range of abilities, some able to sign and learn at lightning speed, others who stare at them dully. Where are they supposed to aim the lesson? Too high, and they will lose half the class. Too low, and the rest will be stupefied. The mix is infernal, guaranteed to produce restlessness in the students, lethargy in the teachers. What they do then is this: dream small dreams, some of them, and by holding on to those visions, challenge the kids. The rest, frustrated, run classes that are holding pens. Mr. Paliwal, he does what he can. And the students, through no fault of anyone's, have no say.

At the end of the hour, I gather up the papers. I bring them home and lay them on the bed. Arching cat after arching cat, identical down to their ears, the exact same stiff repeating cows, but it's the other set of drawings my eye keeps returning to. Not the geometrical ones, but the ones where Anukul called for free expression. In many of them, the boys have drawn themselves—flying through the air in boats, dwarfed by polychrome towers. Something about these is off. I keep thinking I'm looking at space aliens. The kids' heads are too big. They look startled, odd, but I can't say why, and I give it up. I pick up a book, put it down, stare some more, and then I see.

In the portraits of themselves, many of them, the boys have no mouths.

HELAENA AND THE NEPHEW were coming apart. The marriage charts had cleared, and they'd gotten engaged. Helaena began to lose interest.

"Aditya tried to strangle me in the car on the way to school," she'd announce cheerfully in the morning. "Aditya tried to drive us off a cliff," she'd report. Aditya, clearly, was beside himself. Nothing in his life had prepared him to be visited by American dating.

One evening, she and I attended a birthday party. This was immediately after the engagement had gone through—so soon after that, I hadn't, at the beginning of the night, even known it had. Divendra Singh, the celebrant, was someone Helaena had recently met, a lawyer and former classmate of Aditya's. An only child, he lived with his parents on a hilltop estate with a sign that said FORT DIVENDRA.

". . . and we have fourteen antique cars and two temples and a pandit and fifteen servants," he'd said on the house tour he'd given us on our one previous visit. Divendra had the soft, burbling manner of a pampered son, but all the same, sparks were visible even from behind, where I was trailing along, counting.

From a rooftop, you could see the servants huddled around a

cook fire outside huts, looking, from up there, like a diorama. Down-stairs, we joined the family. Mr. Singh, Divendra's father, also a law-yer, radiated testosterone. He was short and scrappy, with the odd-est wig I'd ever seen: black, shellacked Elvis hair. He also had, as Helaena reported on the rickshaw drive up, more money than any-one in town. Divendra's mother, an anesthesiologist, was there as well, along with her sisters, who were all three doctors and seated in the living room with polite, nodding husbands. The room was done in Udaipur modern: a table made of a varnished swan-under-glass, four overstuffed couches and numerous plump chairs arranged in a circle.

"Sing a Hindi song," the smiling relatives on plush sofas had de-manded, but even my Christmas carols were gone. Nearly every song I knew had disappeared into the far recesses of my brain, all but a few left over from one obsessed patch I'd put in with the radio in ninth grade: a Jesse Winchester number called "Yankee Lady," several others from the same year. I was like the people in nursing homes who can remember only the music of their youth, except in my case, I was limited to one narrow band.

"We're supposed to hold hands," Helaena whispered: a Bolly-wood convention; maidens clasped hands when they warbled. We did and fumbled through "Just Yesterday Morning" while the rela-tives leaned forward and stared intently, then I launched into "Yan-kee Lady," and they all resumed talking. *"Sing a Hindi song,"* they repeated when I was through.

Now, on this birthday night, Divendra's friends sat soberly on the doily-covered couches, taking turns breaking into song. Between numbers, one of them, Siddharth, recited *shayers,* Urduized rap, composed on the spot for gentle, tweaking fun. Helaena and I got *"You are fair-skinned and beautiful, but you are leaving one day, so you are not one of us,"* which I'd taken from the reaction, before Diven-dra's translation, to be a minor knee-slapper. Guffaws went up all around when Siddharth rolled the bones at an adrenalized Young

Turk, an engineer who kept whipping out his cell phone. He'd gotten off a good one, you could tell, by the way people were holding their seat cushions. *"What?" "What?"* Helaena and I pled, and Divendra, pausing for air, delivered the English: "If you think your arms are strong, try to shake the building. But if your arms are not strong," and here he had to stop, to brace himself against new convulsions, "then have some wine and watch the building shake." The room broke up all over again, and then Divendra stood. "Now you will enjoy cake and photographs," he said.

The guests filed over to a garage as long as a warehouse, past the Packards and Bugattis and Humboldts and gleaming Rollses that had been reparked outside. Inside, I found myself shivering, then startled into forgetting the cold when I noticed Divendra and Siddharth with their arms entwined, Siddharth feeding Divendra cake. *How homoerotic, and with his parents right there,* I thought, then realized every guest was supposed to grab a sliver and step up to the plate. "Small piece," Divendra groaned when I reached him in the cake line. "I will feed you big, but small for me."

The cake line progressed. Helaena and I hunkered against a wall, seized by the need to exchange a few words about Mr. Singh's hair. For safety's sake, we decided to gossip in Spanish, a language hardly anyone in India knew and which we'd both studied, but when we tried to speak it, something literally dumbfounding happened.

Two words out, the Spanish would disappear, then reappear as Hindi. One of us would make it as far as *"Este hombre"* then continue, as if possessed, *"aisaa lagta hai jaise usne baal chippakke rahka hai,"* thereby remarking, within earshot of the host, "Man looks like he's got glue in his hair." We'd try again: set the sentence up hopefully in Spanish, watch dismayed as it slid back into Hindi. On the fourth try, Helaena opened her mouth to speak and closed it. "I . . . can't," she said. I couldn't either. It was confounding—like one of those party tricks where they get your arms to rise no matter how hard you squeeze them down.

"It's absolutely common, reported by everybody. It's like the new language shoves the other to the background," the psycholinguist Ellen Bialystok said when afterward I canvassed people in the field for theories on how my Hindi could have jettisoned my Spanish like that. Michael Chee, a cognitive neuroscientist in Singapore, mentioned a similar scenario, where English stomps out a rickety second language you're attempting before you've finished the sentence. "*Donnez-moi* the pen, could you?" This will occur if you're monolingual in English and fairly new to lessons, the reason being, Chee said, you've had stronger exposure to your native tongue. "The evidence suggests that when you're processing a second language, you actually have to inhibit the first," he said. "When you switch back, there's a carryover. It takes time."

This switching back and forth may account partly for why language study in later years has been shown to protect the brain against deterioration. Synaptic pathways are strengthened. People who are bilingual and who use both languages every day delay the onset of dementia by up to four years on average, according to one study.

Michel Paradis, when I phoned him, wanted to know how many martinis I'd had "at the time of the incident." When he'd finished joshing me, he observed that if people had been speaking Hindi around me for a while, my Hindi was already primed—the neural voltage needed to activate it would have been far less than what my Spanish would have required. It would have taken a lot more juice, so to speak, to get the Spanish for "looks really weird" up and running than it would have to activate the Hindi. Once you've allowed a second language to lapse, its activation threshold level goes way up, he said. But Paradis thought there was more at play here than the activation threshold hypothesis. Second languages are more likely to interfere with each other than a second is with a first, because, he believes, seconds draw on a different memory system than a first does. They seem to rely on what's called declarative memory—math equations, the combination to a locker, anything that you can declare how you know it—whereas a native tongue draws on automatic memory, which is processed differently in the brain. This is knowledge acquired before the age of five or so—knowing, say, that two cows are called "cows" and not "cow." All second languages, in Paradis's configuring, are run along the same wire, as it were, which is why they have more of a tendency to short each other out.

Back in the garage, our Spanish was fried. "You still planning to head south at Christmas?" I asked. She couldn't, Helaena said, now that she was engaged. "Engaged!" I almost fell over. But she hadn't said a word. Yes, Aditya had asked her to marry him that day, she said in a voice that meandered, as if the thought made her sleepy. A second later she was bright-eyed, awake. Divendra, cheeks patched white, was hurrying over. He stopped and motioned toward the house. "Now you will enjoy the disco floor," he said.

In the dining room, they'd cleared out the table and chairs. Klieg lights flashed from the perimeters. In the center, it was movie star Hrithik Roshan all the way as the guys, faces tense with concentration, reproduced film moves: the arm pump, the shoulder shake, the rapid light-bulb screw. The four sisters in their saris swanned across the floor, executing beautiful, sweeping Rajasthani dance movements against the Bollywood actions. No one was drinking. No one got loud. Servants marched in with trays of warm milk. "Just when you think it can't get any more wholesome, it does," I turned to tell Helaena, but she had taken Divendra's hand, was pulling him toward the door. "Did you say that tape was in your room?" I heard her ask above the bhangra.

By the time Divendra reappeared, his guests had lost steam. They were chatting in groups by the wall. He strode onto the floor. He had something to say. "Now you will enjoy the campfire," he declared, and in the crossed swords of klieg lights you could see, there weren't any crumbs on that boy.

LUCKY SINGH, Piers's friend, calls to fill me in on her multiple rounds of socializing. " . . . I was desperately trying to reach you because we had so many people over for a cocktail party. There was a German man here who was interested in our forjee." Her what? "Our forjee. Forjee. You know forjee?" I don't. "Forjee. Fordjeep." The words chug into view. And how are my studies?

I mention a story I'm writing, about a thousand brides who drowned at a *shaadi*, a wedding. "A *what?*" Lucky Singh says, amused. "A *sha-di*," I say, emphasis on each syllable, uncertain how her comprehension could be lapsed. She's a Gujarati speaker, but even so, we're newly out of wedding season, when we all heard the word night and day; she's got to know it. *"Sha-di,"* I enunciate.

"Oh! Oh! *Shaaadi!*" She says it like a flirtatious taunt, sings it: *"Shaaaaadi."* "Prolong the *a*," she says, and I do, till I sound like a backup singer. *Shaaaadi*, not shoddy. Up till now, the double Hindi *a* has been theoretical, something I employ when reminded. It's taken all this time to fully understand that it's a bona fide, discrete speech sound, entirely different from the short *a*, that it means something and that it's not up to me to correct it with my pronunciation so the native speakers don't sound, to my ear, so whiny, which is what I've been doing. I go ahead and stretch it, feel silly as I do, but as Lucky says, "It's not enough to know the word if nobody can understand you."

Lucky Singh phones often now. I'm glad she does. The conversations we have reach a conclusion. My other attempts at local communication have a circular, stoner quality. Every chat seems to repeat a previous one. They go round and round: *"Does Indian food strike you as good? It does! You like it? And do Indian movies strike you as pleasing? They do? Good! Are you interested in Indian culture?"* I'm always perplexed to be having this same discussion again, like when you think you've made the turnoff but find yourself back on the cindery stretch of highway. Even the videshis are sounding as if they've spent too much time in opium-scented air. "Every molecule you breathe has been breathed by everyone through history, they've shown that," Helaena says one weeknight when we meet to laze around, and we get caught up in a debate over whether we're breathing Queen Elizabeth. Up at Piers's, Ganesh's face spins and spins; the loose ends of the days pull and stretch till they lose all elasticity; my mind is becoming dangerously unfocused. And that's when I remember: oh, the poet.

"WORDS USED IN poems are not only words. They're cultural memories, part of the collective consciousness," he says on one of the afternoons when we meet, in a voice that goes along thin and creaky, then suddenly turns lit and fire-breathing. Nand Chaturvedi's a Brahmin and a social democrat, a combination I'd have thought was contradictory. "Poetry was a social obligation. I wanted to expose the difficulties of my people," he said the first time I came, several visits ago. This was in his study, where the linoleum floor reminds me of a waiting room and where in his unsmiling portrait on the wall, he looks like a raja in the realm of ideas, looks, too, a bit indignant, like he's drawing up against ill-considered remark. Today, there's sun. We elect to go outside. In a small flagstone yard, behind a peeling red gate, we sit and talk while children peer over the fence and giggle, till one by one they drop off and run away.

When I arrived, Nand was on a translation project, putting verse written in Oriya, an eastern Indian tongue, into Hindi. Which is more difficult to translate, I ask as the afternoon light makes thin shadows on the ground, poetry or prose?

"Poetry is harder, because poetry is itself a vehicle for the translation of culture," he says, voice davening. "The poet is trained to convert the inner world into words while creating from the external world an experience of the self. It's a two-way process," he says, and

I'm reminded of something a literary critic at the symposium had said: "Nandbabu invented a newborn Hindi in the sixties." Even in English, when Nand gets on a roll, it feels as if language is being invented in my head.

"When you read a poem," he says, "you forget time, and you forget space, and you forget person. Only consciousness remains. Everything's mixed together. The images and the dreams and the visions of people, all put together." He pulls an oatmeal-colored blanket tighter around him, looks to see if I've put that down. My notebook is out. I'm writing. Even though he's nearly eighty, there's no other position for me to take here than acolyte. He's slight, nearly frail, with a conspicuous absence of several front teeth. Even so, it would be scandalous for me to be simply a woman come calling. Besides, Nand doesn't think men and women can be friends.

"You can't love what is concealed," he's said, a statement that makes sense on this side of the world, where women are always concealed.

Several visits in, I'm still not sure what he is to me, only that his words take kaleidoscopic shape in my head, that I'm happy when the rickshaw drops me off. This afternoon when I arrived at three, the family was still napping. Backing away, I settled onto a stone ledge to wait. A flock of schoolgirls in droopy white socks soon surrounded me. "Why are you sitting where we feed cows?" the tallest inquired. Had me there. "What's your name?" another asked shyly. On this leafy residential street, foreigners are a curiosity.

"Poems exist beyond the limits of dimension," Nand says. In the pale December sun, he knocks his knees to speed his thoughts, sends the word "guru" flying into my head. *Gu* is "dark," *ru* is "light"; a guru takes you from darkness into light. "No poem can be translated completely the way prose can. The language is more charged, more concentrated. A translator can only exchange a word for a word, so a lot of meaning is left out." And that's when I throw in the observation that Hindi has no way to say "privacy," hoping to be impressive. His face assumes the dour expression that's up on the wall, as if someone has slipped him a lemon.

"Yes, but you have only one word for moon. Moon and moon and moon and moon," he shoots back. That's what he thinks about my alleged English vocabulary bonanza. "*I* have ten, and ten ways to say sun, and each one conveys a different softness." The word "guru" that's taken up residence in my head gets poked in the side by another word, one that's pulled itself up from the pit of disuse. Through the rest of the afternoon, "guru" gets jabbed.

"What would he want with her?" he says, throwing his head back and cackling when I report that my friend Renee, whom he met at the symposium, has a suitor her age.

"We have women here who are brighter than you," he snaps, meaning lighter in skin tone. I've never flunked the paper bag test before.

I like that in a woman, he says, essentially, when I tell him that one of my fellows at the school has a bit of a stalkerish propensity with men.

That other word, the one that crawled up and brushed itself off, is "handful."

IT'S ON AN afternoon soon after, when I'm walking with Renee into the hotel where I've moved, everything at the Jains' having jammed, cracked, and smoked, that the man at the front desk stops me. "Madam," he says, "we have received two pieces of disturbing news. The dhobi has put dirt in your laundry. And terrorists have stormed the parliament." Five men, thought to be Muslims, managed to breach the gate and shoot nine employees before they themselves were killed. The date is December 13—12/13 as it'll come to be known, to make the links with the savagery of 9/11 clear.

A few days later at Nand's, a friend of his knocks, a professor of political science. The man is stout, middle-aged, and, as the conversation moves into what's just happened, agitated. "After the attack,

America didn't do anything," he says, not meeting my eye. "Your president hasn't even called." An image of the ragtag peace march back in September forms, the hand-scrawled signs: AMERICA, INDIA IS WITH YOU.

"He hasn't?" I say. Weakly; I don't doubt it.

"America doesn't support their words of nine-eleven—that they are waging war on terrorism," the man says and begins to pace, as a gyroscope, I can see, starts to turn.

A ZOOM LIKE A growl by my ear, then a starfish of pain in my breast. The first time I was punched on the street, the men were on motorcycles. The second time, there was an instant just after when my shoulder felt oddly flat, condensed, as if its weight was heavier than its shape would imply. Like flourless cake, though nothing as sweet as that had happened. When I looked up, two couples were hurrying past, the men's heads pulled down by taut strings, the women's faces turned back to examine mine—laughing, though it looked like they were grimacing.

"Oh, no, I don't think those things mean anything," Renee said when I asked if they didn't seem like signs of some kind of tension massing. Two assaults in one week? Come on. "No—oh, no," she insisted. "I'll ask around, but I am certain that was just teenage high jinks." Renee would brook no suggestion of impropriety in India. Nothing that hinted at any kind of impugnment, no statements even vaguely critical, whether they came from me or her Indian buddy Pauline, the seventy-eight-year-old Brahmin-Christian nurse. Renee had burned her bridges when she came here. She can't ever go back now.

But nationalist fervor was rising, Pauline had said at a dinner the three of us had had just two weeks before. Come on! Renee was forgetting. "In Orissa, they killed a Christian doctor," Pauline said over *idlis.* A doctor from Australia and his two young sons had been sleeping in their car when a gang from the Bajrang Dal materialized, their faces like shards in the thin strips of light. The Bajrang Dal, sometimes referred to as the Army of Apes, is allied with the BJP and is the lunatic fringe of the *Hindutva* movement: Hinduism above all. Bajrang Dal is given to razing Muslim temples and Christian churches and to burning (Western) Valentine's Day cards and is one of several organizations that subscribe to the philosophy of the powerful RSS (Rashtriya Swayamsevak Sangh), an extremist nationalist organization. The RSS despises Muslims and, to a lesser degree, Christians—lesser partly because there are fewer of them to hate. Christians comprise just two percent of the Indian population. In the RSS literature, Muslims and Christians are referred to as "foreigners," even though they've been living in India for centuries and are frequently descended from Hindus who converted. They are, by the RSS's definition, internal threats. The party's ideology is thuggish, to cast it in a good light; hate filled and sometimes lethal, to put it directly. It was an RSS man who killed Gandhi. One of its founders had gone on record in 1939 as admiring the way Hitler dealt with his country's internal menaces. India could learn a lot from how Germany handled the Jews, the founder, M. S. Golwalkar, wrote: "The foreign faces in Hindusthan must either adopt the Hindu culture and language, must learn to respect and hold in reverence Hindu religion, must entertain no idea but those of the glorification of the Hindu race and culture . . . or may stay in the country, wholly subordinated to the Hindu Nation, claiming nothing, deserving no privileges, far less any preferential treatment—not even citizens' rights."

The Bajrang Dal doesn't like outsiders, however they are construed, and what they really didn't like that night in Orissa were outsiders who appeared to be sneaking around trying to convert tribals to Christianity. Investigations later established that the man in the station wagon hadn't, in fact, been engaged in proselytizing. What he'd been doing was ministering to lepers, but on the night in question, that finer distinction wasn't up for discussion. In the darkness, the Bajrang Dal men stole up to the car. Several had thought to bring cans of gasoline. Others of them, matches. Soon light formed jaggedly on their faces. When the doctor tried to wrench open the door, the men at first kicked it shut through the flames. Later, they didn't have to.

"The wife said, 'Forgive them.' She is a Christian," Pauline said at dinner. Renee nodded. That was correct. Yes, that's what she did.

"The man had been helping lepers only," Pauline said. Renee agreed. True.

"And afterward, they had terrible floods in Gujarat," Pauline concluded, making a spectacular leap of karmic reasoning out of her Christian faith. Renee's head caught in mid-assent. Floods? "That's not right. That did not cause flooding," she said, frowning. Renee liked her Brooklyn rationalism challenged, but only up to a point.

The third time would occur in January, a month and a half after the dinner with Pauline. Stones and dirt then made waffles of my palms. This was at a Republic Day performance I'd gone to with Anukul and the kids. I'd ended up in the military viewing stand, surrounded by distinguished-looking men in beige leisure suits, erect generals in sunglasses. On the field, marching lines rippled in navy and white. A brass band in spats left over from the Brits extended their arms as wide as Strum Peter. "India, I-N-D-I-A," a team of school kids holding tinselly horseshoes shouted. The air was so suffused with national glory, I was nervous when I left the stadium early, by myself. Slightly, but not enough to be on guard, and so when the men slammed me from behind, sent me flying, I gasped, partly from surprise.

"If someone comes up from behind and pushes you, the first thing out of your mouth is your native language," Swami-ji had said in class not two days before. Now was revealed, if I'd had doubts: I was a native English speaker. I chased the men, shouting in English and modern-day Hindi *"Poliz!"* till they slipped down a side street. A crowd formed and I hurriedly put on sunglasses, in case I began to cry.

When a middle-aged man stepped forward, to chide me — "Next time, you should be more careful with boys" — I did, didn't care who saw.

AFTER THE FIRST ASSAULT, once I've stopped shaking, I'm sharply aware there's no one at home to say "Tension-free!" There's hardly anyone else on the premises where I live now, in fact, only the thin sad Ayurvedic man who rushes across the lawn whenever I show myself. He sounds more desperate than hopeful when he asks, "Massage?" Except when the wedding field out back is in full swing, there's rarely any evidence of life at the hotel where I've moved. In the musty lounge, rows of mismatched chairs are lined up, as if some merriment has just cleared out. A baby tiger under glass stands beside a TV that shows the cartoon Addams family speaking Hindi. Once when I stayed home sick, I amused myself watching Uncle Fester whisper verb forms we'd just learned in class. I spend hours in the lounge, staring out at the grounds, which are Victorian and leisurely — lawn chairs set in pools of sunlight, latticed balconies hung with flowering plants. I mean to get up and go inspect the slate gray pool, don't. You can do anything later here.

Sometimes I think about calling the Jains, decide to later, don't. The fact is, I can't: I ran myself out of there.

"The father has told them 'She wants a baby,'" Vanita had said the morning I went in to try to figure out whether I was imagining it or not: Were the Jains put out with me? Since the drive to Meena's mother's, I thought I'd detected screwy vibrations around the house. Then again, the baseline for screwiness there was fairly high, and given the paltry illuminations of the language I was operating on, I was reading most situations by candlelight.

In Vanita's office, I laid out my evidence, which grew flimsier as I detailed it. The other evening, when I'd come home late, Meena had cross-examined me brusquely in the kitchen. *"Where, Kathy, where? Where have you been?"* she'd demanded. *And* her face had looked funny. All right, well, not proof of much, but okay, this too: Alka had lately been short with me. Never any time for banter, and one night when we'd all been to dinner, she'd stopped me at the table as I was pulling out a chair. *"No, you sit over there,"* she said and pointed to the other end of the table, *"away from the men."* I said this last with emphasis, then realized: maybe the placement was coincidental to my fears.

"You know, I'm probably just imagining this," I was saying, but Vanita was looking horrified. The Jain family already had the beer-cruising incident on their record. In her book, they'd been on probation, and now they'd apparently added duplicity to suspected deviance.

"I am telling you, he is telling them you want a baby," she said in rising tones that suggested Jain Dad 2 could, at any minute, launch into a full-blown sexual harassment episode. If the guy pulled a stunt like that, her very job could be imperiled. I was about to observe that, really, reasonably, all that had gone on was I'd been placed in a seat elsewhere, but she was already on to evacuation procedures.

"Now that this thing has happened, you have to move," she said as the full realization of how dimwitted I'd been sank in. I'd stay, I said. But Vanita was adamant.

"Now the wives think bad things about you," she insisted. "That's how Indian women's minds work. Kathy-ji, I am Indian. I know."

"I don't think—" I began, when she said the one thing that could have changed my mind.

"Kathy-ji. You do not understand. They only have you there for the money."

All the fight went out of me. "All right," I said. I was stung.

Now I hadn't been so deluded I thought that the Jains were hosting me for the fun we'd had conjugating verbs. I knew they had three daughters and I knew the price of a dowry in India: 5 lakhs, 500,000 rupees, for a doctor, an impossible 10 if you wanted to buy your daughter an engineer. The Jains' whole house had cost 50 lakhs. I knew that, but I'd come to love them and had persuaded myself that in whatever culturally retransfigured way possible, they felt the same. When Vanita said this, I was cut to think what an obvious fool I'd been.

"All right," I said. "Let's go."

I kept my back Rajput-straight while we looked for a rickshaw. When we pulled up to the house hours before the end of school, Meena and Alka were inside and didn't hear us, but by the time I was in my room stuffing clothes into duffel bags, they were at the door. I kept my head down, refused to look at them. Vanita fielded questions. "I don't know why she's leaving," she lied. I bunched the Jaipur curtains into a backpack, still not looking up, though in my mind's eye, I could see the wives precisely. They would be standing side by side, exactly aligned, both with their arms folded, one hip each jutting right. I imagined their dumbfounded expressions, how they'd be casting nervous glances at each other. *What has happened? What thing is this?* I switched my thoughts back to the money: *Hope they're happy. They got four months.* I was trying to find room for a small, glittery basket the girls had brought me from a fair when Vanita said to hurry. "Kathy-ji," she said, "the man is waiting." I set the basket on a shelf, turned to lift my bags, and came face-to-face with the wives. They were exactly as I'd had them in my head, except for one gleaming detail: the line of tears shining on Alka's face.

What an idiot I was, but now there was no going back. Time here could spin, jam, or slow, but even in India, it couldn't reverse itself.

I mumbled a feeble thanks for everything. The wives continued to stare. Vanita and I lugged my things to the drive. The women, with the dumbfounded expression I'd envisioned, trailed after us. They stood halfway down the drive watching as we settled ourselves in and the driver pressed my bags around us, and then he lifted his arm and brought it down on the throttle, and they were already out of sight. As we sped down the road, I knew two things for sure: That even once we'd turned the corner, the wives would still be standing there.

And that from now on, for a long time, I would be lost in India.

"This is a major problem and cannot be disposed of so easily"

 Christmas is coming. We know because Helaena's mother wants to mail a holiday gift basket to her at the school. Raju the cook, however, says no, not if this thing contains meat. It's not just people here who are vegetarian. Entire buildings are, including Antriksh Flats. They get it in writing when you move in: no meat on the premises.

The package arrives just before lunch, on a day Raju's serving his specialty, gluey *saag paneer:* spinach green as an algae problem, tiny gray cubes of cottage cheese.

"But, Raju, there's no paneer in mine," Helaena says to distract him from the box by her feet. Raju peers into her bowl. *"Paneer is not your kismet,"* he says: cheese is not her fate. He returns to the kitchen. Helaena reaches down, and as an oregano-scented cloud envelops us, we proceed to imperil the lease.

Christmas is coming: *bada din,* "big day"—the one when the Raj, indisposed by merriment, tossed their retainers a bone and let them knock off. It's coming, but so dyspeptically, I'm not sure it'll make it all the way. Down in Bapu Bazaar, a blow-up storefront Santa has lost his shape. His head is lolling. He looks beat. Then one day, fresh tidings appear. As my rickshaw passes the folk art museum, I spy, poking up above the wall, a treetop strung with lights. Shaking the driver's seat, I call, "Pull up."

In the yard, children are engaged in a tree-trimming competition. They're working with what they've got, and they don't have the details straight. The trees—peepuls, ashoks, every kind but firs—look more trussed than adorned, with strands of tinsel and flashing lights, plastic garlands that call to mind leis, shiny purple and yellow lanterns left over from Divali. One branch tried to escape its bindings and has gotten piled down with crepe on its way to freedom. One entrant does look vaguely plausible from a distance— blinking star on top, triangular lights—but I prefer the Seuss-like ashok, with its buildup of celebratory detritus on one side, the two banners that proclaim MERRY CHRISTMAS and SALUTE TO THE PEOPLE OF KERALA.

"Wow!" little kids say as they walk by. "Wow!" "Happy Christmas!"

Christmas is coming, trailing leis, dodging cows, plowing straight for Adhikmas, and the days leading up, as they stumble in, will be some of the most haunting of my life.

MY HINDI CONTINUED to rev, so hard, it flew around a corner. "Some people say you've turned the corner when you can make jokes," the linguist Ellen Bialystok says. "Some say it's once they're translating, others when they dream in the language. People put up landmarks of progress."

All my landmarks till now have been more like excavations: bare starts. I've always wanted to dream in another language—to speak one with the same dizzying ease I'd known as a kid when, asleep, I could fly. But so far my dreams in Hindi resemble real life. People natter confusingly, and I'm lucky to get ten words. My translations have been similarly dispiriting: homework that comes back red with corrections. But then one night, to my surprise, I make my first successful joke.

At the Trident, with Piers, one of his posse says, "I saw your photograph in the paper," a comment I'd been hearing for days. When Helaena and I were dragged onstage at the beauty competition, a photographer had been in attendance.

Piers grins. "She's off to be a Bollywood star."

"*Yes. My new film is* Oh What a Fool I Was,*"* I say, punning on the name of a hit movie. The man laughs. I'm surprised. I've been making jokes for weeks, to everyone's befuddlement, but this is the first one that's stuck.

My Hindi careened. My love for Bollywood movies deepened: For the villainous maharajas, draped in fat pearls, who issued adenoidal commands to bring more girls. For the lithe women chained in dungeons, liquid-eyed but bearing up. For one film in particular, *Lekin,* a ghost story set in Rajasthan. The movie is about a woman who's died at the hands of an evil maharaja and is now consigned to flicker in and out as a haint till she can figure out how to be reborn. In some of her apparitions, she sings. Then Vinod Khanna shows up and, between posing homoerotically in just his pants, declares that to escape the netherworld, she'll have to cross the desert.

Every time I watched *Lekin* and the ghost would sigh, *"But I can't go into the desert. I'm afraid of the shadows,"* I'd turn into Swami-ji, choked up and lip-synching. I couldn't stop watching the movie. At home, in the evenings, I'd play the soundtrack for hours. I liked one song especially, "Yara Seeli Seeli."

"I'm lying in bed," I wrote one night, "listening to the haunting 'Seeli Seeli,' and crying, because I'm lonely and afraid I'll be forever." *Beloved, little by little* — "seeli seeli" — *the separation of the night is starting to burn,* the ghost was keening in the voice of the venerable playback singer Lata Mangeshkar. "The taste I've had here, of strong emotion, of being cared for, is seductive and isn't enough, won't last the plane ride back," I wrote, already in longing for India. "'You should have called us when you were ill,' Nand scolded recently after I was down with a bug. 'We would have taken care of you.' 'How do you think I lost my tooth?' Vidhu asked this morning in class. 'I had three sisters and on the street there'd be *chhedna*'—and he used a word we'd just learned, for molestation. 'I had to defend them.' Ever since, I've wondered what it would have been like to have a man protect you."

Uncommon questions have begun to drift through my mind, ones that if I were to say them aloud, would shock me. Such as: But why couldn't you just recede into a gated life, the way the women have here? Why not give yourself over to a man's protection? The feminism I was weaned on was so absolute, these questions, at this remove, seem revolutionary. Breakthrough thinking: *Moka* is "opportunity." *Mauksha* means "release." In giving yourself up, through the release of self, you'd meet with opportunity, wouldn't you?

With shadows looming, I can't make out the forces contributing to this advanced new thought: the seduction of cultural persuasion, the jolts of social disapproval, my own recent street chhedna. Unattached, these thoughts prattle in my head, combine with the Hindi snatches. They'll mumble and trill, *That life is com-ple-te-ly fine*, right up to the morning Vanita's nearly killed. Then every question will be starkly answered.

VIDHU AND I HAD been translating my alarm clock, the Hindu chant that it played, when the door to the classroom flew open. Vidhu jerked his head up. He was filling in for Samta, who'd phoned first thing to say she wouldn't be in. She was too banged up, having crashed her scooter into the gated wall downstairs the afternoon before. In plain view of anyone who might have been looking, someone would later point out.

"Praise . . . be . . . the lord of the world," and with a crack, Helaena was in the door frame.

"You have to come. Something's wrong with Vanita," she said. "I mean, really wrong. She's saying she fell off her scooter." This odd detail—two spills, so close together—hung above the confusion, bumping and skimming but not taking root, even when Vidhu said softly, "Something's fishy." We took off at a run.

In the back office, Vanita was pressing her head, moaning and swaying, so small at her desk, she looked like a filament.

Swami-ji arrived in a blast of air. *"The ambulance will be here in an hour,"* he said. He'd waited to file a report with Delhi before phoning the hospital.

"An hour, no way," Helaena cried. Vanita sunk her head down.

"We can't let her go to sleep," I said. Reluctantly, she pulled back up.

"She has a head injury," I argued. "She has to go now."

"You are supposed to register at the police station first. Even if you have a head injury," Vidhu was explaining, but we were already coaxing Vanita onto her feet, steering her toward the door. The others caught up with us at the elevator.

In the rickshaw, Vanita bumped between us, while outside, India turned surreal: two yellow dogs by the side of the road were tearing at a dead one's chest. A nursing pig with a thick, long face stared balefully at us above her young. Black tears were running from her eyes. The rickshaw came closer. My vision cleared. The tears were revealed as blood.

"Hurry!" I called to receding backs in the hospital lobby, from the benches where we'd all assembled. "Hurry! Her arms are going numb!" We sat and watched hospital personnel ignore my commands, and after a while, we'd been there so long, Vanita began to revive. She asked Swami-ji to call her father, started to tell me what had happened.

"For months I have been getting threatening phone calls," she said, related how beginning in October, one month after she'd come to the school, her starched, orderly life was repeatedly yanked into some overwrought Bollywood film. A man with a muffled voice began phoning her at home. "Your health is in danger," the goonda would say. "Quit the school," he'd purr through fabric. "You had better quit the school. Stay out of Sector Eleven unless you would like your legs to be broken." Indignation squeezed her voice.

The calls kept coming. Vanita was rattled but refused to back down. She had every business being in Sector Eleven. She kept showing up there with the same diligence and show of certainty she applied to her master's, even if all day she'd worry herself into an enervated trance state. But this goonda wala could only be crazy! She could go wherever she wanted. Then this morning, he'd made good on his warnings.

Vanita-ji had been putting along on her scooter toward the school, mulling over a host family matter, when just past the Paras Theater, "oh, my God," she snapped to. Two men, faceless behind helmets, had jumped into her lane and were speeding straight for her. Before she could yank the wheel sideways, they'd already slowed and were slamming her to the ground.

"Never in my whole life have I thought this thing would happen to me," Vanita said with a wail as an orderly came to escort her back. "Something's fishy," Vidhu said again, with such a showboating shake of his head that I did a double take as I realized: he had some kind of inside scoop. Around the classroom, Vidhu had a reputation as a man who could be made to spill. Usually, it took three questions, but today he needed only one: "What's going on?" And that's when I found out who'd tried to kill Vanita.

Samta's husband.

The story came pouring out. As soon as Vanita had been hired, she'd acquired the high-gloss, immutable shine of a golden girl.

Swami-ji had been dazzled by her crisp efficiency and appearance, by her determination to get ahead, by the way she took notes on everything he said. This girl was meticulous, a comer, just like him. Samta, meanwhile, was left to suck up the injustice of this: to seethe. She'd been on staff for years, but her star had never risen this high, and what's more, she'd come to be regarded as a bit of a dim bulb, one with any number of limitations. Unlike Vanita, who turned up for every one, she couldn't, for instance, go on field trips. Her husband, Manesh, forbade it.

Samta had lost whatever luster she'd had, and it was all that upstart's fault, she realized with greater acuity as she grew increasingly distraught. She took to weeping about this unfairness at home, thereby getting on Manesh's already frayed nerves. His nervous system had been taxed by a long stretch without employment as either an astrologer or an architect and by the well-founded suspicion that the whole town sniggered about it behind his back. Although Manesh did hold a well-placed position with a local right-wing Hindutva organization, it was honorific; organizing thundering brownshorted nationalist marches didn't pay. The nightly sobbing, then, emphasized two unpleasant facts: One, his wife was the sole breadwinner in the family. Two, his mainstay stream of support was about to be cut off, if there was anything to Samta's bawling. It was all he could do not to hit her. Sometimes he went ahead.

When the threatening calls to Vanita started, the finger of suspicion quickly tapped Manesh. "A conference was held at the school, and he was brought in," Vidhu was telling me when a disturbance in the hospital lobby drowned him out. "Till now, I have not interfered in the affairs of the school," a burly man was shouting. "But now I am going after that chap! That chap does not even have a job!" Two men calmed Vanita's father down and showed him to the back. Vidhu continued.

The year before, Delhi headquarters had begun receiving letters accusing another, now departed female teacher of gross misdeeds. When Manesh was accused of mailing them, he hotly denied the charge, even after it was pointed out that the letters had been signed with his name. Vile slander, he maintained, and offered as proof the fact that whoever had sent them had spelled his name correctly, while he, Manesh, preferred to spell it incorrectly.

This struck me, as it had the others, as a less than airtight defense—a feint, perhaps, to throw off suspicion, as Samta's scooter crash had almost certainly been. Although Samta, in the strained state of protection she inhabited, had likely been ordered to enact her own accident, Manesh would have been acting of his own volition.

An academic adviser was flown in. He was from the U.S., but not high ranking enough to have a tilak shot on the wall. "We are taking culturally appropriate measures," he announced, but the troops were in no mood. The troops were in revolt. "I've had it with this overgrown study abroad program," I said. We'd discuss it over dinner, he told me.

At dinner, the adviser outlined what the culturally appropriate measure would be. A policeman would stop by Samta's and give the husband a warning. *Bas:* that was it.

We finished up with polite conversation, and at the meal's end, I caught a rickshaw home. *"Mera yaha,"* I told the driver: literally, "My here," though the expression meant more like "That's my place, there." *There* was now irrefutably *here,* where for months I'd wanted to be, and even so, the next day I quit speaking Hindi.

IN SCHOOL, I BEGIN to use only English, casually, defiantly. I don't want to make the laborious Hindi sentences anymore, which now strike me as fetters to thought. The teachers, who didn't do anything about Harold's death threats, don't do anything now. They answer me in Hindi, as if that's what we're speaking. I reply in English. Conversations are really quite comfortable this way, each doing what we do best.

> VIDHU: *Kathy-ji, are you planning to have literature class tomorrow?*
> ME: Yeah, sure. That's what we agreed.
> VIDHU: *Of course, Kathy-ji. You are the students. We are the teachers.*
> ME: Good. Then let's meet at three.

In immersion-only Antriksh Flats, this is the equivalent of flipping the bird.

"WHAT MADE ME REALIZE how much I dislike the sound of French was the continual, unctuous, caressing repetition of 'l'oiseau' (the bird). It is a word that cannot be pronounced without simpering. I did not want to speak French because it gave me the bird." Several weeks before I boarded the plane to come over, I'd read a book containing accounts by people who, hell-bent on learning a second language, had ended up in far-flung destinations. Called *The Neurobiology of Affect in Language,* it was an exploration into the ways motivation affects the process. Many entries were rapturous, like this excerpt from Alice Kaplan's memoir *French Lessons:* "There was chocolate in every store, on every corner, chocolate bars with colored wrappers showing roses, bottles of milk, nuts in rows of six, three deep. For each bar of chocolate I didn't eat, I learned a verb. I grew thinner and thinner. I ate French."

Heady with the prospect of transport, I concentrated on those entries. I ignored the selections like the first one above, which I found when I rechecked the book. It had been written by a man, age fifty-five, who'd taken to the Alliance Française in Paris with great enthusiasm till he was repeatedly referred to as *imbécile* by his teacher and snubbed by students who considered him ancient. Some diarists, I discovered on the second read, had been faded by frustration until they were blurry presences in the classroom. Others had launched confrontational language strikes, same as I had.

The author of the book, the linguist John Schumann, had wondered back in the sixties why some people stall with a language, while others bulldoze all roadblocks. The deciding factors aren't necessarily tied to natural talent, he'd realized during a stint as a Peace Corps volunteer in Iran. Some of his fellow volunteers had earned blazing scores on the MLAT, the Modern Language Aptitude Test, then gone on to have only middling success with Farsi, the language of Iran, whereas others who'd placed in the midrange on the MLAT ended up speaking circles around the rest. Their assignments, he realized, had had a lot to do with this: The most promising volunteers, the ones who'd swept the test, were mostly stationed in cities where, with English speakers on every corner, you could blow off Farsi practice at every turn. The others had landed in flyblown outposts where, if you wanted to say anything—and often you desperately did: *The well water's green; you sure it's potable?*—you had to work to be understood. You had to learn Farsi.

This observation got Schumann to wondering what other factors influence performance in a foreign tongue. When he returned to Boston, he got a job teaching English as a second language and discovered "the same thing" as he had in Iran. "Social and psychological factors made a huge difference," he recalls. The Italians he taught outshone the Puerto Ricans. The Italians had access to established Italian communities in the area and "got jobs right away. The families became socially integrated. The Puerto Ricans didn't. They were agrarian, they went back to Puerto Rico often."

Schumann had started this job around the time second language acquisition studies were beginning to take off. Most foreign language teachers back then were still using the lockstep approach: pattern practice drills, which were supposed to replicate what the main theorists at the time, the behaviorists, believed was the way infants learned a language—one grammatical structure at a time. "Little Tommy is hungry?" the mother would ask, and gurgling Tommy would supposedly file away the knowledge that in that particular linkage of noun and adjective, the copula should be singular. This produced a lot of laborious French and Spanish classes, where kids were hammered with rote lessons, similar to how they were taught science and math.

Things were about to change radically, though. Noam Chomsky had, not long before, launched a salvo at the collective thinking when he proposed his theory of universal grammar. In it, he maintained that we all have access to some kind of natural wellspring of grammar, that we all have something like a language acquisition device in our brains, that it doesn't make sense to beat example after example into children's heads, since language begins to expand on its own, almost as if it had a life of its own. That was the end of the "I tie my shoelaces, you tie your shoelaces" form of French and Spanish instruction, the beginning of understanding that language study is a more human operation than, say, trigonometry, and so subject to psychological forces.

"There is no question that learning a foreign language is different to learning other subjects," the English psychologist Marion Williams writes, summing up the viewpoint that holds now. "This is mainly because of the social nature. Language belongs to a person's whole social being: it is part of one's identity. It involves far more than simply learning skills, or a system of rules, or a grammar; it involves an alteration in self image, the adoption of new behaviors." If language is arguably what makes us human, then learning one has to be, by definition, messy, frustrating, glorious, cause for despair, unnerving in how it obscures itself and also for what it reveals.

Not to mention subject to the whims of motivation. A lot of studies into that aspect of SLA were being launched in the late 1960s, when Schumann enrolled in Harvard for a doctorate in human development. The Canadian psycholinguists Wallace Lambert and Robert Gardner had just come out with their observation that people learn languages from one of two broad motivations: either they're doing it to make a living, or they have some compelling desire to slip into another community. Sometimes this second aspiration stems from the fact that they feel masked in their own. "Why do people want to adopt another culture?" Alice Kaplan writes. "Because there's something in their own they don't like, that doesn't name them." Sometimes the underlying factor is less urgent. Next year, if they can keep up with Wednesday nights at the Y, they'll haul off and surprise the proprietor of that little café in Provence with their stream of bons mots. Then he'll really think they're sophisticated. Then they will, too.

These fast-talking personalities of the future—the one who startles and delights the friends in Rome, the one for whom Mandarin flows like sweet wine—are what the Hungarian psycholinguist Zoltán Dörnyei calls the "ideal L2 self" and are essential to long-term success. Motivation, he believes, consists of the desire to reduce the discrepancy between your actual self and your ideal L2 self. In India, after Vanita was attacked, I seriously contemplated leaving. Once I did that, the whole enterprise was derailed, for I was not seeing myself there anymore. Lose your future self, you lose all motivation with it. It's a truth that applies in every area.

To this day, motivation is the subject of more academic papers and discussion than any other aspect of SLA, partly because it's the only area in which a consensus can be reached—namely, that motivation is sheer firepower. Had you taken our motley group at the school and gauged how much of it each individual had, you could have predicted on day one roughly how everyone would do by the end of the year.

Harold, whose main incentive to come to India was not, shall we say, driving—to get out of grunt work, far as I could tell—scored, essentially, zero on the year-end improvement test, his being shipped out early having precluded him from taking it.

At the other extreme, you had Helaena, whose motivation was compelling: she could only be fully Helaena, the avatar version, in

India and in Hindi. Her motivation was the greatest, and, indeed, she got top scores in the test: 25 percent more advanced than at the beginning of the year.

The Whisperer was there, she said, "to communicate better with my father," a goal that was, possibly, less sustaining, for in addition to Hindi, her father knew English. Since a bridge of communication already existed, that might have cut the impetus some. At any rate, at the end of the year, she came in 13 percent improved.

As did I, on the button. But since the Whisperer had a strong base of Indian language to start with and I had years of brain rot on her and Helaena, I have, in brooding moments, tried to make the claim to myself that my improvement was, relatively, stratospheric. No, *I* was the shooting star. In my dreams, perhaps. But as far as motivation went, all I knew going in was that it felt like rocket fuel—I wanted that language like I wanted life itself, it seemed. Later, I'd see this was true.

WHEN SCHUMANN WAS still at Harvard, as part of his dissertation he began meeting twice a week with a factory worker who was Costa Rican, illegal, living with other Costa Ricans in a Portuguese neighborhood of Cambridge, and basically only there to make money. Schumann wanted to document how the man's English had developed at the end of a year, but he couldn't, owing to the fact that there'd been little progress. The man, he found, had settled into an obdurate, entrenched kind of pidgin.

Through these meetings, he came up with a theory that's now widely accepted in the field: all language learners, early in the process, go through a "pidginization" stage. But while some build their fragmented sentences into full language, others never progress. "I became interested in what makes someone get stuck," says Schumann, who went on to become chair of applied linguistics at UCLA.

It was because he was looking for clues that he asked people, in the late seventies, to document their experiences learning languages. But when the journals came back, he found he had nothing useful. One girl encountered bug troubles so bad she looked like a "small-pox victim"; another ended up teaching English to the children of a Japanese gangster, and terrified to be. But mostly, as far as he could see, the journal entries were all over the place. The only repeating theme he or his colleagues could find was competition. Every correspondent mentioned it. A little competition appeared to act like a spur, too much turned them off. And that was it for unifying principles.

Till twenty years later, when Schumann came across an idea, called stimulus appraisal theory, that the Austrian scholar Klaus Scherer was proposing. According to Scherer, there are five broad ways in which you appraise an experience, the stimuli that surround you: how pleasant it is; how compatible it is with your self-image and social image; how relevant the undertaking is to your needs and goals; how able you are to cope with it; and how novel it is. This last factor has a more variable impact than the other four, whose effects are more straightforward. If something is pleasant, you like it, end of story, but novelty goes both ways. A little of it adds fizz, makes the experience enjoyable. Too much produces confusion and anxiety, similar to competition. These five variant perceptions combined, Scherer argued, are responsible for every take you have on anything.

In reading over the theory, Schumann was struck by a thought: Every one of his diarists had, in fact, been evaluating their studies according to these criteria. There'd been five strong repeating themes running through the journals. He just hadn't seen them. He set about adapting stimulus appraisal theory to the business of learning a language, got to thinking how one person's interesting experience with Italian is another person's wipeout. Scherer, he began to think, had left out an important consideration, one that applied double time to second language learning: the enormous set of likes and dislikes that you have, over time and as the result of your experiences, stored in your brain. The new way to say "sky," for instance, contains a remembered threat of leopards, and since you have traveled this far in an attempt to show that you're unafraid of anything, the word strikes you as thrilling. Or you loathe cats, big or small: the word provokes a thudding feeling. These responses would draw on different neural sites than the ones commonly regarded as the crucial language sites, and here Schumann sketched out a possible ancillary network. The amygdala would have to be involved: the site that mediates fear and anxiety is the emotional center of the brain. Also, the orbitofrontal cortex, which has a lot to do with judgment, along with the nervous system located in the body proper.

On the phone, when he and I spoke, he elaborated on how the stimulus filters work. "Going to France, where it's Christian and Western, might provide enough novelty to interest some people, but if that same person went to India, it might be too much," he said. I'd been describing how, after Vanita's assault, for a time I'd bowed out; the place had grown too surreal, was too much.

"A Peace Corps volunteer I know was in a country where she'd lived before," he said. "She'd gone back, and things had changed. It was the same city but different this time when she encountered it, and she found it really disorienting. Novelty's a funny thing: you want just enough to make it interesting and not too much to make it overwhelming." You can perceive French as punishment the first time you take it, as thrilling when you try again. A similar split reaction occurred at the school around the time of the hit on Vanita.

In the days after, Helaena continued to blitz happily in Hindi. I gave out stony looks and English, thought, *They're idiots.* Perhaps my recent experiences in the street had made me feel a kinship with poor, alarmed Vanita, had retooled my amygdala in ways Helaena's hadn't been. Or maybe, being from New York, I was quick to link Manesh's political affiliations with the events that had occurred in my hometown in September, to erect a wall between me and Manesh

and any associates of his I knew. And likely, as Schumann specu-
lated when I related the story, "when the cultural differences really
made a difference, you had to take the position *They're idiots and I'm
going to speak differently.*"

Whatever the reason, pleasantness soured, my ability to cope
eroded. My self-image stopped short of being able to encompass
an association with a fanatic who'd been plotting murder. Novelty
turned to anxiety, immediately, and I quit speaking Hindi. I sized
up the stimuli and beat it out of there, for a time at least, in my
head.

· 13 ·

"After a long time, I have
the honor to see you"

 It's 10 P.M., and the niece of the maharana is saying she will not bring children into this marriage. Not with the way things are, she says, as a back-and-forth whoosh of cold water on marble contradicts her. *Wiiill, beeee,* it votes, slurry, mournful, muffling the faint rumble that's been tickling my feet. I give the room a fast scan. Everything's stationary.

Over in one corner, the maharana is bending heads with his bull-necked adviser, Shakti Singh. Earlier, Sri-ji had posted himself by the door, but he'd wandered off after an hour of sporadic arrivals. It's four days before New Year's and what should be the height of tourist season, but you'd need just two seconds to count the Americans in the room. Four, plus one constitutionally confused. Four point five; I'm the half.

The niece, seated beside me, is picking at her sari. At the buffet behind us, men in white stand motionless. The spread's the same one they served two nights back at another rent-a-royal party, in the other palace in the lake, one floating mirage over. Glistening roast pig, exquisitely perfumed puddings, desserts both massive and frothy, but the niece will have none of it. She's twenty-six, raised in London, and now deposited in a frustrating arranged marriage here. The concentrated sight of Western faces must be hurtling her back, must be creating deep feelings of affinity, for remarkably, given the fact that no Indian normally would, she's decided she wants to spill.

"My mother-in-law expects me to wear the five compulsory proofs of marriage," she tells the Americans, who've each plunked down the equivalent of one month's local rent to say they attended a party at a palace. Oh, she tried—donned the ankle chains, the nose ornament, the bangles, the special necklace; streaked the part in her hair vermilion to show she was wed—but she'd been in London too long. She reverted in less than a month.

Wiiiiiill, be, the water shushes.

"Huhhhh," says a thin woman, from Los Angeles and in her thirties, whose air of self-satisfaction does not appear to have been curbed by two weeks on the road in India. She assumes an expression of intense concern, nods from time to time like a shrink.

"Reeaally?" breathes a middle-aged woman from Long Island, who's momentarily confused by the marital compulsions part of the talk but knows a confessional moment when she sees one.

"My in-laws don't approve of me." The niece attacks a wrinkle. "I don't want children till I see if I can bring them into this," she says, and soon the Americans are bringing the weight of decades of collective national therapization to bear on the situation.

"Have you tried journaling?" the California woman says. "You need to work out your feelings about your own identity. I ask because I started keeping a journal, and it changed my life."

"I do like to write," the niece allows softly.

"You know who you have to read? Naipaul. He had conflicts about *his* identity, and he's worked them out through writing. You should think about writing like him."

We're in a country where rapid personal makeovers are inconceivable; where everyone likes to wear the same thing, go into the same business as their parents, touch their elders' feet; where disgruntled husbands, in many areas, have the cultural power to torch a wife and say she fell into the stove. Why don't you try a little Nobel-level upgrade now that you're not wasting all that time putting red gunk in your hair? the LA woman seems to be suggesting. I look to see if the niece is insulted. She's drinking it all in.

"You know," Long Island says, "there has to be trust in a marriage. It doesn't sound to me like you feel a lot of trust toward your husband. This is my second husband," she says, glancing at the hefty man on her left, who's been eyeing women all evening. "In my first marriage, I couldn't feel comfortable, but now we're very, very happy." And the niece is signed, sealed, and delivered for life, a fact that doesn't seem to have registered with LI, who proceeds to deliver a long story about a daughter who got off on a wrong first marriage but spun around and remarried, her gardener. With help from her, he now has the largest landscaping business in the county.

The niece is pumping it, basking in the attention — "But could I . . . ?" "Do you think?" — when LA, who'd assumed a glazed expression, jumps back in.

"You have to be able to express your feelings," LA says. "You have to be your own person. I'm serious, you have to think about writing," she goes on, till Long Island stops her cold by asking my opinion about a local sight. "Oh, you don't want to go there," LA says sharply, and the niece and I are left to converse on our own. But it can be so hard here, we agree. No, really it is, we say. But you can't know till you've lived here, and the sentence establishes our true affinity. She, I, we understand, and so I'm persuaded to lower my voice and tell her about something that happened three days ago, when I went to the villages with Renee's friend Pauline.

"Oh, God, and then we found out, the girl had been only fifteen."

The niece nods, her face impassive. "It was meant to be," she says, poking daintily at her baked Alaska.

"It was?"

"Yes. Those things are meant to be," she says, as the whoosh builds to a shout, as the rumble becomes a roar. As Christmas comes barreling in three days late, sporting crimson horns, and in the collision with Adhikmas that occurs, time is sent reeling backward.

FOUR DAYS BEFORE THIS, Christmas Eve, at a palace up the hill.

"Come by my flat around nine," Sri-ji had said when I phoned that morning, following the instructions he'd issued at his birthday party. I'd just come off a camel safari that had fanned a cold into a flu. In my feverish state, I'd taken the word "flat" literally, imagined all day that the maharana lived in an atelier, in the spirit of Marie Antoinette, perhaps. With potted palms, but no, at 9 P.M., his directions left me in front of a building the size of a small embassy. A maroon MG roadster was parked outside.

A barefoot servant in a formless gray suit answered when I knocked. He led me into an anteroom, where I signed my name in the guest book beneath someone who'd added "prince of Slovak" to his. In this town, any deposed royal was welcome to take back the title. The servant left. I sat on the edge of a thin gold love seat and looked around. Across the room, a cast-iron lion, a *singh,* was tearing apart a deer. On the walls, stark-faced rulers of Mewar appraised each other from their large gilt frames. In his portrait, Sri-ji was in a long white tunic and explosive red plumed headdress. One eyebrow was raised in a way that could look affronted or amused, depending on how you craned your neck.

In the chandeliered reception room, his attire was more relaxed, red-and-blue-striped T-shirt over pants. "Yes, yes, have a seat," he said when I was brought in, frowning as if to place me. The aides perched on chairs shot each other glances. He cleared his throat. He nodded gravely. He cleared it again. Then no one said anything.

"And what do you do for Christmas?" I ventured when the silence stretched on.

"We drink," he said.

He proceeded to tease a thin aide, a new girl from Delhi. "She's a Parsee. They're like elephants, an endangered species. There are only ninety-nine thousand in the world," he said, and everyone laughed helplessly, except for the aide, whose shoulders seized up. A radiant-looking young woman rustled in, Sri-ji's daughter, on break from college in the States. "I was just telling Bobi she's like an elephant," he said. "Endangered." At that word, Bobi inhaled sharply.

His daughter took a seat. "Show them what I found in the vault," he said. Eyes downcast, she lifted her arm to display the Yuletide trinket, an emerald the size of a kiwifruit set in a white-gold band.

Sri-ji held forth on the endless rounds of dinners and parties he had to attend in his two official roles: kingdom figurehead, CEO of several palaces that had been reoutfitted as hotels. "I can talk to someone all night and not know who they are," he said. "He can. I've seen him," his daughter said fondly. His stories began, rose, swelled, were delivered in a baritone as persuasive as any movie maharaja's. "Bin Laden has had plastic surgery to look like a woman," he announced, and no one questioned this, though maybe that wasn't entirely the voice.

He talked and people twittered, and periodically nervous-looking retainers would appear carrying trays laden with envelopes. He'd hold up one finger, then he'd tear them open, scan the contents, and toss them back on the tray. At the time, I was wide-eyed. Around town, common knowledge held that Sri-ji had godlike abilities to know what even the smallest citizens were doing at all times. Now I was seeing the source of these powers, I assumed—these were missives from his network of spies. Later, though, I got a better idea of the kind of intelligence the envelopes contained. Toward the end of the year, Sri-ji had me to dinner with the maharani, his wife. All through the meal, servants scurried in with cell phones on trays, and then, because my Hindi was firing, I could ascertain what variety of secret communiqués were being exchanged. *"Just add more ghee,"* he was saying into the phone. *"Yes, more ghee. It will make it much better."*

A man appeared and said the cars would take us to dinner now. We all piled in and the cars slowly made their way down a drive wide enough for two passing elephants, past stone pachyderms trumpeting from high fortress walls. The procession inched along like this for about two hundred feet, till we reached a pavilion above the lake, then we all got out. "You are studying Hindi?" Sri-ji asked in the royal skiff over to the Lake Palace.

"Haan-ji," I said, in the clipped tones of deference the jigri had taught me: "Yes, sir."

"Well that must be boring," he said.

In the open-air courtyard of the hotel, a holiday party was in full swing: glittering Indian couples from other states, boys in dry-ice clouds dancing to a live band, one badly dressed magnate from an Eastern bloc country and his wife. At our poolside table, Sri-ji pulled a chair up next to mine. We all hit the buffet, then he took my photograph, had me repeatedly look into the camera to see if I liked the preview. All I could see was that my cold had made a chapped butt of my face. He passed around a PalmPilot displaying a joke: "Women and hurricanes are similar in that they're wet and wild when they come, then take your car and house when they leave." He knocked back a few, made booming remarks, got up and touched my shoulder. "Come," he said. We switched tables. He had some further analysis to deliver about Helaena.

"She is mentally crazy," he said with a note of wonder, picking up where we'd left off. "She is cunning and too smart for her own good." The band went into an Elvis medley. "What?" I had to keep shouting.

"She does not like you," he said. "Why do you think she didn't want you to come to the palace?" I widened my eyes in the hope this would qualify as a response. "Over and over, I said, 'Bring her.'" His tone was sorry, shocked. He paused to let me reflect on the opportunities that had been lost to me. I considered that I had come up, about a hundred times, but since he had that many rooms at least, how would he have known? I wasn't going with this line.

He offered proof of Helaena's scheming ways. "My brother is looking for a guest, and you were looking for a place to stay? You went to see him? Yes, she told me that." All right, now I was going to kill her.

It was a well-known fact, as far away as the Great Thar, that Sri-ji had been on the outs with his brother ever since their father died. The brother, being older, had been in line for the throne. But in some tricky bit of business, upon the father's death, the brother had been ousted and sent to live on a dairy farm at the foot of the palace. Sri-ji had become the possessor of the head plumes. "Sri-ji is not the rightful maharana," people snickered behind his back, inaccurately, because ever since the royals lost their titles, no one technically was. Nonetheless, all of this amounted to cryogenic social ostracism for anyone who stepped one foot past the dairy farm gate.

I'd made it all the way up to the door after learning there was a room there for rent and having heard one too many 4 A.M. rounds of the "Brazil" song, then considered what life would be like with an embittered exiled ruler for my host family and beat a fast retreat back to the hotel with the wedding field. Helaena, when I told her, had been sworn to secrecy. "You see, she wanted to keep you away," Sri-ji said. Okay, I was giving him that one. Clearly, there'd been some perfidy.

He cocked a finger for an adviser to join us, a woman whose job responsibilities evidently included gasping and looking disbelieving. "Do you know Helaena wanted to get married?" Sri-ji said, and the adviser clucked. "Do you know she wanted to marry my nephew?" The adviser appeared stricken. "Do you know she never said goodbye?" he said tightly, and without another word rose and rejoined the table.

At the end of the evening, we all reboarded the skiff. "There's snow in Kashmir," everyone kept saying. Dressed as we were in thin saris and light coats, the night air off the lake was cutting. We huddled down as the boat circled out toward the other floating palace, a hulking gray form now. The boat curved back, and as it did, it set off rippling splashes: flapping glinting balls, coruscating disturbances in the dark. Almost at the dock, I figured out what they were: sparks of light off the wings of spooked ducks.

EIGHT DAYS BEFORE the evening with the niece, somewhere in the middle of the desert.

"Tiger will eat you," the camel drover's son was saying, one dromedary over to my left, through the fog of a cold I'd contracted in a sleeper train north.

"Not the tiger!" I cried and sneezed.

"Tiger eat you," he repeated. From one camel to the right, my traveling companion, a shock-jock radio producer, gave us a look. Her ride kept making gurgling noises and twisting to bite her, which was not boosting her appreciation for the tiger dialogues. The boy and I had hit on this rewarding colloquy by day two of the camel safari.

"No, not the tiger!" She and I had saddle sores from three days of rocking past snake holes and lime green flashes of parrot, the occasional tiny donkey. I was keeping my mind off my tenderized behind by practicing Hindi. Away from the school, I forgot I refused

to speak it. The boy was going for the squeals the exchanges produced. I was going for the mastery of the aspirated Hindi *g* you could get by repeating *baagh*, "tiger," about a thousand times.

"*You tiger.*"

"*You tiger.*" The producer was going to kill us.

"*Tiger eat girls.*"

"*No! Not the tiger!*" The producer sighed. She and I had met only once, the year before, at a wedding in Manhattan. Over dessert, we discovered we'd both be in Rajasthan. "Well, we should travel," she said in comradely tones, for this was back when I still resembled someone who might be a comrade to her: someone edged and shaped by New York, who could be counted on to know the drill and not to exclaim, "Hey, why don't we sing songs!" as the car pulled out of Jaipur on day one of a trip together. *That's what we do here! It's how we have fun! We do that and then we drink warm milk!* I didn't specifically say any of that, but it had been fairly implicit in my tone.

"I'm not much for songs," she'd said quietly. I was in violation of hip.

"*Tiger eat girls.*" Gradually, we'd both come to see that our winter vacations had been invaded by an alien, in the person of the other one. I'd arrived at this conclusion when in a grease pit, I'd become reacquainted with a word that had faded from memory: "co-dependent." The sullen driver we'd signed on had been muscling us into restaurants I knew would be flyspecked. The producer had been overriding me. "Hey, what can I say, I'm co-dependent?" she said in singsong, as across the room, our driver glad-handed the manager for his kickback. I glowered at him across the lentil-encrusted table. Then, next, at her.

"*Tiger eat boys.*" The look was similar to the one she'd given me when I was in the middle of the Indian bargaining dance with a hotel manager. "How long are you going to keep doing that?" she'd interrupted. Her speech, the fast, sharp, rejoindering talk that's entirely ordinary in New York, was, over here, unnerving: suddenly naked and direct, like a streaking. In a place swathed in veils—veiled references, displays, emotions, half the women—directness was shocking.

"You tiger." By the camel safari, she and I had arrived at measured silence. But I'd been primed for imitation for so long now, I quickly fell into an automatic groove with the boy. With each round of tiger frights, I caught what felt like his exhilaration.

"You tiger." Giddiness flowed, one to the other, with each exchange.

"Tiger something-something-that-seemed-to-mean-'boogers.'" I held off on that particular rep. I wondered dimly if my cold wasn't affecting my brain. I considered whether something hadn't wormed in that caused the afflicted to pack Buddy Holly hiccups compulsively onto their *g*'s. And years on I decided that while what had been addling me was most likely not a bug, one could argue with some conviction that it was catching.

"I think the process might be better called contagion," Chris Frith was saying in the course of an interview I was conducting with him after I'd returned from India. Frith, a professor of neuropsychology at University College London, was discussing empathy, the fact it's now commonly believed to be produced by the subtle, reflexive, neurologically induced mimicries we all engage in throughout the day. At the start of the conversation, I'd mentioned the tiger rounds I'd engaged in back in the desert. I was curious to know how important he thought imitation was to learning another language. From there, the talk had quickly veered into this other stretch, about contagion. The two topics were, believe it or not, related. Or so Frith was making a strong case.

"There's clearly a tendency in all of us to imitate other people automatically," he said. It's a pull that's expressed when you're with a colleague who limps and you find, to your horror, that you've started dipping alongside him. Or when you look up and see you've adopted your dinner companion's exact pose in reverse form: her head's tilted onto her left forefinger; yours is propped up by your right. This monkey-see reaction begins as far back as the cradle. As many a gleeful older brother or sister has discovered, if you stick your tongue out at a baby, the baby will automatically thrust hers out at you, as if she's been possessed by rude, controlling forces. Later on, the impulse is curbed enough that we don't go around spontaneously aping other people, but nonetheless, it remains, and throughout the day our bodies briefly reenact gestures we've just seen.

This innate drive isn't so odd when you consider that infants, unable to ask questions, have to rely on imitation to learn how things are done. A researcher once got toddlers to turn on a light box with their foreheads after producing a woman who leaned down and did just that. One week later, when the group was reassembled, two-thirds labored to bop the light box on with their heads, though it would have been easier to use their hands. "Mindless Imitation Teaches Us How to Be Human," a *New Scientist* article about the study was titled.

"We don't just pick up other people's movements, but their expressions and emotions," Frith said. "If I see someone smiling, I'm more likely to smile myself." In one study, when participants forced themselves to smile artificially, they reported an improvement in mood as a result. Given our tendency to synchronize with other people's gestures, moods, it turns out, really are contagious. "It's one aspect of the mirror neuron story," Frith says.

This mirror neuron story, at the time he and I spoke, was one of the bigger headliners in the field of neurology. Mirror neurons are brain cells that seem to download other people's gestures—to encode the movements, so that they're then patterned in the observer's head, for the observer's own use. When your friend is demonstrating with an air key the tricky half turn her actual key will require, your mirroring system will, without your awareness, be recording the sequence of motions. Later, at her apartment, you'll draw on the template that was laid down in your head to jiggle the lock with prepatterend ease. The cells create an automatic link between the observer and the observed. "They're not so surprising when you think how social humans are and how important the intentions of others toward you are in the development of a sense of self," says Istvan Molnar-Szakacs, a cognitive neuroscientist at the Brain Mind Institute in Lausanne, Switzerland. "Almost everything you do is a reaction to something someone else has done, or you're doing it to affect someone or something."

When the mirror neuron system is damaged, some scientists believe, the result is a condition that imposes isolation. You get people who are unable to read emotions on a face, who balk at human contact, who can't feel empathy. You get autism, in short, according to one theory. "They're Martin Buber's I-thou space," Nancy Isenberg, an autism researcher at Princeton, said in a fervent moment when we were discussing the cells. The I-thou space, as Buber, an Austrian theologian, described it, is the deep psychic realm where humans meet in their most authentic forms. Mirror neurons, Isenberg was saying, provide a place of unshielded connection, are how we take each other in.

There's no consensus on how, precisely, mirror neurons affect us, on what their limits of influence may be. Many neurologists say that the cells code hand or mouth gestures, that's it. But there's one camp, to which Frith belongs, that suspects the mirroring system may, ultimately, turn out to have a broader range—that it may in fact link up with other neurological networks to produce, for instance, empathy. Another crossover area has received a large amount of attention: language. "When you look at the literature," Molnar-Szakacs said, "the language functions are located in the inferior parietal lobe, the superior temporal cortex, and the inferior frontal cortex, which incorporates Broca's area." Broca's area is involved in speech production. "These are precisely the regions that are now considered to be the human mirror neuron system. I don't think it's a coincidence they overlap."

Language is dependent on the brain's motor strip, which controls actions. In fact, language likely evolved from gesture. Some scientists believe that the protolanguage our earliest ancestors used consisted of sequenced gestures and that they're what gave rise to grammar. We literally talked with our hands then. Given all this—that language resides partly in gesture and our brains contain mirroring cells that automatically download others' gestures—does that mean language is, to some extent, catching?

No one has anything like a definitive answer to this question. Going on my own experience, I can say that body language certainly is. Within three months in India, when I spoke Hindi with someone, it was in physical concert. They'd head-wobble; I would, too, without thinking. This synchronization gave me a near-visceral conviction that we were engaged in more than just talk, that we were coming together. The joined motion was a little like dancing together as we spoke. It left me with the belief, later confirmed, that these connections would remain deep within me for years. Most likely, reduced down, though, it was simply the side result of mirror neurons, which automatically try to synchronize people. Because of these, the more you're exposed to someone, the more you'll feel the same thing. And the more, if you're abroad, you'll assimilate.

Does learning a language promote imitation? I'd asked Frith. He'd put it the other way, he said. "The more you're trying to interact with someone, the more this kind of imitation would occur. We take in culture through the mirror system." We become aligned with the person we are talking with to the extent, he believes, "we start imitating words and sharing concepts." If that's true, language is indeed catching.

But through the automatic response, you can take in more than you'd expect to. "Inevitably, when going into another environment, you absorb values that aren't yours," Frith added, something I'd observed firsthand. Even by the time of the camel safari, the values of the place I was from—hipness, reflexive edge—had come to seem, when I encountered them now, galling and strange. In turn, I'd begun to feel I wasn't myself, although at this point, I could still believe that really, I was only playing at that.

THREE DAYS PRIOR to the evening with the niece, the 25th of December, early.

Christmas dawned colder than any day since I'd been here. At quarter to seven, when I left the hotel, the rickshaw walas around Jagdish Temple were nested in blankets. In the eidetic winter light, their outlines were precise, as if they'd been caught in a flashbulb. Two hurried over to supervise my order when I stopped at a tea stall. *"Chai, brother! And anise sticks, there! There! Wrap them in news-paper. Madam will take those with her."* A man in a gray vest dropped me off at Renee's. If I gave him 30 rupees, he'd be happy all day, he said.

Renee, at her front door, was the color of putty. The burning chill that rose off her unheated limestone walls had braised her lungs, turned her cough to a burble. "I just stopped breathing last night, nothing dramatic," she said. Inside, her apartment was shadowy. She waved off my offer of antibiotics, purchased the day before when I'd stumbled out of the desert after days of febrile travel. The cost of seven pills was roughly the same as daylong happiness: 20 rupees, 57 cents.

We placed wicker chairs around a stool to make ourselves a table. She'd changed her mind, she said. Her knees were bad; she didn't need to be tromping around in the villages with Pauline. We'd made plans to head out with Pauline on her annual Christmas run. "You go," Renee said, would not admit the bronchitis was stopping her.

I felt in my backpack for the package with the anise sticks, paused to tell her about the latest chapter at the school. Samta had been dismissed, then Vanita was, too, on the grounds that her family had brought a lawsuit against Samta's. Samta's family was now counter-suing: one big mess.

"I don't know what I did to her," Vanita had said the day before when we'd gotten together for tea.

"Well, she's insecure," I'd replied, repeating the adviser's observation for want of anything better to say.

"And killing me would have made her more secure?" Vanita wailed. She had a point there. "And I was trying so hard," she added.

So hard?

"Yes, I was trying so hard to learn Hindi," she said, and I started.

"You're not a Hindi speaker?" I asked my erstwhile Hindi teacher.

"No!" she said lightly. *Of course not.* "No, I am a Bengali speaker."

Renee twisted her mouth out of a grin. Well, that was just like the school.

"No wonder none of her sentences ever worked," I said. I asked how much Renee thought I should give Pauline toward her expenses. Pauline funded these trips through the kindness of expats and fellow congregants from the Church of North India. "Whatever you give her, watch that she keeps it," Renee said. "If there are people around, they'll take it."

I found the package, set it on the stool. She reached over. The power cut off. We ate breakfast that morning by candlelight.

A cool blue light was driving shadows from the room when we heard a car pull up. We stood. In the alley, Pauline got out, long and tall, to greet Renee, and I was struck again by Pauline's stubborn beauty. Neither age nor the hairy-black-socks-under-sandals she had on could diminish it. Even at nearly eighty, she had an elegance that was preserved in the bones.

Her hefty driver polished the windshield while Renee made her excuses. Pauline and I slid into the back seat. On the way out of town, we stopped to collect a parishioner. Mrs. Bishwas, round as a robin, with a precise gray bun, had the brisk air of a lieutenant. "Happy Christmas!" she trilled, marching down the walk. Settling into the back, bumping Pauline to the middle, she smartly slapped possible dust motes off her knees.

We stopped once more for supplies. Pauline's white bun was already coming undone. Before we got out, I handed her a 500-rupee note, about ten dollars, enough to cover food for the three villages we'd be visiting. Returning to the car, we resumed the same formation. We stared out the windows as the buildings grew lower to the ground, then sang Christmas carols, "Dashing Through the Snow," but I forgot the words and, after all the years I'd spent in malls, had to hum. The town fell away. Pauline taught me a hymn that began *"Kushi, kushi, manaanaa"*: "Happy, happy when we praise him." I thought about how the word *kushi* had resurfaced in English, and how odd that variant, "cushy," would seem here.

The car slid by scrubland, by people huddled around a fire. We passed two peacocks that had commandeered a hill. "Scabies, lack of water, conjunctivitis due to flies. In rainy season, malaria," Pauline was saying, tallying the ailments she'd encountered in the seventeen years she'd been going out to the villages.

Pneumonia, bronchitis, cough, diseases of livestock. Once someone had asked her to pray for a cow. "I thought about it and thought, *Well, God created cows,*" she said, so she did.

Hunger, a white-hot, brutal anger after four years of drought. With the crops shriveled to paper, men's tempers flared. "The last time we went," Pauline said, "a husband had just thrown his wife into the well. The body had just come out." Mrs. Bishwas nodded at a stone fence.

Night blindness from vitamin A deficiency; worms from bare feet; malnutrition, terrible malnutrition. The list thinned down as the land grew sparser, shot up higher, turned rocky. Anemia among the women. We rode for a while in silence. Pauline said, apropos of nothing, "You must miss your family." To my surprise, I started to cry.

Pauline had experience living abroad. As a young woman, she'd gone to college in the States, a spectacularly improbable turn of events, given how bleak her life had been till then. In the back seat, she told me the story again: She'd been born into a rich Brahmin family, but then her father had died and her mother had converted to Christianity, and her father's family, outraged, had kicked them out. Pauline and her sisters had ended up in a Christian orphanage. The conditions were stark. She had to rise at 4 A.M. daily to start breakfast, but at some point, Jesus or Ganesh intervened. A nun, remarking on the quickness of her mind, applied for a scholarship to the nursing school at Syracuse University on her behalf. She got in.

At this point in the story, I was always startled for I always forgot that Pauline and I were fellow alumnae. I'd graduated from Syracuse, too, but these two aspects of my life refused to converge in my mind: SU Orangemen/Pauline. In the back seat, I tried to picture her as a coed on a snowy upstate New York quad in the 1950s, got only an image of her there at the age she was now, hurrying along in her black socks and worn purple sari.

In the years after Syracuse, she'd taken jobs at health clinics in Thailand and Laos, trained nurses in Fiji, worked for decades in Delhi before a sister who'd settled in Udaipur wrote and offered her a room. "I come from a poor family. I know what is hunger," she said, bringing us up to the present and her missions to the villages.

A truck emblazoned with the sign HORN PLEASE screamed past, causing the car to swerve. We righted ourselves, and Mrs. Bishwas started a long story in Hindi, something about a mutual friend who'd suffered dire misfortune and was languishing in an ICU. I was able to follow until the road rushing toward us became a ribbon. When next I glanced over, Mrs. Bishwas was folding a 500-rupee note to tuck into her purse.

At the first village we came to, a dozen mud huts on a rise, eighty people were waiting, mostly women and children, a few old men. Anyone who was younger and male was in Udaipur looking for day work. The women were veiled, with heavy iron ankle rings above cracked bare feet. The children, too, were barefoot in the sharp cold, though many were wearing bulky sweaters. These had been Christmas gifts one year from a now departed expat who'd set her relatives in England to knitting.

"You will sit," Pauline said, and they did, in tight rows. In the car, her voice had been quavery and small. Now it was commanding.

"We will sing," she said, and led the assembly in *"Kushi, kushi, manaanaa,"* after which she went to see about the supplies. "Perhaps you can teach them English," she said as she left.

"My name is Kathy," I began. "My name is Kathy," everyone repeated. The women in front were grinning shyly. "No, *my* name is Kathy," I said, tapping my chest. "No, *my* name is Kathy," they all boomed back.

Pauline returned with the driver, who was huffing under vats of food. Two villagers followed with a charpoy on their heads. They set it down near a pair of dogs that were sculpted ovals in the cold light, and Mrs. Bishwas and I took seats on either side of Pauline. People lined up. We distributed Christmas presents, which this year doubled as Christmas dinner: salty flour sticks called *namkeen*, white dinner rolls, the sugary flour balls called *ladoo* that are the favorite sweets of the Hindu god Ganesh. "Last year, I gave them soap," Pauline said. "The trouble is, there's no water."

A frail old woman came and sat by the bed. "She has fever and diarrhea," Pauline said, taking two Advil from a canister. The woman was joined by a boy with a fat belly. A fly landed on his face. He didn't blink. Pauline pressed on his stomach. "He has a high fever," she said, and diagnosed malaria.

The procession of people suffering ailments continued: a boy with a deep burn on his buttocks, a tiny girl who clung to her brother's leg. Mrs. Bishwas and I helped dispense medical provisions. I learned the Hindi for "bottle," how to say "measles." I practiced sentences: *Who has not had a biscuit?* Mrs. Bishwas poured gentian tonic from a jug labeled GOLD CREST. "Shhh, whiskey bottle, don't tell," she said with a giggle.

A skeletal young woman in a dirty cloth approached. She leaned down, whispered something to Pauline. *"Any cough?"* Pauline asked. The girl shook her head, whispered something else. Pauline pressed on her chest. "She has been beaten," she said.

"Beaten! How old is she?" I asked.

"They don't know their age, so I look at their faces. She is very young. She must be recently married."

A while later, I saw the girl talking to a young man, about eighteen, who had short, sharp cheekbones and a checked shirt that hung on him. He said something I couldn't hear. She took off at a run in the direction of the sky, till she grew very tiny and was swallowed up by yellow dirt.

People continued to stream in from the horizon. Before we left, I took a count: 130. But at the next village, only 10 people were waiting, mostly children whose brown legs were gray with dirt. One girl could not contain her amazement at seeing a videshi. A boy, the youngest, was staring at us expressionless as tears ran down his face.

Pauline said she'd go look for the others. Mrs. Bishwas and I waited beside an enormous ad that was plastered across a building. Water was cascading down a Western man's ecstatic face: LIFEBUOY, FOR HEALTH! the slogan read. Underneath that, someone had attempted a translation in scrawled Hindi: *"Take water,"* it said. *"It's good for your health."*

Pauline reappeared, out of breath. "A young girl has died just now," she said. "A Christian. From an infection. She was fifteen. They are all with her."

On the bumpy road out, we didn't speak. Then Pauline broke the silence. "They come together if one is in trouble, or in sorrow, or in joy," she said in a high voice. "From them I have learned to be satisfied with so little. They have so little, and they are so happy." I started to say something, as an image came to mind: dense black hair, gleaming, eely, rippling above a body in a well. I thought better of it, nodded. "I knew this before, but I learned it again," Pauline said dreamily.

At the third village, we sang gleeful songs in Hindi and counted to twenty in English, and the whole time I couldn't stop thinking: of the girl who'd just died when fifty-seven cents' worth of antibiotics could have saved her, of the emerald bauble that would be stashed back in the vault as soon as winter break was over, of how this was the truest Christmas I'd ever had. Even if it was sort of Hindu.

Part III

· 14 ·

"I can understand you quite well now"

 In the square near my house, the haveli where I live now, in noontime sun so severe it can prick like sharp ice, the fruit wala wants to know all the code words. Please can I tell him? But honestly I can't, even though it's a matter of some urgency—clear from the fact he's on his feet when he asks. Other than me, he's the only one in town who is.

A fierce heat has come on Udaipur, changing everything. "Come at five, not three-thirty," Nand says now when I call; earlier, he'll be too groggy. In the high, open shops in the ancient quarter where I've moved, shopkeepers curl up on mattresses half the afternoon, the soles of their feet on display. Out on Bedla Road, dogs loll in the shadows of brick mounds. Cows sprawl in a way that looks drugged. The heat puts down people, dogs, cows, but I don't mind it during the day. In full sun, the colors on the old homes are vibrant, even the palest lavenders, which grow so vivid, they could break your heart.

At night, though, the heat is churlish: petulant and demanding, of air, of attention. I sleep under a window on a marble floor, wake drenched at dawn with the call of the muezzin.

A fidgety loo wind has blown in from the desert. Its hot, frenzied ions make everyone cranky. Two days ago, a baby cow tried to charge me on the street. I bopped it on the head with my purse. There's no air conditioning here, only air coolers, gargantuan contraptions that take days to fill with water. I bought one and discovered that what it does is turn the hot air humid, then aim it over your bed. By noon, the air cooler has scattered all my papers around the room. By 1 P.M., a mango shake is the only recourse possible.

At the fruit vendor's, I take a white plastic stool. His neighbor, the gangly photo wala, hurries over to join me. They watch intently while I nurse my drink. *"Madam,"* the fruit vendor says when I'm finished, *"what are the* code words *to use with foreigners? Like you say,* 'Hello! Hello!' *I think."*

"The expression 'code words' *is not known to me,"* I tell him. Other than "code words" and "hello," we keep it to Hindi, easier all around. For the men, because they don't speak English. For me, because I stay mainly on this far side now. Sometime back, I crossed a fast black line I never actually saw. The new language didn't judder into view, the way I'd imagined when I was scrambling across stones toward it. It was just suddenly there. One day I couldn't tell what the woman on the other end of the phone was saying. The next she was clearly reporting that all lines were busy, try back later.

"Yes, yes!" the photo guy says. "Hello! Hello!" He nods vigorously.

"Or I think you also say, 'Excuse me!' *when you want to call them over,"* the fruit vendor says, carefully extending "excuuuse."

"Or sometimes you say 'Ki-yu! Ki-yu!' *"* the photo guy says.

The fruit man and I look at him. *"I don't think* 'Ki-yu!' *is a word,"* I say, but the photo guy looks so crestfallen, as if he's suddenly realized why his business has been so bad, that I relent. *"Well, not in English. Maybe* 'Ki-yu!' *is French."*

"Yes!" He brightens. *"It is French. Or Israeli. A lot of Israelis come here."*

"So, madam, what are some other words for the foreigners?" the fruit man asks, but the photo guy is on a roll. *"Or you can say* 'Weee-Ooh!' 'Weee-Ooh!' " he's exclaiming, sounding like he's making a birdcall.

"That is really *not a word,"* I say with some annoyance, imagining an entire street doing that as I walk by. *"You cannot say* 'Weee-Ooh!' " The fruit man ignores him.

"But, madam," the fruit seller says, *"what can we say? Can you tell us more code words for foreigners?"*

And I try, but I can't come up with a single one, at least nothing that won't put people off, so I tell him I'll think, then add, *"But there aren't any foreigners here anyway."*

They both sadly agree. No there aren't.

IT'S MONTHS ON, decades if you factor in perception. Early April, if you go by the calendar. A while ago, the language began to set, and as my accumulation of words sped up, so did time. Back in the fall, when I had to name the world from the ground up, time slowed, then stopped so I could. I existed in eternity. I had been here forever. I'd found a worm hole. But inevitably the extraordinary became ordinary — classes, tests, dinners with the same people, all routine — and life resumed at the speed of sound. You can only get exemption for so long.

Months on, and mostly now, I stay in Hindi. In Hindi, people tell me things they wouldn't in English. When I stop by the travel sundries store near my house, Govinda behind the desk drops the practiced English weather talk he uses for tourists. He pops me open a Coke, and we discuss how bad the year has been, all the scattered terrorism and invasions. Before, they could count on the Israelis, but now that Israel and Palestine are throwing the solid stones again, even the Israelis aren't coming. We talk about how many people have died in this heat: five hundred, all poor, people forced to work for hours under a sun so brutal that if you lay down under it, you'd be dead in an hour. Five hundred early casualties of global warming, I consider. I wonder how anyone will possibly survive here at even five degrees more. We talk about how movies are making Indian girls dress immodestly, which gets us onto the subject of impropriety in general—how Govinda for years has seen the women around Lal Ghat, the Western tourists, dressed in short skirts, no sleeves. *Shameful!*

"Not like you," he quickly adds. *"You are fine,"* and I nod. For I am, absolutely. I'm so *"fine,"* in Govinda's sense of the word, that yards of fabric flutter around me when I walk, enough to swathe a beekeeper. So *"fine"* you can just about see my nose.

We discuss how kids understand everything these days. And on and on, and every so often, I realize it's full Hindi. Glee shoots me up above the words.

The language increased exponentially after my main English cheat source relocated to Jodhpur, the Blue City, a hundred miles north. Not two months back, Helaena was still engaged in her usual approach to Hindi language acquisition: causing serial breakdowns among the male population of Udaipur. It's an apparently fast-forwarding technique, for she'd achieved dizzying heights of fluency while only sporadically cracking a book. Aditya, on the other hand, had reached new depths, of despair. He's been regularly calling his friend Karni to weep over their breakup, unaware it was Karni's handprint he'd detected on Helaena's breast once after a wedding.

Then a month and a half ago, Helaena met her match: Sumair, a minor prince from Jodhpur who, to the detriment of his personality, had placed fourth runner-up in the Mr. India competition. "People will say a lot of things for this face," he informed her. She reported this with a wry smile. But Sumair had many glittering qualities. He knew people in Bollywood, could arrange introductions. Sometimes in those movies, they used Western girls. He was a Rajput and a first son; he stood to inherit. He was also a man with hormonal gumption, something I'd observed firsthand the time we met.

This was on a trip that she and I made to Jodhpur, for Holi, the Indian springtime celebration, when revelers toss colored powders at one another. The plan had been a soigné party at the palace, but the weekend, as Helaena's India often did, turned rambunctious when competing festivities set up down the street. I hesitate to use the word "debauched," since that would imply wholesome fun was not had, and it was, for a good two minutes. After which we ended up getting flung repeatedly into a tub of water and rubbed with powders, by four princes from Jodhpur dressed in jodhpur pants.

In the driveway, turbaned servants played flute music, alongside the family Rolls-Royce. "Down, tiger!" the most square-jawed of the celebrants shouted each time he pushed us under. Sumair had perhaps been made a bit addled by the opium the retainers offered on trays.

From an upstairs window, a round woman dourly surveyed the proceedings. "Oh, mother!" the prince whose place this was would call up. "Don't be in such a bad mood for Holi." "Oh, mother! I phoned that man back," and then we'd get dunked again.

A servant held out a hose. Another soaped his master's face. A dachshund ran by; we broke for lunch.

All in all, a blue time was had in the Blue City, in the film sense of the word. The next morning, Helaena put me on the bus. "Tell them . . . I know, say I'm up for a part in a Bollywood movie," she said. She'd decided to stay on for a while.

The bus down passed bedraggled donkeys covered in purple Holi spots. A young cow was the same glaring pink as my face. A sticker beneath the window caught my eye. *"There are only two ways to be happy,"* it said when I leaned down to examine it. *"Choose work that's indispensable, and be in harmony with your circumstances."* I settled back smiling—I had, I hoped; I was, for sure—then did a double take. But I'd just read that, casually, easily, like cutting through clouds. In Devanagari.

ACROSS THE LINE, on the far side, my sign language has also revved some. Though not enough for the day I arrive at the deaf school and find Anukul leaving. Rita is going to have a baby. He has errands to run. "You can take the class for the rest of the day," he says—till three o'clock, and it's only ten to two. I panic. But what will we do?

The question's soon moot. I've brought sweets, and in no time, word gets around. My classroom and the hall outside are a mess of kids. *"Aren't these a lot of boys for this class?"* I ask Mr. Gupta, a teacher who's wandered in with a group of itinerant students, but my Hindi, in crossing over, jams.

"No, we have one hundred and five students in this school," he says. All of whom are in here now. Kids are arguing with their hands, making high-pitched cries, signing insistent questions I mostly don't understand. When I don't, they tap my shoulder again to draw my attention back from the next one. I'm getting tapped from all sides. Hardly anyone is drawing. No one will sit down. Anukul, when he hears, is going to kill me.

Attrition sets in when a volleyball game starts up in the court-yard. I'm left with a core group, six guys eager to discuss any subject, any way. *"What is your name?"* one asks in sign, and when I frown, he inquires again using chalk. *"Your name?"* I ask back. *Your town? Your age?* All ground we've covered before, but it's invigorating; we're sparking. One boy can speak some answers. *"Sixteen,"* he says. In Mewari, but no problem. By now anything goes.

Bits of India wink as we talk. Someone mentions *"Wednesday,"* Ganesh's day: two-fisted elephant trunk. A boy says he's about to take a wife: line along the part of the hair, the vermilion mark that shows a woman is married. I ask for names for things around the house. *"Cupboard"* is a cognate to English: door described, then opened, then many lines or boards. *"Radio"* is easy: dial being tuned. I haven't seen radios at the school, wonder if the kids know them from their visits home, which, according to a teacher named Mrs. Punamaya, are infrequent. The parents rarely come, she told me when I went to her house. "In India," a visiting daughter added, "the feeling is *Well, he's deaf; we'll just have another.* Even if you threaten and say, 'If you don't visit, we'll send them home,' they say, 'Fine, send them home; we'll just leave them in a room.'" In the classroom, I notice a band of dull metal on one boy's finger: iron, for protection. I hope a parent slipped it on.

We talk so much, my senses are compressed into gestures. Later, my brain will imbue the gestures with sound. *"You are Christian? Me, too!"* the slant-eyed tribal boy says in memory, in spoken words, prompting a fascinated colloquy from the Dustbin on how Jesus got his hands nailed. Feet, too. The Dustbin demonstrates. *"You will take me to America?"* he asks me slyly, makes a face: *Don't like it here.*

"That boy's bad," a little boy complains.

"Yes," the kids all say. *"He hits him."*

"You shouldn't hit him," an older one chides.

When I look at the clock, it's quarter to three. I've forgotten all about the art. I quickly hand out pencils and paper. Draw your house and your family, I instruct the boys, and ten minutes later I get back six Shaktimans. Six Supermen. Family in, action figure out—about how it goes with my Hindi, too.

One crayoned hulk is in a hot-pink jump suit with the maharana's crest on the front. *Who says chivalry is dead?* I think, placing him on the stack, then can't remember what exactly that meant.

LUCKY SINGH PHONES. She asks me over for a party. When my rickshaw gets lost and I call for directions, her husband thinks I'm a teenage Hindi-speaking prankster. "We get calls all the time asking 'Where's your palace?'" he apologizes when we establish it's me. His wife is listed in the phone book under Rani Sahab: "Madam Queen."

In the living room, ten guests hold plates of mutton. The women are on one side of the room. They're all in their late forties, except for a beautiful young wife, early thirties, who touches toes all around, then meekly listens, head covered, from a side chair. The forties are when women here come into their own. Before that, they show obeisance.

The pistol to my right, a woman with a comfortably assured air, tells me about her arranged marriage. "I didn't get married till I was twenty-nine," she says. "I was running a school and happy. But then my parents said, 'You are going to.' I hadn't even seen a photograph of him." She shakes her head, smiles. "The day of the wedding, my sister told me, 'You have to look shy' — you know, Indian brides are supposed to look shy? I said, 'But how will I? I've never looked shy in my life.'"

When Rani Sahab and her best friend leave the room for a minute, the woman makes a beeline for the men's side. She kicks up a conversation about India and Pakistan. Should India invade or not? Tensions have been increasing since the attack on the parliament.

I lean forward to listen to the men's response, hear dirty-Mussulman talk, with plummy accents. I catch mutterings of it everywhere now. *India should attack:* the men say this with huzzahs. "We have taken enough nonsense!" one exclaims.

"Even the Hindu religion says you should not take nonsense from other people," a second adds. "You should not do harm to anyone, and that includes yourself."

"That man Gandhi was talking rubbish," says a third, a statement that to me, of course, sounds like sacrilege. But every one of the men nods: *Oh-yes, oh-yes, that man was.*

AT THE TRIDENT HOTEL with Piers and his entourage a few nights later, I told his Nepalese houseboys the story about the Shaktimans, partly because I thought they'd appreciate the word-confusion, partly to distract them from the flinty looks a waiter was giving them. "This is not done here," Lucky and her friends will say when the startling subject arises of how Piers brings those boys to restaurants. "He does not treat his servants properly"—with the proper decorum and strictness. "This is why they eat all his bread."

I was up to the detail about the royal crest—Bharat, the one who did a perfect deadpan Mr. Bean, got the twist—when I remembered I'd promised Anukul I'd report in on how my solo teaching day had gone. I ducked into the hall.

Not good, he said when I called. His mother was sick. Hepatitis. Our voices slowed, found unshielded grooves. His mother had begun to vomit blood.

"Oh, Anukul. What's her name? I will pray."

"What is Rama's mother's name?" he said, his spirits rallying on pedagogy. "You don't know?" he scolded, ever the teacher. I mugged mock exasperation at a potted palm, saw Piers through the glass door watching.

"I will give you a quiz," Anukul said. "Is it (a) Parvati, (b) Durga, (c) Lakshmi, or (d) Kaushlya?" I picked (d). The others were too well-known. *"Haan,"* he said. "That is her name. Good."

"Anukul, I am so sorry." In India, a turn like this wasn't temporary.

"We will see what God does," he said. He sounded so forlorn that I told him my cancer history, which I'd kept almost entirely to myself. Over here, through omission, I'd regained my health.

". . . and that was ten years ago," I said. "And I'm still alive."

"You know why you are still alive?"

I didn't, actually.

"Because you help people. When you help me, I say only thank you, but every cell in my body is happy, it is going to you. We call that a boon. Every cell is giving you a boon."

Back at the table, I tried sending boons to Anukul's mother, felt only air. The waiter brought new plates. Bharat and the boys looked stiffly miserable. They shook their heads hard when Piers offered them nan. *Maybe when nothing about you translates out, all you can show for yourself is goodness,* I thought, the idea of goodness still playing on my mind. I was still slightly surprised to have been referred to as someone who helped people. Last I'd looked, in the States, I'd been as self-absorbed as anyone. For years, I'd stayed juiced on career preoccupations and passions. That kind of spree produces a pleasing buzz that keeps your focus from straying from what's important: you, after a while, if you keep at it too long. But change your passions, you change yourself.

Last week, in this town I'd come to love, I'd been returning home one afternoon when I'd felt someone seize me from behind at the elbows and drag me to the side — out of the path of stampeding sacred cows, I saw when I turned. I hadn't, till that moment, been afraid, just confused. In New York, adrenaline would have flooded me the moment the person grabbed me, but here I'd reflexively known that whoever it was (a rickshaw driver) had only good intentions. There was a goodness to this place that sank into the reflexes.

At the Indian end of the table, a policeman said something to a jigri that I could tell had been barbed. Contempt flashed across the jigri's face. No one else at that end seemed to catch it.

Maybe out of translation, I thought, you kept the pragmatics part of your brain, the right side, constantly fired. You kept the pathways that handle inference sparking, as you constantly had to rely on dog vision—the clear sight you gain without words. How high you kept the burners probably had to do with how much of your old life had stalled at the line, how little of the familiar you had to rely on. I considered, again, which parts of my former life wouldn't cross over.

Words, of course. My ex-husband, the fact of him. My age, which in Rajasthan didn't match my face and made people, when I gave it, look like they'd seen a ghost. Women that old were papery-skinned grandmothers. "Don't tell anyone at the school," Anukul had all but shouted recently when he'd asked, sounding as startled as if I'd been exercising sleight of hand. The next week when I came in, every staff member converged on my classroom: Was it true? Was I really that old? But how could I be that old and not be married? Did I want to get married? I stopped to consider what the correct answer would be, decided to go with yes. A bride at forty-five! Everyone gasped. "If you get married now, all Indian peoples will laugh," Anukul said cheerfully.

Looks, however much I had. While Helaena's went through the roof here, mine cratered through the floor. In India, not to put too fine a point on it, I was a dog. I knew this because I could see it in the mirror and because there were no cultural proscriptions in place in Udaipur against offering hot-or-not appraisals on the spot. I knew because people told me. The other day, Nand had broken off in the middle of a soliloquy on Sanskrit-era notions of beauty, to stare thoughtfully at my face. "Your features are not very beautiful," he said, then added helpfully, "But in India, inner beauty counts." It was the second inner-beauty pep talk I'd gotten from a geezer that week.

Most jokes, most aspirations, most everything trivial. Over here, I had a different zodiac sign, every bit as accurate as the other one. And on and on, till I realized that all I had to go on here, the only thing that would register, was goodness. That's the only trait I could find that people could perceive—when I went, for instance, to volunteer at the deaf school, the act was clear, it wasn't fogged. India was causing me to amplify goodness if I wanted to be seen—about the last turn I'd ever expected.

In the dining room, Piers stood and walked over to me. He put a hand on the back of my chair. Everything was all right, was it? he asked. I smiled, gave a light, brushoff answer. Out of translation, you lose the habit of explaining yourself to anyone, including yourself. The lightest answers, the thinnest stories can suffice. They can tangle and mat, torn nets on the water—but they'll be nets, covers, all the same. This far from home, nearly any story will hold, or it will for a while. Your son hasn't phoned due to covert obligations. Or: You're on an adventure; this is one big lark. These nets will keep everything below, unless the real explanation is blasted up despite you, exploding the skeins all at once, revealing them to be as poorly made as they really were all along. Of course, this can happen at any time, but if it occurs at the end of what linguists call the silent period, this timing, then, later, will seem ironic.

HANUMAN LOOKED LIKE an orange blob the afternoon I began to understand what I was, deep down, really doing here. The temple keeper had been repainting him when I'd hurried past the shrine and through a door to the left. Hanuman, lieutenant to Rama, is the erect-tailed monkey god, but in street shrines, the statuary can amount to no more than rounded daub on the wall, just the divinity's head. The temple keeper hadn't gotten around to applying his eyes, and so Hanuman's head was still a large lump when I went by.

Upstairs, past an Indian-style toilet, outside the room where jars of fetuses were displayed, I explained to the pathologist that my oncologist wanted the blood tests done again. For most of the time I'd been here, my doctor had been e-mailing patient, reasoned replies to questions I'd hit on when I'd lain awake too long. My right hip hurt: could that be progression of the illness, or did he think that was from a rickshaw ride? But when I'd sent the results of the last blood tests, he'd written back just three words: "Run them again."

The pathologist listened, nodded. Yes, that would be very good. We would do them over. I could call in several days for the report. He brought me to the other room, where a nurse lit a rusty Bunsen burner set beside a jar of needles. She threw the match onto the floor. *"Aapke pas bandaid hai?"* I said when blood began to trickle down my wrist. She stared at me blankly: no Band-Aid, no comprehension. Masking tape over alcohol-soaked cotton, what she tried, canceled each other out.

The temple keeper was pasting flowers onto Hanuman by the time I came back down. The god's new eyes had gone on skewed and given him a fun-crazed look. Would I like *prasad?* the old man asked: sanctified sweets? I took the opportunity to inquire whether Hanuman handled health. The man made bulked-up monkey arms to suggest strength, a yes, then perhaps registering how my face looked, reconsidered and suggested I go straight to the top, to Hanuman's boss, Rama. That sounded prudent. My tumor markers, the blood tests that measure cancer activity, had come back ten times higher than normal.

"Does Rama do health?" I asked.

"Madam, Rama-ji does everything," he said.

I went in and knelt down.

IT WAS IN THE 1980s that the phrase "silent period" first entered the lexicon in linguistics, around the time an argument started in the field over whether people who are trying for a second language follow the same physiological sequence, the same stages of development, they did the first time. Do all subsequent outings retrace the sturdy, straight-shot, original highway to fluency? The debate has never been fully settled, as no debate in linguistics ever fully is, but the two sides are now well defined.

The camp that believes second-time learners recapitulate their linguistic infancy points as evidence to, among other things, this so-called silent period. Every student of French/Cambodian/Lithuanian, teenager or adult, has passed through it. So has every baby. It's the frustrating early period where you understand infinitely more than you can say, where you recognize five hundred words tops and your surest bet is to point. It's typified, the ESL Web site I consulted said, by "performing actions, gesturing or nodding, saying yes or no," but the reactions mount from there. Staring glumly at a woman shelling peas while being hurtled back to the infinite powerlessness you'd last known in fifth grade—that could be another one. The silent phase is also called the "shock stage," for a reason.

On the other side of the debate, you get the camp that weighs in with a resounding "yes and no." Yes, you obviously go through a mute passage. But while it can feel as if you've been dropped back onto the playground, there is one huge difference: the second time, you have the fully formed brain of an adult. You're setting out to learn a language with a head full of language, with prior comprehension of all kinds of rules of grammar and syntax that can be used, if necessary, as handholds along the way. Yes, you've kind of been dropped back, but no, not really. Because you remain the age you are, you're more accurately, this group thinks, going sideways.

If the debate could be moved into the realm of metaphor, a third, compromise position might be possible. What you're doing in the silent stage is making yourself like a child, in the Buddhist sense. Buddhists believe that in meditation, you aim to become like a child. And language study, as anyone who has stayed with it knows, becomes a form of meditation as you chant the alien words to yourself. In both instances, meditation and language study, you try for a state of receptive infancy, usually with variable success.

The 1980s, when this debate started, was also the time when Noam Chomsky advanced his principles and parameters theory. Babies' brains are hardwired for language, he and a number of other linguists had long maintained, but in the eighties he fine-tuned that theory. What infants are hardwired with, Chomsky proposed, are fundamental principles, the deep structures of a language. From there, in time, through parents' and bystanders' cooing and baby talk, the parameters of the local tongue get set. Spanish babies absorb the patterns of Spanish, that it's fine, for instance, to dispense with subject pronouns—more economical to say *"Was going to the store,"* since the pronoun is implied by the verb, than *"She was going to the store,"* which infants born to English-speaking parents learn. They're fundamentally drawing on inborn knowledge of a universal grammar, Chomsky's belief, just adding local embellishment. And it's at this point that the debate begins: if there is, in fact, a well you had access to when you learned to speak, can you return to it for a second language when you're older?

"That's where it gets interesting," Martha Young-Scholten, the Newcastle professor of second language studies, said. The field, she said, splits evenly: "Fifty percent think adult learners are using general problem-solving mechanisms, the kind of thinking you use with chess. Fifty percent think they're using the same mechanisms young children do." She puts herself in the second category. Having more than once, when studying with Gabriela, known with surprising assurance the answer to a question about material we'd just begun, I'm open to persuasion. In those early days, I'd sometimes have the brief sensation of just knowing Hindi, and studies indicate that's not uncommon. When adults and older children learn languages, it turns out, they convert directly from their native tongue far less often than anyone had assumed.

"We're using much more detailed questions and finding adults get implicit knowledge of things they weren't taught, very subtle things that weren't present in the input," Young-Scholten said. I thought of the scanning studies Lee Osterhout was conducting, the ones showing that language students' brains know the right answers long before their slack selves do. "*Homo sapiens* are born knowing things about human language. It's just part of the genome," she said. Then why, she and others argue, couldn't that knowledge carry over to foreign languages?

Here are some other characteristics of the silent period, as outlined on the ESL Web site. Many so-called silent students are actually engaged in private speech. They're rehearsing survival phrases to themselves. Chittering snatches are running through their heads, while the whole time, they appear mute. This phase, the Web site said, can last between ten hours and six months—on the shorter side if the student is enrolled in an immersion program, longer if there are extenuating circumstances. These calculations jibed with my experience. In India, around the time I crossed the line, I was then about five months in.

HANUMAN STARED AT A point above my head, through disappearing curls of smoke. He looked like he'd seen someone who reminded him of the good times. On my knees, I was perplexed what to say. Pieces of old Episcopalian doxologies rose up, were smoked out by the incense. I could hear an arriving worshiper beyond the door invoke Rama's name in greeting to the temple keeper. The shrine was big enough only for one. *Just speak from the heart,* I told myself. Under Hanuman's sideways gaze, I remembered the psychic who'd said I'd witness a spectacular healing and thought, *I'm sorry, Rama, but I'm taking it.* As if in the ozone, you could wheedle your future into place. *I'm taking the spectacular healing,* I thought. I heard how craven and arrogant this sounded, but that was the extent of what I came up with.

Five evenings later, when I phoned the pathologist, I saw that this truculence had been ill-advised. "I am very sorry, madam," he said. "The lab has told me they have already done them twice."

AFTER THE SILENT PERIOD, there are other stages in adult language acquisition that parallel the first go-round. Older students use a "no" construction similar to the one toddlers do—they say things in the new language such as "No want that" or "No do that" before the correct form takes over. Adults, like young students, over-generalize rules. They make irregular verbs regular, the way preschoolers do: "Mommy wented to the store." Adult learners have to struggle to pull themselves upright. It's only after repeated bruising and scuffing that any flowering will occur.

"RUN THEM AGAIN," my oncologist wrote back. A third time. The pathologist immediately agreed, professional courtesy. But he also sent me across town to a general doctor, the man, apparently, people went to here when they needed to know about their chemo-therapy options in India. "There is no reason, madam, you will have to return home," the pathologist said on seeing me off. "You can fly to Bombay."

The second doctor's waiting room was an enclosed front porch. I sat down next to a thin, young tribal woman, recently in from the country. A veil covered her face; she continually tugged it back into place, appeared ready to flee. A baby in her lap stared agog at my face, at the unfamiliar color. His mouth trembled. When I cooed, *"Nam-as-te!"* he started to bawl. The mother swung him away from me.

In the inner room, the doctor gave me the number for the hospital in Bombay. The phone booth I stopped in on the way home was next to a Rama temple. In my prayers, this time, I was humble.

The third test came back. The numbers were normal. Forever since, I've had to wonder: could that just have been a matter of two bum test tubes? My doctor, I've noticed, neglects to include the miraculous Rama healing in my chart. Lab error, I'm certain, is what he concludes. But *twice?* Twice, the blood was mixed with God knows what? Or was there someone, somewhere on the subcontinent, celebrating her indisputable good fortune—two clean bills of health, who could argue with that?—at the very moment, perhaps, the baby started to wail. Someone who, months after receiving the two reports, felt a nagging pinch, followed weeks later, perhaps, by the same ominous electric buzz in the bones I'd had ten years before. Catastrophe almost certainly would follow: tumors expanding, biting into bone, blackening and ossifying tissue. Perhaps, or perhaps the spectacular healing was so potent, it swept through us both. Maybe the woman in Bombay recovered and got on with her life. I had—or, at least up till the moment of the second bum test, that's what I'd been telling myself.

THERE'S ONE FINAL stage that exists in children learning a language and is often repeated in adults. This phase, called "the naming explosion," happens the first time around age three and is like a sluice of passion. Young children are suddenly, ecstatically deft with words—woefully fluent, their exhausted parents might say. Adult learners sometimes find the same thing occurs with them—they cross line after line, come into the far world they've been hankering after. Passion is what has kept them going during the long, grinding silence, and now that they've been rewarded for their determination, passion intensifies. In his book *Seeing Voices,* Oliver Sacks refers to this stage as it occurs in children when he describes the "love affair with the world" that the nineteenth-century German wild child Kaspar fell into on being taught to speak: "Such a rebirth, a psychological birth . . . is no more than a special, exaggerated, almost explosive form of what normally occurs in the third year of life, with the discovery and emergence of language." The world, till then chaotic, uncertain, becomes lovely through the order imposed by words.

My silent period, coincidentally, ended just before the three markers were run. It was followed, not long after, by a naming explosion. In that fertile state of mind, I was able to cross the desert. The blinders I'd used to narrow my life fell away; I came face-to-face with the reasons why, exactly, I'd withdrawn from a career, pulled back from romantic engagements. The physical illness I had was treatable, and for years, but it wasn't curable, and while I didn't constantly register that fact, my psyche, apparently, did. My psyche, I saw now, had been prompting me to respond the way animals do in the face of danger: if fight or flight isn't possible, they play dead. Playing dead! When I'd been given this extraordinary gift of so many extra years. I saw how preposterous that was, saw, too, how I had, without realizing it, begun to free myself from the bind.

It was only in the scented air of Rajasthan that I perceived the connection between the illness and the passion that had been propelling me for so long. First time around, language jump-starts the brain, Russ Rymer says in *Genie.* "The organization of our brain is as genetically ordained and automatic as breathing," he writes, "but, like breathing, it is initiated by the slap of a midwife, and the midwife is grammar."

In going back for seconds, I was trying to replicate the process. At the edge of the desert, surrounded by camels and pleasure gardens and high palace walls, I'd been slapping myself back to life.

· 15 ·

"You will be taught. He will be taught.
They will be taught."

 "Behosh. be. hosh," Swami-ji says in my vocabulary class of one now. The Whisperer has permanently barricaded herself inside one of the small classrooms. Helaena has never returned from Jodhpur. "*Be*—means 'out of.' *Hosh* is 'the senses.' This is how you say 'unconscious,'" he says, and I consider whether I've gone unconscious over here or come fully awake. Across the line, I'm out of all senses as I knew them. My skin continues to absorb the smell of heat. My ears fill with color, for in India, the seed, or basic, mantra of each god has its own shade. Toward dawn, when I wake into musty light, I can hear the soft red sounds of Rama's chant from a temple by the haveli where I've moved.

A friend of a friend named Rashida, a Muslim woman who makes batiks, steered me here after two lodging arrangements back-to-back grew irrevocably strained. After leaving the hotel, I'd moved into a house where the patriarch was Sri-ji's priest and where his son was a live example from the orientation seminars: *A man insists on lurking outside the three-quarter-length shower door. He is standing there silently. You can see his shoes. What do you do?*

At the next guesthouse, volubility was the problem. The mother embraced her mission to help improve my language skills with urgency. As her thin, gliding daughters, Minki and Chinki, stopped and stared balefully, Mrs. Prasad conducted hysterical Hindi lessons at 7 A.M. *"Did I want pancakes? Paranthu? Porridge? Toasti? Sweet carrots? Would I like to try saying the word 'carrots' with her? Was I familiar with the word 'sweet'?"*

At the haveli, the batik artist had said, they'd grown used to Westerners and their perversely solitary ways.

The haveli, to a Westerner, looks like what Gaudí would have designed if he'd been seized by Gothic inclinations. Its high fortress face is so old, it appears to be sliding to the ground. The last time any touchups were done, the *Octopussy* crew was in town. The house had a cameo. Payment was a paint job. Since then, flakes have appeared. An air of genteel poverty hovers over everything, though at one time, the Rajput family that lived here was so stupendously rich, when anyone opened the massive front door, gold coins spilled onto the street. This is just one of the many interesting tidbits that the owner, Mr. Singh, a resort manager and impoverished descendant, delivers along with breakfast. Once, with the chai, he brought the news that a Hindu nationalist group had been calling him at the office and rebuking him for answering "Hello."

"You should say 'Hare om'!" the anonymous voice scolds. *"Are you so westernized that you say 'Hello'?"*

"But this is a resort," he tells me he replied. We both titter. Twice, on days the phone bill has come due, he's tried to sell me the haveli. He smiled amiably beneath his wire-rim glasses when I had to decline — regretfully, for I love the new place.

Most of the time, I have the whole top floor to myself, a gallery with marble floors and peacock arches and a small bedroom at either end. Bats flit through the long hall at sundown, and you can sense the ghosts of the old Rajput women who lived here, but on the whole, during the day, it's cheerful. Afternoons, tinted glass casts a confetti of light across the floor: red, green, and blue, colors of the seasons. (Spring in Rajasthan is so abbreviated, it doesn't get a shade.) Plants fill the tinted bay windows in the gallery. Seventeenth-century paintings of tiger hunts festoon the walls. In my bedroom, an elephant has a tiger by the tail and is hoisting it into the air.

Late at night, though, the bedrooms become convection ovens. That's when I drag my bedding out to the long hall, arrange it under one of the bay windows missing glass. The bedrooms are essentially hermetically sealed, for the windows in there are no bigger than a woman's head, large enough only for someone to watch a passing parade below without being glimpsed in return. They were designed when no one dreamed that throughout the world, temperatures would begin a steady, beating rise—were expressly ordered at that size, in fact, and for functional reasons: to further conceal the already veiled residents. The original inhabitants here were all in purdah. I'm living in what was the zenana of the house. This is where the language has led me: not into the heart of India, not exactly, but into ancient women's quarters.

Up in Jodhpur, Helaena's Hindi has deposited her in a zenana as well. Sumair's family took one look and dead-bolted her into theirs. "I am so bored in here," she sighs when my cell phone rings in class. The family won't let her out. If their son is seen on the streets with her, a Western woman, he will get a reputation. Sumair, it seems, is in accord with this assessment. He's out most nights on his own, Helaena says with exasperation. But the next time she calls, her mood is lighter, despite the fact Sumair has ordered her not to "increase" the marriageable young sister who's in lockup with her.

"*Badhaana,* that's the verb he used," she says lazily into the phone.

"*Badhaana?*" I ask.

"Oh, you know, 'to widen,' 'to increase.' We had it in class, I think. He was talking about her mind." She sounds unruffled. Days in modified solitary have given her penetrating insight that the other members of her haveli lack. What the family, even Sumair himself, doesn't understand is that his kismet has taken up residence in the house. Helaena has come to see that's what she is, knows it the way she knows that the black-tongued goddess Chamunda Devi turned her tongue black the first time Helaena prayed to her. She just woke up that way the next day, and it wasn't the result of Pepto-Bismol, the way some people tried to claim. This new understanding has allowed her to settle into the small rhythms of the floor: tea at four, Sumair's secret visits after midnight. That, and hand-held video games. "Things are much better," she says, "since I discovered Nintendo in the zenana."

In mine, I occasionally discover that a German or French backpacker has moved into the other bedroom for a night, dragging in annoying reminders of the current century. But otherwise, it's always the same time here as it is up at the palace: four hundred years ago, not one mote different.

At sundown, the ghosts' chattering can drive me out into the streets, which smell the same at that hour as they have since the Mughal era: scents of cumin and fennel and fenugreek condensing into one muddy brown rill. The light slanting down soft yellow makes the lanes look like misty stage sets. Women in filmy *lahenga* skirts come toward me in the haze, a few balancing copper pots on their heads, and it's easy to believe that they're phantoms, or else I am, that some vectors have crossed and as a result, my own mind has been increased. My senses have doubled: that's the only reason I can see them.

The idea that the senses could be multiplied was planted by Nand last week. "In Sanskrit times, they had ten," he said one afternoon when I visited. This was a day when the loo wind's ions were whirling at a frantic speed. In the morning, a rickshaw driver, driven mad by the whine, had pulled back a fist when I'd objected to his price. The other drivers gasped. His body shrank down. When I got to his house, Nand was out of sorts.

"But Kit-ti, how will you ever pass it?" he said when I mentioned I had a test coming up. He made his voice squeak to suggest incredulity. He widened his eyes in disbelief. Nand is of the freely displayed and often voiced opinion that my language advancement remains undetectable.

"Your father doesn't think much of my Hindi," I'd said to one of his sons as I was leaving on the last visit, after he'd said, "Hey, you're really getting good." He'd smiled conspiratorially. "My father thinks *my* Hindi is bad," he'd said. This son, like Nand's other eight children, is a Hindi professor.

"He believes he is your father in India," Mrs. Singh, the proprietress of the haveli, said when I described how Nand is always on me: How do you not know bhakti poetry? Why are you not married? *"He thinks it is his dharma"*—his duty—*"to say these things,"* she decided. In the event that Mrs. Singh has had Freudian training, I neglect to say that my flesh-and-blood father back in the States has just been moved to a ward for people who can no longer stay anchored in time. I keep this piece of information to myself for another reason, too: I know how bad it would look here. People tell me things in Hindi they wouldn't in English. *"We think Westerners are animals in the way they raise their children,"* a man I'd gotten into a conversation with at the train station had said. *"They raise them, and then when the children are eighteen, they have them leave. Who does that but animals?"* It wasn't a leap in understanding to guess how the man would view grown children who had their parents leave for assisted living, even if the move had been the parents' idea.

"Did you get the birthday check I mailed?" my father wrote back in November. "You probably didn't," he said, "because I sent it to Mexico." Mexico was where we'd all gone six years ago when my mother was still alive, but the whole time I've been stockpiling words, my father has been losing them. *Maybe,* I think, with every disjointed letter and phone conversation, *it's time to go home.* But I can't get a bead on where my dharma lies here. My father, who's lived his life in one place, has always taken vicarious pleasure in my drive to light out for parts unknown, has always encouraged me. I'm either being true to him in India or I'm an animal of a daughter, I can't tell which. Probably both.

On the way to the cybercafe, I calculate how much longer till the school year wraps up: not that much. So I put off the decision and phone my father instead, tell him about the astonishing sights passing before my eyes, even if I have to make them up. "Oh, man, Dad, an elephant just went by," I say, hoping to bring him into my present. But my present doesn't match anything he's ever known, and as usual, by the time we hang up, we're both more confused.

"FINE" AS I'VE BECOME, in Govinda's use of the word, the new neighbors aren't able to see it. In fact, when they learned that a Western woman had moved in next door, they began to see pretty much the opposite: me performing acts so degenerate on the third floor, they were forced to come over and speak to Mrs. Singh about it. Mrs. Singh defended my honor, though the week before, I think, she wouldn't have bet on it.

"Kathy, you are alone up there?" she'd called me in to ask. She and her daughters were lounging on pillows in her bedroom, which resembles a harem room, all furnishings draped and low to the ground. Of the four, only Mrs. Singh has the requisite curves for the décor. The three daughters, bespectacled and thin, look dutiful even when they're sprawled. One other woman lives on the premises as well: a bucktoothed *dadiji,* a grandmother, who has a room on the ground floor. Whenever I come in, she peers out at me through a crack in her door.

"Yes, ma'am," I said in Hindi. Mrs. Singh is in a complicated state of purdah that has curtailed her English. She doesn't wear a veil at

home, but on the other hand, she never leaves the house. In her grandmother's day, if a woman of her status, a royal, was required to go out, servants would creep along beside with silk panels to shield her on her way to the litter. The masses would not have been permitted to see her. Mrs. Singh probably wouldn't need panels nowadays, though it's hard to know for sure, since she keeps confined to the second floor. This limited mobility hasn't prevented her from knowing, to the rupee, what everything in town should cost. When I'd gone out to buy the air cooler, she'd commandeered the bargaining by cell phone.

"You are alone?" she repeated dubiously.

"Ji," I told her: Yes, I was. *"Ji."* For sure.

She cocked her head. *"Alone? You are certain?"*

"Ji," a third time, as the daughters glanced at one another nervously. She and I were at a stalemate. The daughters tensed to see what I'd say, then the oldest one whooped with relief.

"It's a tape!" the girl cried, and everyone laughed, including me, once I saw what the problem was. Vidhu had given me a Hindi tape that used a man for the call and response. I'd been repeating after it up there. They'd assumed they'd been hearing sordid love talk. *Kitna achchhaa mazaak tha!* What a good joke! But a week later, I'm back to account for myself again.

"Kathy," Mrs. Singh says, her tone uninflected: she will brook no nonsense. *"You have been throwing condoms on the neighbors' roof?"* The daughters lean forward.

Uh-uh. Can't say I have. No, that is one thing I have not been doing.

But the neighbors, it seems, have complained about this. They've marched over to report that they've seen me flinging rubbers from my window onto their terraced roof. Needless to say, they want this behavior stopped. Mrs. Singh defended me and told them to beat it. Now, though, she's, well, wondering.

"You have not been?" she says hopefully, on my third denial.

I summarize the situation as it stands: *"I have not been bringing men up to my room. I have not been throwing condoms onto people's roofs."* She grins. *Of course not!*

"The neighbors are dirty people," she rushes to explain. *"They are very bad. The man sits out on the deck in women's clothes. And they are jealous of us because we are royals,"* she's saying, but my smile is going flat. I suddenly have a good idea what's gone on just now. The neighbors have seen an apparition. A product of the times. One state down, in Gujarat, just a four-hour drive, sectarian tensions have boiled over, warping people's perceptions there and here.

What had happened to cause this is still hazy knowledge to me. Later, I'll piece together facts. On February 27, a train carrying Hindus was attacked by Muslims. The Hindus, right-wing activists, had been returning from Ayodhya, the temple town where extremists had razed the mosque a decade before, setting off waves of violence. For ten years, the site had been rubble policed by guards. But the passengers on the Sabarmati Express had gone to Ayodhya with the intention of doing puja, of worshiping, and thereby sanctifying the grounds, so that in the months to come, a temple to Rama could be built on the site. They'd been planning to take back the land. Incendiary business, and like other BJP contingents before them, they'd been turned away.

If the puja had gone on, it would have had the effect of gasoline on sparks. The prospect of a temple to Rama being built on what, to Muslims, was now a desecrated site was not only outrageous but ominous: a threat. For years now, the Hindu right had worked to recast Rama as a symbol of triumphant nationalist identity. Rama had been victorious in vanquishing the rakshasa demons, just as, the RSS and other right-wing parties made clear, the purified Hindu nation would defeat their own latter-day threats: the Muslims. In case anyone missed the parallels between Rama's struggle and the *shudh* Hindu nation's, when the popular made-for-TV movie of the Ramayana aired, various party leaders spelled them out in articles and speeches.

In areas where sectarian tensions were running high, in conservative precincts such as Rajasthan and Gujarat, Rama's name was now often used menacingly. *"Jai Ramji ki,"* people said increasingly all through Udaipur: "Victory to the followers of Rama," what used to be a greeting transmogrified into a threat.

Or *"Jai Sri Ram"*: "Hail Lord Ram"—what Bajrang Dal workers traveling on the Sabarmati Express had forced Muslim passengers to say when the train neared Godhra station in Gujarat, on February 25. The Bajrang Dal brandished iron rods, to emphasize the immediacy of the request. Two days later, when the same train, now carrying the spurned *karsevaks,* "spiritual volunteers," pulled into Godhra station, a mob of angry Muslims was waiting. Words were exchanged. Stones were thrown at the carriages. The passengers locked themselves in, so that twenty minutes later, when one of the coaches went up in flames, people were trapped inside. Fifty-nine Hindus were asphyxiated or burned to death—the result, later forensic evidence would suggest, of a Hindu passenger's malfunctioning cookstove. But at the time, shrieks went up throughout Gujarat: the Muslims had done this thing. Party leaders led the howls.

They had done this thing and they would have to pay, the party leaders declared. If the Muslims wished to be safe, an RSS official said once the state had gone up in flames, "they will have to earn the goodwill of the Hindu people." Madness reigned. There was no means for the Muslims to obtain goodwill. Mobs of Hindus prowled the streets, their faces contorted by the leers of the righteous. *"Kill! Hack! Burn!"* they screamed as they fell on Muslim families trying desperately to hide. Children were stabbed to death. Mothers were set on fire.

Oh, but Gujarat, people would lament in the months to come, as the violence continued at a slow, steady boil till nearly two thousand had died, most of them Muslims. *Gujarat!* Gujarat was Gandhi's state.

At the Singhs', I can perceive only the vague outlines of this. I can sense something very bad is happening, but I'm trying to decode it with my slippery Hindi, from snippets, body language, and intuition. My newsgathering abilities are sorely tested. In America, the papers are still concentrating on the country's own perceived threats. Gujarat barely rates a mention from what I can tell at the cybercafe, during the five minutes the computer stays up. That leaves me with several options, none ideal. I can try to navigate the Indian papers, but Hindi newspaper language is byzantine, as I've learned to my frustration. The last time I tried to decipher current events this way was when a friend e-mailed, horrified, about something that had occurred in this part of the world. What happened? I wrote back. "You don't want to know," she answered. I found the story in the *Dainik Bhaskar* and, with a dictionary, tried to make sense of it. Twenty minutes on, I was one paragraph in, and dawning understanding was freezing my mind. Numbed, I contemplated words instead of meaning. So odd how the word *galaa*, "throat," contains a letter that looks like a long, exposed neck: ल. And isn't the hard clacking *t* sound in *katna*, "cut," exactly like the one we have in "machete"? And then I couldn't look anymore at what had happened to Daniel Pearl.

The Hindi papers are out. By default, my chief news source becomes the clipped *Times of India,* which runs short, sterile accounts that in their terseness convey the message: whatever is happening in Gujarat is unspeakable. SIX MORE KILLED, a headline reads, then just names, ages, and towns follow, never the details, never the full reports that have begun to cause cries of "Genocide!" to go up in Europe. "Six more": one a Muslim man who was first beaten so bloody, he could no longer move his arms, at which point someone produced a tire and placed it on his chest. Someone else found a match as the crowd shrieked with laughter.

FOUR MORE KILLED: among them a pregnant Muslim woman

who was gang-raped. Afterward, one of the participants sliced her belly open and impaled the fetus on a sword.

FIVE MORE DIE IN GUJARAT: most likely from burning, the preferred method of slaughter, a pointed reference to the train deaths. MUSLIMS, LEARN ARSON FROM US, graffiti on the walls of Ahmedabad sneer.

One, five, ten more. In our town, a curfew is imposed when violence threatens, but then it turns out that the trouble was just a rumor; we can all go out again. A Muslim shop owner in Udaipur is nearly lynched when word spreads that he's molested a Hindu girl. Shops shut down. Then they reopen. Apparently, he didn't. Apparently, what that was, was one more apparition. On the streets, on the roofs, the bogeyman's appeared.

"IN SANSKRIT, they had sight, taste, touch, smell, hearing—oh, yes," Nand said as the afternoon waned, carrying on his examination of the ancients' ten senses. Once the whirling particles began to slow, a pale focus was restored to the mind. Sanskrit speakers had the same five we do, he said, called collectively the *jnanendriya,* the agents of perception. But perhaps the path to sensuality was twice as wide then, as Sanskrit speakers had five senses more—the *karmendriya,* the agents of action. These were grasping, walking, excretion, sexual reproduction, and one more so obvious that it's astonishing to think we haven't made it a sixth. For if the senses are the means by which we take in the world, then this one, speech, has to be the ultimate. Consider: In one language, you have five. In another, you have twice as many to speak of. Speech is so powerful, it can double the senses.

Now that my own have been altered, I'm beginning to understand how interconnected all the senses are, all five, or ten. Change one, and the others are transformed with it. Change your speech— the word for "fine," say—and your sense of vision may be altered, too.

I discovered this when I passed a Western woman on the street. There still aren't many tourists here, so she was immediately visible from a distance. I tensed on a side glance. Her movements were bizarre. At first she looked like she was stomping. All around her, women in saris moved in a glide, in slow fluid lines, but the Western woman's legs chopped the air. And what legs! Hard and knotted as a laborer's, blatantly exposed by high shorts. *Slap in the face to all decency,* a singsong voice in my head pronounced, the new language having apparently tamped down all memories of the high shorts in my bureau back home. Passing the woman, men on the street looked nervous, as if they had caused this sight. They glanced away. A few gawked or giggled. Most of these men had never seen their wives naked. ("The women lift up their saris at night," Helaena, working toward an off-label degree in Sexual Mores in Rajasthan, had explained.)

The woman came closer. Worse, the shirt she wore was sleeveless. A word, unbidden, flashed in my mind. It was one Govinda had used. *Sharmnaak.* "Shameful."

If the word had lodged in English, another, reproving one would no doubt have followed: "priggish." But because it hadn't, a tracery of all the others to which it was linked in its network flickered: *Pakka:* "proper"; more specifically for women, "demure," "restrained." *Shudh aurat:* a woman who's devoted in her worship of the gods, a group that, quite literally, includes her husband. Her *patidev,* exact translation: "husband-god." There are no "wife-gods" in Hindi, but there are *patrivrata,* "one who fasts for her husband." In Hindu belief, women are born so sinful that they stand less of a chance of coming back as a man than an animal does of returning as a human. Though a woman does have one route to salvation open to her. If she accepts her husband as her god, the way Sita did Rama, she can achieve *moksha,* "liberation."

"Fine," like most every other word I've learned, leads straight into religion. I'm perpetually bemused by how entwined this language

is with Hinduism. Sometimes I think I can't begin to speak it without a thorough grounding in the religion. Sometimes I think that's what I get in vocabulary class. It is my *dharma* to visit my father, I find myself thinking. The shower is now religious purification: *snan karna* is both "to bathe" and "to cleanse oneself spiritually." They say there's no conversion rite into Hinduism, but there is: learn Hindi.

Now that I'm *"fine,"* I've achieved double vision. On the street, for a minute, I can see the woman the way she would have looked to me before: healthy, tanned, in shape, striding tall through the town. She would have been all these things back when I was who I was before: a woman who came by independent thinking naturally, whose great-grandmother had been the mayor of a town in Florida, whose grandmother was an artist, who'd strode up plenty of hills and so would never have tsked audibly at a woman in hiking shorts. Which, to my delayed shock, as she came within hearing range, was precisely what I'd done. It was as if I'd been possessed, and I have been: by words.

Over the line, I have the second sight I've been dogging ever since those first heady glimpses I had of a far world. Half the time now, I can see what they're talking about. Half the time, what they're talking about are only the kinds of concerns people expressed in the textbook the first months: How many rooms are in this hotel? Are they large? Or are they small? Still, ordinary as much of it is, this double vision is always slightly spooky. A straight view into places that were once off-limits? There's something taboo about it. A sacrilege, perhaps, for this new sight comes at a price.

I'm an accidental Hindu, and I'm an Episcopalian. I'm not like those women, but of course I am. Daily, truths crash, and for the divine experience that follows, of being rattled into new sight, a price must be paid. As one sense is altered and changes the others, the old senses are suspended, including one that's an amalgam of all the rest. With each collision of worlds, for a time, I lose my sense of self.

THE LOO IONS CONTINUE to spin down as Nand and I pick up speed. We talk about the Indian sense of speech, how it has to be the most acute in the world. "In India, we have been criticized for our verbal hobbies," he says. The British had made digs about how they went on. "We have an oral tradition," he says. "Therefore, much was put into poetry. Even books of astronomy and medicine. Poetry can be learned swiftly." English, he observes, has a written tradition, and so "it is informative in nature. Its knowledge is encyclopedic. Other languages explain the world more celestially."

We talk about how the international boom in Indian novels has been confined to books written in English, how many extraordinary Indian writers, because they can write only in their own tongues, are consigned to obscurity. The first group's "money is always talked of," he says, "and that has created a frustration among the Hindi writers. The writer is supposed to be a crusader against the evil designs of a society, but what I find today are writers who want to be crusaders and at the same time become businessmen. If I see a prosperous neighbor, a prosperous market, a prosperous life—how big a crusader will I be? Writers are part of the social ambitions in which they live." We talk, as always, with a sense of urgency, with the understanding that there's still so much to say, with the belief, I'll think later, that if he can keep it to eternal truths, he can keep us both here forever.

We talk, and when a silence finally falls, it sounds like an exhalation. "Kit-ti," he says after a while. "When do you leave?" I give the date, only weeks away now, and he takes such a quick breath, I change the subject and tell a story.

I tell him about the fine hot day lately when I'd traveled out of town to a poets' conference with a new friend, a writer named Ruby, someone I'd met through Renee. I omit Ruby's name; like poets everywhere, these two spar. Why don't you try not writing lyrical poetry? Nand had inquired the one time we'd all met up. I leave out her name but report how I'd traveled for miles to the town of Nathdwara, where poets were gathering in a community hall. When I'd walked in, Ruby jumped up to introduce me. "Now the conference is international!" the poet whose recital I'd interrupted had exclaimed. Out the window, a singer in an off-key wedding band was belting out the refrain: *"I want a hi-fi wife!"* The poet began again and, above those lyrics, sang a plaintive ghazal he'd composed, which, like all ghazals, was about an illicit affair. I told Nand how I'd delivered a speech in Hindi at the poets' urging. I omitted the part about how it had collapsed into the usual dada muddle.

I said that after all the poems had been sung, after all the exclamations of *va! va!* had been made, we had walked through the early-evening streets, past slashes of neon and rickshaws with hearts on the back, till we came to an ancient inn where waiters circled our tables with pots of fragrant concoctions. Dozy, I listened to the poets discuss me: *"She is studying in Sector Eleven." "She has written a book." "No, no, in English."* I mumbled a sleepy account of my life. "You speak like a poet," the poet I'd earlier interrupted said, the nicest spin anyone had ever put on my Hindi. Then everyone picked up their forlorn-looking suitcases and headed for the bus, and Ruby sang ghazals to me all the way home, and at this point in the telling, I'm lost again in India. For Nand's the person I'm closest to here, and there is no way to make him understand the punch line: Out of my old senses, the five I arrived with, I'm a poet and don't even know it.

· 16 ·

"If a change takes place,
we shall inform you by cable"

My life at that time was full of poets. I visited the pathologist, and when I wasn't with Nand, I spent a lot of time with Ruby. In many ways, she reminded me of my friends from home: stealth-bomber sense of humor; possessed of smarts she'd arrived at on her own; resilient; engaged in a career. In addition to writing poetry, she worked as a journalist and an announcer at festivals. But then, too, there were the ways she didn't, the chief one being that, from time to time, she was possessed by the spirit of a prostitute from Jaipur. Ruby first told me matter-of-factly about Phulkumar, the name the ozonic floozy went by, in between ghazals on the bus from Nathdwara. Three months later, back in New York, I'd have occasion to think of Phulkumar again.

To understand how Ruby came to have a shade popping in and out, it's necessary to know a thing or two about her, mainly that she had the deep voice and beauteous heft of an old, black blues singer,

and along with them, more man appeal than a crateful of super-
models. Ruby was big. Pheromones rolled off her. Although occasionally at a poetry meet, some mean-spirited male versifier would
yell, "Get the sack of rice off the stage!" much more frequently she
had to beat the men off with a stick. Her magnetism was such that
the entranced would often show up at her house in the days following a conference, hoping to get better acquainted. These suitors
were annoying in the extreme, especially since Ruby was married. In
her gossipy Jain neighborhood, visits like these could lead to no end
of talk. It was during a week, in fact, when one too many had turned
up that she was first possessed by Phulkumar.

Initially, Phulkumar confined her activities to getting Ruby to
make monkey lips at people. Soon, though, she graduated to induced monkey lips combined with rude noises, followed by slat-
ternly poses. "Like this," Ruby said on the bus and demonstrated:
legs akimbo. The priest at the Bhairuji temple she consulted said she
was just depressed, though who wouldn't be with the uninvited calling the shots?

Ruby's housework had gone to hell, she was in a bad way, when
Phulkumar decided to shape up. This happened after a swaggering
doctor from one of the conferences appeared at the door, a guy
who'd not only tried to make time with Ruby but had attempted to
lay hands on her. Phulkumar took one look at his leering mug and
evidently grew incensed. She beat him with shoes and put red-hot
spices in his eyes, Ruby reported. When the next Romeo came
around, Phulkumar again made herself useful and tried to strangle
him. After that, she confessed that she, Phulkumar, had been the
one who'd been casting come-hither looks at the men, using Ruby's
eyes. She also claimed that she'd been the one writing all of Ruby's
poems, which at first I thought was mingy of her, but when I considered the kind of flak Ruby took for pursuing the arts as a woman,
I had a change of heart. After a time, Ruby and Phulkumar reached
a comfortable accord. Lately, there had been no growling.

All the same, Phulkumar was a hungry spirit. "Aren't you afraid?" I asked Rajendra, Ruby's husband, one night when I was over for dinner.

"No, no," he said. "Now it is habitual."

"But Phulkumar is a prostitute?"

"Yes, yes," he said brightly.

Phulkumar was never in action when I was around. Soon enough, she slipped my mind. I had reason to remember her, though, on a day when I was newly back in New York. My computer had developed several untidy problems, the biggest being self-cannibalism. After it had finished consuming its own address book, it began devouring other pieces of itself, though not the 800 customer service number, which I called. A man by the name of Jeff answered, made diagnostic inquiries, delivered the news.

"Madam, you will have to buy a new computer," he said.

I didn't think so, I replied. Nothing was wrong with the computer itself. Only the software was affected.

"Then a new hard drive perhaps. We cannot help you."

I voiced one more polite objection, then leapt for his throat across the phone lines, began slapping him around long-distance. "What kind of nonsense is this?" I said with full-force hauteur. "You are entirely wrong. You will get me someone who can fix this. You are incapable of performing this job," I said, my vowels stretching into weird twirls.

It was as if I were hearing someone else, someone who could reflexively curl her voice and signal *I will not listen to any more monkey chat.* Someone—and suddenly I understood—whose tone sounded suspiciously Indian. A little like Jeff, in other words.

"Wait a minute," I said. "Where are you from?"

Bangalore, he admitted after a pause, and that's when I saw that I hadn't been the victim of some flash reincarnation by an aggrieved woman from India, had not developed my own Phulkumar. I was simply being myself, or one of my selves—one that had come into being in a place where notions of hierarchy are so entrenched, it's perfectly fine to address service personnel in the caustic tones otherwise reserved for servants. It had taken only a hint of Indian prosody, the faintest singsong, to trigger in me a whole neuronal constellation of a self that had formed the year before. "For every language a man learns, he multiplies his individual nature," Charles V of France said, to which one could add: and ends up becoming an actual multiple, if he doesn't watch it.

"I was someone else in that other language," I'd say often during that time, and while the split I was experiencing sometimes seemed like psychosis, this perception is common. When a Temple University researcher named Aneta Pavlenko posted a questionnaire online asking bilinguals whether they felt as if they had different personalities in their different tongues, 65 percent answered yes, a quarter said no, and the rest put themselves down as "ambivalent."

"It was as if in Hindi, I became another person," I'd say, though with a certain degree of caution if I was talking to a linguist. Linguistics is a contentious business—is "arguably," the journalist Russ Rymer writes, "the most hotly contested property in the academic realm. It is soaked with the blood of poets, theologians, philosophers, philologists, psychologists, biologists, and neurologists, along with whatever blood can be got out of grammarians"—and of all the claims you can make that could lead to bloodshed, this one, in particular, is fighting words.

"FOR THE LAST TWO DECADES, the hypothesis that language affects thought—generally known as the Whorf hypothesis—has been in serious disrepute," cognitive scientists Dedre Gentner and Susan Goldin-Meadow write in their book *Language in Mind*. "Admitting any sympathy for, even curiosity about the possibility was tantamount to declaring oneself to be either a simpleton or a lunatic."

Up until the 1960s, people had been freely admitting curiosity about this possibility and for years, even before Benjamin Lee Whorf made his mark by arguing that the language you speak helps shape your worldly perceptions. Whorf was a linguistics scholar and fire inspector; he worked for the Hartford Fire Insurance Company at the same time the poet Wallace Stevens did, though the only evidence that the two ever met is a letter about language that was sent to Stevens and mistakenly delivered to Whorf. "We dissect nature along lines laid down by our native language," Whorf wrote in the 1940s, part of the theory that goes by the full name the Sapir-Whorf hypothesis. (Edward Sapir, a linguist, was Whorf's champion at Yale.) "The categories and types that we isolate from the world of phenomena we do not find there because they stare every observer in the face," Whorf argued. "On the contrary, the world is presented in a kaleidoscope flux of impressions which has to be organized by our minds—and this means largely by the linguistic systems of our minds."

The world is a rush of stimuli that each language makes sense of uniquely, meaning that the speakers of each language comprehend the world differently—he was extending a line of thought that the German anthropologist Franz Boas had taken up forty years earlier. Boas observed that every language contains grammatical elements that are "obligatory" and that these determine "what must be expressed." In other words, within a particular language, you can only say things a certain way. If you were to come upon a rhinoceros demolishing your car, to give an example, you would, if you were a Turkish speaker on the phone to the police, be required by the verb to convey whether you yourself were witnessing the rampage or someone had told you about it. In Turkish, verbs of observation are formed differently, depending on if the speaker saw the event firsthand or had it reported to him by someone else. Were the rampage occurring in Russia, however, you'd be obliged, morphosyntactically, to indicate whether the animal was male or female and whether it was finished flattening the car or still in the process of doing so. In

Mandarin, you could speed things up. Mandarin has no past or future tense, so the exact stage of trampling would likely not be addressed. Each of these reports would relate the action, but with different shades of meaning.

Boas laid the groundwork for what would become a clash that continues to this day. The crux can be expressed in one question: if, as they do, individual languages make people focus attention on some aspects of a situation and ignore others (for instance, time and gender), does this shade their perceptions of the event? In other words, does language shape thought?

Any answer to this question will depend on the answers to several other questions, one being, How much, truly, do languages differ in how they describe the world? "No two languages are ever sufficiently similar to be considered as representing the same social reality," Edward Sapir declared, to which a lot of people have since responded with a sound *total nonsense*. Does language exist independently of thought—and if so, how would it be possible for language to affect thought? Which comes first in order of their importance in cognition—concepts or words?

Words, absolutely, according to Nietzsche. "Unspeakably more depends on *what things are called* than on what they are," he wrote, italics his. "Creating new names . . . creates new 'things.'" No one got overly excited about this idea when it appeared in *The Gay Science* in 1882, but when, one field over, Whorf came out with a far milder version of the idea in the 1930s, the hypothesis was first lauded as a breakthrough, then two decades later trounced. This pummeling occurred after MIT professor Noam Chomsky skewered the behaviorist B. F. Skinner in a book review. That attack sent linguistics spinning off its axis (or so it seemed to the then reigning behaviorists) and led to the downfall of Whorf and his theories. For years up till then, behaviorist assumptions had shaped how foreign languages were taught. Skinner and others thought that children arrived at fluency in their native tongues through the positive and negative reinforcements they received when they spoke. "Do you want milk?" the mother says as she pours some, and click—the information is filed away: "milk" is the right name for the white liquid that comes in glasses. "Isabella were eating cat poop," a child reports, and her mother screams, "Isabella was eating *what*?" "Were," it's ascertained, is wrong usage. Children were fine-tuned, word by word, into proper speech, the behaviorists thought; ergo, that's how language students should proceed. The assertion was accepted as common knowledge for years, until 1959, when Chomsky wrote his critique of Skinner.

In it, he made a number of points, one of the central ones being that it's ludicrous to suppose children learn to talk solely through the influence of "primary linguistic data"—how their mothers, fathers, and kindergarten teachers form sentences, or don't. If kids had to wait for chiropractics to be performed on every single utterance they made, they'd still be babbling into middle age. How was it, he asked, that by age six or so, a child automatically knows that sentences he's never heard before—"The man don't want that banana"—are grammatically incorrect? Because, Chomsky argued, we all have an inborn facility for language—something he later called a "transformational generative grammar"—which allows us to generate grammatically correct sentences endlessly, based on finite samples. In short, humans are hardwired to speak.

Language is innate: that became the rallying cry of the school that formed, called, logically enough, the nativists. In no time, their views held sway, and Skinner was removed from the fore. Whorf was sent to the corner, for the nativists were of the strict (some have said tyrannical) belief that concepts aren't shaped by names and, furthermore, that since all languages operate on one universal, innate grammar, any differences among them are superficial—mere wallpaper, "so much noise." Once these ideas became governing propositions, the question of whether differences in language affect thought was moot, since, perforce, there weren't any.

For a long time after that, if you were engaged in the serious study of language and you were foolish enough to speculate publicly that maybe old Benjamin Lee hadn't got it completely wrong with his theories, which had become known as "linguistic relativity," you were considered to have the same keen mental faculties as people who believed in UFOs. "Discussions of language and thought were about as respectable as discussions of flying saucers," Gentner and Goldin-Meadow write in *Language in Mind,* in the part of the book where they point out that the same academicians who rejected linguistic relativity were, invariably, careful to embrace politically corrected speech—were, for instance, assiduously using "senior citizen" for "old," presumably because "old" had pejorative connotations and *could affect the way people thought.*

Whorf's case certainly had not been advanced by the fact that, from time to time through the years, his ideas were hijacked and used to press racist points by academics with murky agendas. They'd begin with the pseudo-Whorfian observation that certain words— certain words, in these instances, used by Westerners and particularly Anglo-Westerners ("right," "wrong," "blue," "gray")—were missing from the vocabularies of certain people (in the category described in times past as "primitive people"), then pole-vault from there to the conclusion that the people in question were, ergo, incapable of complex thought. Perhaps the deficits in complex thinking lay with the authors, since not one of them ever questioned whether the Papuan lexicon, say, contained words that were missing from English.

In addition, Whorf was proved wrong on several fronts, one being in his argument that the Inuit (formerly, Eskimo) have more words for snow than anyone else. They don't, subsequent analysis proved, a correction that linguists were quick to register but that's never fully made its way into common wisdom. (Not long ago, the novelist Christopher Buckley inveighed in a book review, in order to make a point, "The Inuit have—what?—seventeen words for snow?")

There was also the color study upset. In the 1950s, the researcher Eric Lenneberg set out to show that the more words a language has for basic colors, the better the speakers will be at remembering shades: words affect thought, fundamental Whorfian analysis. The range of basic color words that languages use is fairly wide. At one end, you get a count of eleven (the tally for English), at the other end, two. Some tongues have no direct words for colors, but use instead adjectival nouns such as "smoke-smoke" and "grass-grass." Originally, English (and Turkish and Hindi and Rajasthani Sign Language, among others) took a similar approach with "orange"—borrowed the name of the fruit to represent the previously unnamed color. The word "red," to digress some more, turns into *rudhira,* meaning "blood," if you take it far enough back to the Sanskrit. "Blood red," then, strictly speaking, is a tautology.

When Lenneberg investigated this link—between number of words in the vocabulary for colors and ability of the speakers to recall the shades—he found that there was one, suggesting that words do anchor concepts, that language affects thought. But about twenty years on, around the time linguistic relativity was being called into question, another researcher upset these findings—ran tests showing that the Dani people of New Guinea were no more slack than Anglophones at remembering colors, despite the fact that the Dani's basic color vocabulary consisted of two words. The feeling by then was that Whorf had long ago had his day. And that, looked like, was that for him.

To cut to the present: a new movement has taken hold in the field, based on the theories of, yes, *certainement,* Benjamin Whorf. Since the mid-1990s, his beliefs have undergone a renaissance, as a backlash against Chomsky has gathered steam and many earlier studies of linguistic relativity have, on retesting, proved to have merit, Lenneberg's color investigations among them.

Researchers today receive grants to explore every conceivable neo-Whorfian proposition. Does the way a language treat space influence the way speakers think? In Spanish, to give an example, you're *in* the bus for five hours; in English, you're *on* it. What about when a language obliges you to ascribe gender to nouns — does that make a difference in how you see things? At MIT, one linguist applied scientific principles to investigating whether there was a connection between gender use and people's thoughts, with surprising results. Or maybe not so surprising. The researcher, Lera Boroditsky, got two groups of people — one Spanish speaking, one German — to describe photographs of various objects. The items seemed to have been randomly chosen, but in fact, each of them had opposite genders in the two languages — a key, for instance, is masculine in German, feminine in Spanish. What Boroditsky found was that with items that were linguistically feminine, she got largely feminine descriptions; masculine items prompted adjectives that were more traditionally masculine. To the Spanish speakers, the key was "intricate," "lovely," "shiny," "golden"; to the Germans, it was "hard," "heavy," "jagged," "metal." A picture of a bridge — feminine in German, masculine in Spanish — struck the German speakers as "beautiful," "elegant," "fragile," "pretty"; to the Spaniards, it was "big," "dangerous," "long," "strong."

"The private mental lives of people who speak different languages may differ dramatically," concluded Boroditsky, who didn't venture a guess as to what all this meant for people whose nouns don't have gender. Are English speakers' chairs free of sexist overtones? Or is our natural world missing a certain overlay of lyricism?

There's been something of a stampede on to reopen investigations into what influence, if any, color names have on thought. In one study, people who spoke English, which makes a distinction between blue and green, were compared with people who spoke Tarahumara, a Mexican language that doesn't make such a distinction. (So many tongues, in fact, refer to blue and green by the same name that researchers invented one in English for it: "grue.") When shown color chips, the English speakers reported that the samples that were bluish green (i.e., a grue with more blue) were dissimilar from the ones that were greenish blue. The Tarahumara speakers didn't. Other studies like this have come up with the same general results, with one very intriguing methodological exception. If, in the course of the study, you engage people in verbal interference tasks at the same time that they're being quizzed on blue and green—get them to count backward from eight to one, say, while they're trying to identify colors—you find no Whorf effect whatsoever. English speakers will perform about the same as the Tarahumara speakers.

"This suggests that the effect is mediated by some kind of online verbal representation, as opposed to it being a permanent part of your perception," said Terry Regier, a psychology professor at the University of Chicago who's worked on several color studies. "People who want the Whorf hypothesis to be right will look at those results and say they strongly support Whorf: 'The results tell you we took language out of the picture and the effect went away.' People who want Whorf to be wrong like the findings, too. They say, 'Look, this isn't some long-lasting worldview. When the verbal resources aren't there, the effect isn't there.' The findings are like a Rorschach."

Regier reported that there are a "ton of color studies going on." Not all the new research categories are as crowded. There are fewer experiments being done on whether a language's words for emotions shape how its speakers feel, perhaps because the possibility for racist interpretation is wider here. Does the fact that the Chewong of Malaysia have just seven words for emotions, not one of them describing "sadness," mean that they are a simple, happy people? Or that they have more advanced control over their emotions than do English speakers, who, with two thousand names (by one count) for feeling states, might be viewed as emotionally sloppy down around Kuala Lumpur?

The number of emotions a language contains varies widely. Feelings that exist in one tongue don't in others. It can be disconcerting for a therapized citizen of the English-speaking world to learn that there are places on the globe where people never talk about their anger because they don't have a word for it. People who are monolingual naturally tend to assume that the emotions (i.e., theirs) are universal. Well, aren't they?

Charles Darwin thought so. Emotional expressions are innate and the same for all, he wrote, but then again, Darwin was operating on English only—no basis for comparison. The writer Milan Kundera—who speaks Czech, French, and English—has named one that's not the same for everyone, at least to the extent that no one but the Czechs have anything remotely similar to it in their dictionaries. "*Litost* is a Czech word with no exact translation into any other language," Kundera writes. "It designates a feeling as infinite as an open accordion, a feeling that is the synthesis of many others: grief, sympathy, remorse and an indefinable longing . . . I have never found an equivalent in other languages for this sense of the word either . . . [It] is a state of torment caused by a sudden insight into one's own miserable self."

As soon as you read that, you begin to imagine you know exactly what Kundera is talking about, and that reaction is one of the points of contention that arises in this debate. "Why . . . do so many people think that emotions differ from culture to culture?" Steven Pinker asks. "The common remark that a language does or doesn't have a word for [an] emotion means little . . . I have never heard a foreign emotion word whose meaning wasn't instantly recognizable." To which the outspoken Polish-born linguist Anna Wierzbicka replies,

"The 'instant recognition' of the meaning of foreign emotion words often takes the form of wrongly identifying foreign emotion words." You may think you've recognized the *angst* that lies within, when what you really have in your soul is anxiety.

Several studies have suggested that bilinguals' emotional perceptions of situations may change with the language they are thinking in. A psychology professor named Susan Ervin-Tripp ran some experiments. In one test, she asked a man who was bilingual in Japanese and English to tell a story off the top of his head about drawings she showed him on cards. One, for instance, was of a woman sitting on the floor, head resting on the couch. In the story he came up with in English, the figure was a girl who was finishing a project for sewing class. In the story in Japanese, which he was asked to invent several weeks later, she was a suicidal woman weeping for her lost fiancé.

ANNA WIERZBICKA ARGUES that emotions derive from "cultural scripts," and as such are learned in the language of the culture. Perhaps this explains why, months into learning Hindi, I become keenly aware of a feeling I've never experienced before. It comes from outside me, fills me and the room. It's longing, in a shade I've never known before: for something I can't name but that I know viscerally is unbounded, an object or state that's protean, divine. In English, the closest word for this emotion would be "melancholy," but it's a melancholy laced with joy and expectation—more like the Portuguese *saudade*. These opposite qualities make the feeling nearly unbearably bittersweet, and also so transporting that I never want it to end. Even if I could figure out what it is I'm in longing for, I wouldn't want the desire to be satisfied, as that would kill the feeling. The feeling is sharpest when I listen to certain haunting Hindi songs, and for a while I wonder whether the melodies—like pleas themselves, like milky amber in my head—aren't producing it. Before long, though, I suspect that it's the lyrics, the words I decipher after many rewinds and with the help of Rashida, the Muslim batik artist.

"*Beloved, little by little, the separation of the night is starting to burn,*" the great playback singer Lata Mangeshkar croons in my room, till I know each word by heart, its general meaning. One of the words, *birha,* is the Rajasthani pronunciation of a word that means "separation": *viraha.* I know that much, but not the full definition, which I will find out later on. *Viraha,* the anthropologist Owen Lynch writes, translates as "love-in-separation": longing. And though it can be used in a purely romantic sense, like a lot of Hindi, it has a religious meaning, too: the near-unbearable yearning that the *gopis,* the cow maidens, felt after Krishna multiplied his body and made love to them all, then disappeared. The purest form of love, many Hindu sects believe, is incomplete love: viraha. "The frustration of the emotions' desire for immediate union with Krishna," Lynch wrote, "becomes the closest possible encounter with the divine." A transcendent longing, unable to be fulfilled, that becomes desirable in itself—this description fit, exactly, the emotion that suffused me.

The song lyrics focus my attention on viraha, but after a while I see there are reminders of it everywhere. The landscape here, cultural and physical, is shaped by this amber shade of yearning. It's apparent in architectural details on the haveli's top floor—the tiny windows intended to enforce separation, the faint outlines of what had been a hole in the floor. Mr. Singh tells me his grandfather used to pull himself up through the ceiling of the kitchen below in order to have clandestine late-night visits with his wife. Even when married, men and women were separated. This yearning is apparent in the Bollywood films, in which couples are never allowed to kiss; in the myriad words that translate roughly as "longing." *Chaahanaa:* "to want," a basic desire. *Tamannaa:* "to desire," "to long for." *Aramaan:* "desire," "longing," "heartfelt wish." *Hazrat karna:* "to long for." *Khwahish:* "longing." *Iccha:* "longing." *Viyog:* "separation." *Vi-*

rasa: "unrequited love," a situation in which there is not fire on both sides.

Viraha is evident on the streets in the form of purdah; on a drive with a male storeowner, who has me sit in the back seat and talk to the back of his head "so people do not get a wrong idea"; on an afternoon when I first visit Ruby. My rickshaw circles endlessly through her neighborhood till I call and she comes down. Outside her building, children are flying kites above the carcass of a car. She unlocks a gate and leads me up a grimy stairwell to her apartment. Two thousand rupees a month for two hospital-green rooms—it's more money than they have, she says, "but my things grow."

Most Indian apartments are spare, but Ruby's is a veritable emporium. Books are everywhere: toppling from an old sewing machine trestle; piled on the floor; squeezed into long, felt shoe holders on the walls. Above a black shag sofa, a shelf is crammed with so many trophies and awards, a seated guest is in danger of getting cracked on the head. A feng shui consultant, Ruby says, has just been by and directed her to take the shelf down. Feng shui guys do a land-office business here, while yoga teachers languish, reduced to teaching the salute to the sun to whatever tourist girls they can hoodwink into donning Lycra and sitting in their bedroom while they give short shrift to downward dog. Transcendence always kicks in faster if the catalyst isn't from your hometown.

"You like hills now? Hills? Hills? Hills?" Ruby asks once we've removed our shoes. She's speaking in English, staking out which language we'll use. Ruby hates it when I make her speak Hindi with me. "Your Hindi is making me very, very uneasy," she complains. Though one of us could say the same about the other one's English.

"Hills?"

"Hills, hills," she maintains. "You are liking hills."

"I don't *not* like hills. Ruby: *What?*"

"Yes, hills." She points to the beat-up Manolo Blahniks I've left by the door, remnants of my magazine days.

"Ye 'heels' *bolte hai,"* I inform her in a superior tone: "The way you say that is 'heels.'" Her failure to make herself understood in English has allowed me to seize the moment and reroute us into Hindi. We get about the same results there, however, so in the bedroom, lounging on the bed she shares with Rajendra and their two daughters, we switch off, back and forth and when we get stuck—*Prabav?* "Influence"? "Force"?—we call out to the girls watching TV in the other room: *"Prabav ka matlab?"* ("What does *prabav* mean?") "Effect!" they shout back, over a swelling soap.

On the bed, she hands me a library book, pages to an earmarked passage, translates over my shoulder. "A good man always stands alone—" she begins.

"Ruby," I interrupt. "How did you not become like the other women here?" She isn't; not remotely. For one thing, she's the only one I've met with a real career. The fact that Rajendra has a negligible-wage job in his father's card shop has turned out to be a blessing and a curse. A curse because most weeks, his father refuses to pay him, and then Ruby's and Rajendra's fights grow rancorous. Why can't he get a real job? Whenever she introduces the question, he threatens to throw himself into Fateh Sagar lake—so evaporated now from the drought that he'd only hit his head on the religious statuary people have tossed in, but all the same, a concern. Things for a while got so bad, they had to take it to a palmist. "Palmist said husband should support his wife and children or they won't survive," Ruby said in her throaty contralto when I checked in later. It wasn't hard to figure out who was paying the bill. "Palmist said, 'If you suicide yourself, you will suicide yourself your next seven lives.'" Fallout over multiple lifetimes—that is not something our Western marriage counselors have to work with.

She was lonely, she answers, after her arranged marriage, but discovered that when she traveled to poets' conferences, she found other people to talk to. She did, more and more, and one thing led to another—newspapers began publishing her work, she landed a correspondent's gig with a major daily in Bombay—and now, she says, "I have fame and a name." In that respect, Rajendra's job has been a blessing.

Her oldest daughter brings chai. Ruby pulls out a photo album, and we flip through, past poets declaiming at podiums, Ruby addressing crowds, smiling broadly, again and again, magnificent at two hundred pounds. ("When she got on my scale, it read ninety-six kilos. She said, 'I'm not stopping till I hit a hundred,'" Renee had said with pride.) We turn pages, and she offers illuminating commentary. I learn about the older woman in town who allows young couples to conduct trysts at her house on the condition she be allowed to watch, about the prominent local figure who has village children brought in for sex play. That's another way Ruby's not like other women here: better gossip. Like journalists everywhere, she has all the news not fit to print.

On the bed, miraculously, the tea doesn't spill, and miraculously, she gets a joke I make in Hindi. She slides a Hindu New Year's greeting she's composed from a pile of blue notebooks that rise high above the bed, after that a ghazal she had published in the paper. It's written to her friend, Shahid, a Muslim poet. "Ruby's a nice Hindu woman. Shahid is just a friend," Renee explained when I asked who he was, but he's the kind of friend who demands vast amounts of psychic attention and obeisance. Ruby stands her ground, which leads to fights and inordinate analysis of the situation with friends. After Ruby and Shahid's last dustup, I'd learned how to say "son of a bitch" in Hindi: *brother-in-law.*

"He is telling me to come to Nathdwara," she says, waggling her brows. She asks if I'd like to hear another ghazal, reaches for the papery blue tower that stretches toward the ceiling. The journals are so close to our heads, if someone flew a hand up without thinking, Ruby's innermost hopes and desires would come raining down on us. "What if your husband looks at those?" I say. They're right there, like bedside reading.

He won't, she says. And if he did, he wouldn't understand them. I remember bucktoothed Rajendra congenially asking me at dinner, "And you are a bachelor?" I think for a minute, she'll be fine.

But what if he did? I say, suddenly afraid. The ghazal to Shahid had been a growl.

She swings her head around, says something I don't catch. Only one word, *purdah:* "curtain."

"What?" I say. In Hindi, signal to stay on that side. She obliges till I have to cry uncle.

"What?" I say. In English: okay to cross back.

She leans in, stares, bites her lip, smiles. "But in the curtain," she says—if everyone keeps it under wraps—"all things are permitted."

THE END OF THE YEAR closes in, drawing with it heat from the future that's so violent, any grapes purchased on the street explode in your mouth as if they've been microwaved. So fierce, if a woman leaves a lipstick in her purse, it's melted by the end of the day. So blasting, no one in their right mind gets together with a friend just to talk, though Nand and I do. We're bidding again for eternity.

The talk this afternoon starts off like a shot. "This terrorism is only a word here," he says when I mention how frightened everyone in my country still sounds. "People here say, 'All right, it will pass over.' They rationalize things, because after all, how long can you go on fighting if nature doesn't smile and you have famines again and again? If you have deaths and diseases over and over? You eventually decide, 'Oh, all right. These are the wishes of the gods. All right, but we will have good days also.' In Sanskrit, they say *chakravat*—'it's like a wheel.'" He presses a finger to his chin as if to slow himself. "Younger nations are afraid of evil situations, especially if they have seen only prosperous times. America is very much afraid of facing evil days," he says, but soon this smooth-flying talk smashes up.

"Kit-ti, you are a guest here," Nand snaps when I say something about how the economy in India has never been better. "You are not seeing. If you are a guest, you come to my house, and I give you tea. I don't tell you what my thoughts really are." The expression in the portrait is on his face. "You are not in the game," he says. "If you are in the game, then I don't give you tea." He pauses to brood. "I kick you. I try to take your advantages. I am not very nice. There is so little money. I will try to take your money. India is corrupt. Indians will cheat you. The country has so many problems; it's not in good shape. Kit-ti," he says, "you are a guest; you are not seeing."

"But I am," I say, and Nand rebuts every proof I offer, till it's established beyond dispute: I've seen nothing all year; I know nothing about India; I'm like the *Angrezi,* the English, before me, skimmers of the language. I may know the words, as some of them did, but I will never write poetry. *"Angrezi"* does it. I stand up to go.

"It's late," I say, already mentally out the door, already on the main street, where turbaned vendors will be hawking tubers by the rickshaw stand, where bikes will be propped at crazy angles in the dirt, where the Muslim storeowner will be hovering above the Shogun tissues display. Where, if I skid back often enough in my mind, they will always be.

"Kit-ti," he says, two falling, high-pitched syllables that stop me, though for a second I still mistake his tone for irritable.

"Kit-ti, you know, you could have tried harder to learn Hindi," he says quietly. "I could have talked to you so much better then. You can only really speak intimately in your native tongue. In Hindi," he says, "I could have told you how I loved you."

Out past the vendors, past the crazy-angled bikes, the rickshaw men will argue about which rickshaw I'll take. They'll select a beat-up one with velour seats, and I'll get in. The driver will rev us forward; the wind will sting my eyes. *But Nand is full force enough in English,* I'll think each time. *I wouldn't want to see what he could do in Hindi.*

· 17 ·

"Who are these people?"

 It's late spring now, and some days when I arrive, Antriksh Flats, the fifth floor, looks nearly abandoned: an outer-space station where most of the inhabitants have been mysteriously vaporized. On the frequent occasions when the Whisperer doesn't come in, the head count is three, down from eight at the start. I sit in the main room, and Swami-ji and Vidhu switch off. Without the hubbub from before, the rooms sound hollow.

Down to three, there's an awkwardness among us, as if we've all just met. I'm glad for the extra attention, happier still when the school day ends. The hours on the fifth floor are interruptions in days that stretch out luxuriously, are golden hued, lofting, and laced with tranquility, that fill me with peace. More than alien concepts sink in with the language. The town's sweetness has, too. It steadies me.

In New York, where the constant hum of aspiration produces ADD, it's impossible, ever, to really calm down. But here, where the screech of the street is even louder, it's easy to sink into a meditative state. Half the homes here don't have phones; people weren't raised on TV. At this pace of life, from some other shuffled era, my synapses slow. Any sight can become a mandala. Afternoons, I watch clouds streak the sky rose above a low slope of the Aravallis and feel one of those aches of happiness so light, they seem remembered even at the time.

Mornings before school, I lie on the mattress beneath one of the small, square haveli windows and watch the Indian family across the street get ready for the day. After months of life without it, the concept of privacy is growing alien. On a pretty rooftop arranged with planters, the mother sets a newspaper aside to clip her daughter's nails. She leads her son, pants still down around his ankles, out from a small rooftop bathroom, and he squats down in front of her. I turn to check the time, and the children are now rushing out the front door and into the street, where two rickshaws are waiting to take them to school. The mother waves goodbye from the ledge. A German shepherd sees them off from the front door, but then, in a blink, he's up on the roof. Duties discharged, he settles down as the city cranks awake under a pale yellow sky.

On a weekend out of town alone, I find myself in a town by a lake that's vibrant with life. Shocking-blue kingfishers ripple the surface with their beaks as they skim the water. Proudy Siberian cranes command the shoreline. Two thousand tons of fish every day are pulled from these depths, the brochure in my hotel room reports. An impressive feat, given that the leaky rowboats plying the lake need one guy onboard just to bail. The nearly deserted hotel looks out over this sanctuary from a small spit of land. It has a pool with a supply of loaner swimsuits that appear to be imports from the Soviet Union circa 1982, a general manager with a lascivious grin. Every four hours the first night, the phone by my bed rings: a not-so-mysterious heavy breather. When I march down the next morning to complain, the manager claims he was similarly plagued.

"Was it one call, madam? Two? Yes, in my room, too. Why didn't you telephone me?" he says. Because yesterday, I'm tempted to say, when I was reclining poolside in a red-star bathing suit over orange knee-length loaner shorts and a complimentary in-room shower cap, you crept around behind bushes and ogled me. But the ache of happiness is too strong. Instead, I give him a look and go out to find the orange shorts and lie by the pool. I close my eyes and smile. I eat the sun.

RUBY BECOMES THE first person ever to figure out what good all this Hindi can do me. Others have politely indulged me the obsession, but Ruby has keyed in on where the hidden cash and prizes lie, and not just for me, but for her and Priyanka, the young journalist she's brought along to the Rose Garden restaurant tonight. Ruby has a plan. She's come up with a scheme that's foolproof, she's decided, but all the same, she waits to spring it on me. No doubt because the plan involves substantial public humiliation on my part.

"Have you heard from Chirag?" Priyanka asks once the two of them are seated, with such obvious nonchalance, my chest tightens. Priyanka, lanky, with incandescent skin, is twenty-four, the age when the eligibility clock for a woman here starts to tick. To my increasing horror, I said I'd help her get hitched. Power had gone to my head on our first meeting, when she'd said, "No, do you know anyone?" after I'd asked if she was married. *You could arrange a marriage for someone just like that,* I realized then. I offered up Chirag, the computer student who, back in the States, used to come to my apartment to practice Hindi. Chirag was a Brahmin like her, I began, then tried to think what else. Uh, handsome (well, he wasn't ugly; I would have remembered). Smart. Eager to land a wife before embarking on the lucrative business of Java programming. The realization that the wife part was supposition faded as Priyanka and I imagined me helping her settle in the States. And so when Chirag, via e-mail, blithely dismissed his fate, I was a little stunned. He hadn't seemed reckless like that. "You've found a woman for me to marry?" he wrote back. "Interesting, but I'm nowhere near ready to get married." He didn't ask, How are your studies going? That much was clear: around the bend.

"Yes, he just wrote. He's been asking about you," I tell Priyanka at the table. "He's going to write you." He'd rushed off with a mention that he might. A mosquito coil by our feet is sending up lazy wisps of smoke. Yellow lights are strung overhead. Monkeys are scampering through the trees. In the romance of the setting, Chirag has come through, and she's the one who needs convincing. "You know, Chirag is really terrific," I say. "He's a really nice guy."

"He is a cow?" Ruby suddenly, mysteriously chimes in. "Do you mean Chirag is a bull?" she cries, funniest thing either of them has ever heard, judging by the way they're rocking and snorting. "What?" I ask, irritated. The joke has sailed over my head and rear-ended a monkey, which hoots and bares its teeth.

"You have said Chirag is a 'guy'?" Ruby has to dab her eyes to explain. "But 'guy' in Hindi means a 'cow'?" Spelled *gai,* but all right. "So I am saying Chirag is a bull." More rampant hilarity ensues, then she takes off into rapid-clip Hindi, reprising some of her best lines from the Indo-Pak conference she just moderated: *"The blood of our concern should remain in our veins." "As much as we know, that much we have to learn."*

The conference, attended mostly by Hindus, repeatedly erupted into outbursts against Muslims, she reports. Relations between India and Pakistan have grown ominously strained. The threat of nuclear confrontation is on everyone's mind. India seems to be on the verge of going to war with Pakistan over the attack on the parliament last December. The Hindu right, furious that the invasion was almost certainly carried out by Muslim militants based in Pakistan, has called for Pakistani president Pervez Musharraf to crack down. Musharraf's response has been viewed as tepid. For months now, Indian and Pakistani troops have been massing at the border.

"At the conference, a poet got up and said bad things about the Pakistanis," Ruby tells me, breaking for English to be sure I'm still with her. "Everyone clapped. But when I suggested understanding, there was silence. You can't win at these conferences if you don't say you hate the Muslims." Then she slips back into full-fire Hindi, and I remember how, beginning of the year, the necessity for tolerating ambiguity nearly killed me. I'd never cried as much over a man as I did over Hindi then, I'd just told Vidhu in class. He'd just confessed that I was, on arrival, one of the worst students they'd ever seen.

"We don't often get people with so little Hindi," he'd said. "When we have, they didn't make it. They lost heart. But you didn't. For three months, you hardly made any progress, and then your Hindi went straight up." He'd soared his hand into the air. "Six more months, Kathy-ji, and people would take you for a native," he'd said with courtly exaggeration, and the sentence fractured me. Six more months? I didn't have six weeks.

Below the table, smoke from the mosquito coil is lowering mosquitoes down onto my feet. Distracted stabbing my sandals to try and shake them off, I miss the unveiling of Ruby's plan.

". . . is what I am telling you, this thing could be very, very good for you," she's saying when I tune back in. Priyanka is nodding emphatically beside her. "And it will be broadcast on the Mewar channel," Priyanka says. None of this sounds good.

None of it is. Something called the "Videshi Competition" is coming up, an event held each year at the puppet museum. The name says it all: hapless tourists lured into a stumbling salute to Rajasthan for the amusement of the locals. "I'm not doing that," I say preemptively, in case that's what they're getting at.

They are. "But all you'd have to do is wear traditional Rajasthani dress and sing a traditional Rajasthani song," Ruby says. While everyone in the audience snickered.

"But you will win," Ruby says, noting the look on my face. Hers is lit with the brilliance of the plan, which she proceeds to spell out. But do I understand who my competitors would be? Tourists! Tourists, who do not speak Hindi! Do I see I could wander on looking clueless, as if I were one of them, then open my mouth and blast them off the stage? The idea makes Ruby cackle. "We will win," she says with verve and confidence, using "we" because she's going to be writing my speech, and Priyanka will help with the coaching. "No way, Vijay," I tell her.

Undaunted, she proceeds with the bombshell inducement: "But first prize is a night at Kumbhalgarh," she says, her face now 120 watts. Kumbhalgarh is the mountain resort where Helaena used to meet Aditya, the place where the students gathered at the start of the year, back when leopards, all manner of retransfiguring wildness, were just about to appear. Ruby says the name with such low reverence, memories come flooding back: of attar-scented water glasses, of silver chandeliers, of stone steps rising and falling through the greenery, rising and falling like a song. It's a king's existence, all right, for as long as you stay, which in Ruby's life, will be not ever. She could host a thousand panels, could sell a million poems, could force Rajendra to get a real job, and she'd never have enough for even one night at Kumbhalgarh. True, yes, but still: the year is coming to an end, and exams are coming up, and I'd sooner eat the algae in Lake Pichola than parade around like a tourist.

Ruby is staring at me, calculating my response. I shake my head, firmly. In the yellow light, her face dims. "But you would win," she says slowly. "You would win, and then you could take Priyanka and me with you." She laughs quickly to show *That was just a joke,* but her expression is serious. Coaching, speechwriting, don't I see? She's proposing an even trade. Ruby has never let the fact of my relative wealth—the vast comparative sums I have as a Westerner—come between us. She's made it emphatically clear: in this friendship, we're equals. She's always met me halfway: cooked me numerous dinners, taken me to poetry meetings and journalism conferences. This thought makes me consider all the boons I've received here all year: how Vidhu frequently stayed on for hours after class, unpaid, to help me resolder my sentences, all Nand's fussing attentions, the way Anukul has thrown open the doors of his classroom.

Really, all Ruby's asking me to do is to make a fool of myself, which I've been doing all year anyway.

"Well, I do know a song," I say. "And it is Rajasthani." I demonstrate my mastery of "Yara Seeli Seeli."

"That is Rajasthani with a pop beat," she says in a monotone. I smile at what I think is a compliment, then remember she'd specified "traditional." She takes it from the top, sounding a lot more like Lata Mangeshkar than I do. I try again. She shakes her head. "It is a song by a woman who's died and wants her lover. You're supposed to sound sad," she says. I thought I did.

"And you shouldn't do that with your head," Priyanka pipes up, indicating my head wobble, which I'd assumed could mean grief. It means everything else here. I try again. "No, sad," Ruby says. "You come to my house, and we'll work on it."

Late that night, tape player on the bed, I tell myself, *You can do this.* But when I put the cassette in, try not to head-wobble to the first keening line, alien phonemes and morphemes and nasality trip me up. Lata Mangeshkar's voice trembles, and I can imitate her for one word, but I can't push it into longing without sounding like a dog that's had it with a squirrel. My howl cracks. I lose my bearings. Swelling emotion has never been big in American music, so God knows when swelling is good or when it's bad. Except I do. I do because I can hear it when she does it right.

I listen, again and again, because the singer does it in a way I can tell is perfect, because the music on its own terms is haunting. I will figure out how to sound naked and pleading and to ignore my American notions of decorum. But up against my own cultural reserve, I can't. I play the first four lines over and over, and each time her voice gains power. Each time, I see a little more of what she's doing, injecting despair into the word *"night,"* going low then rising in protest on *"burn."* I listen, and finally I can come into the music unshielded, un-American, not with anywhere near her talent or grace, but I can make my voice slide and plead, beg; I can restrain a shriek, though not for too long. I don't wince as my reserve peels away. Reserve has always been protection and dignity, but it can be reclaimed anytime. What I've never done before is to wail—express full pounding sorrow at all that happened to cause my ghost life—and now, with the fan set on High, I do.

"AA-O, KATHY," Mrs. Singh says when I poke my head into the television room. *"Aa-o!"* Come! Her daughter Ritu has made a special Gujarati dish, sweetened grains. *"Bhaitiye,"* sit, and I do, to lots of food and TV. Not the Indian *Weakest Link* tonight, too bad, but Hindi movies that freeze from weak cable and no one cares. Ritu serves me, serves her mother, who's a temperamental cook, she says. *"She can't give cooking lessons. She has to be alone in the kitchen. If anyone else is in there, the food will be spoiled."* The word she uses, *bigaad,* is one Vidhu just taught me. Words lately keep magically appearing the day I learn them. I show the women where I've written *"spoiled"* in my notebook, which occasions a vocabulary quiz.

"What does dil *mean? What does* ghar *mean?"* Ritu asks, nabbing words from the film.

"'Heart.' 'House.' *Bahut asan,"* I say: "Too easy," which I've pronounced like "too is-ee."

"Asaan," she corrects.

"What does muhabbat *mean?"* Mrs. Singh asks, Asiatic eyes crin-

kling in a grin. Okay, she's stumped me. "Love," she says, and smiles triumphantly, though I'm not sure why. *"Main aapse muhabbat karti hun,"* she says: "I love you."

Mrs. Singh exhibits the same equanimity my mother had, has the same wry regard for life. I've become fond of her, in all aspects but one. When this one appears, I make myself think of it as a tic. The troubling part of Mrs. Singh's personality is that she's not terrifically fond of a number of nationalities. Can't take the Israelis who sometimes stay here: they lock the room and leave the fan running. Could do without the Americans. When relatives stop by, she insists on telling them I'm French. And Muslims . . . Mrs. Singh's eyes narrow. I'm exempted, however, and so's her Muslim friend Rashida, the one who helped me find this place. Rashida is all right; *"she is a good Muslim."* For a while, the tic can be like when someone burps in the West—the conversation pauses, you look away—then in no time, around the afternoon I go to a homeopathic doctor for a sleep remedy, exemptions are revoked. On both sides.

Can a homeopathic cure take effect after just one dose? I wonder the morning after the visit. The whole time I've been here, my sleep has been largely barren—snippets of unintelligible Hindi, never a fast glorious ride, or else dreams in my own tongue so weighted, they can't unfold, they sink down as soon as they begin. I rarely have the sensation of having dreamed, as if most of my energies need to be siphoned into the task of laying down language, at all times. But on this particular night, I dream in vivid rushing images, of men murdered with their hands bound and hospitals where the doctors are wasps and dwarves, scenes so horrifying I bolt awake several times.

When my brain continues to heave up gruesome images over several nights, however, I have to conclude it's not the homeopathic pills that are the cause, but most likely the nightmarish stories that are arriving here from Gujarat. I catch bits and pieces now, enough to haunt my dreams, not enough to understand that the nocturnal imagery is tame compared to what's going on a hundred miles to the south. It's anarchy down there, I'll learn later. I'll hear the full stories in time: Several Muslims, racing to escape a howling mob, made it to what they thought was the safety of a hospital but were captured on the third floor and thrown to their deaths. In one village, a family of eleven Muslims tried to escape after their homes were destroyed. They hid in a field under a large tree, but by nightfall a mob of five hundred had found them. The men in charge reassured them, *"You will not be killed."* People gave them water, asked only that they leave. The family made it twenty feet down the road when they were set on from behind. A thirteen-year-old girl was gang-raped first. Then they were all hacked to death, and in a "conversion" to Hinduism, their bodies were burned on a funeral pyre.

The official death toll has now reached nine hundred, or that's the number that appears in the papers. The official death toll, however, is meaningless, since only intact bodies are being tallied, not the many that have been incinerated by mobs with gasoline cans. Eighty percent of the official dead are Muslims. The other 20 percent, the Hindus, have, for the most part, been shot by police while they were rioting. That particular figure has been kept low by the fact that the police often stand back and do nothing. "We have no orders to save you," they frequently tell the Muslims who beg them for help.

Cries of genocide, of ethnic cleansing, have gone up around the world, as representatives of human rights organizations begin to arrive, to tour the refugee camps where an estimated 175,000 Muslims without homes are living. The BBC has sent reporters. The outcries and concern have come from any number of countries, though not the United States. There no one seems to be aware that any of this is going on. My country, it appears from over here, is in a vacuum of self-absorption, dissecting and analyzing what happened to it months ago, endlessly, to the exclusion of others. Meanwhile, the anti-Muslim rhetoric that started up then has mutated into something equally savage here.

"It's terrible down there. Don't go in that direction," a woman, the wife of an NGO head and a friend, says when I call. Her husband is touring the camps, where conditions, she reports, are miserable: a single toilet for five hundred people, inadequate food and water, outbreaks of disease, fragile security. At one camp, loudspeakers set up outside the walls by Hindus broadcast the chant "Kill! Kill! Kill!" through the night. The state government, she says, has refused to donate even one rupee toward the camps.

"It's so terrible, I worry all the time," she says. "During the earthquake last year, people could get help. But now people's homes have been burned with their insurance papers inside. The insurance companies will not reimburse them. The companies say, Where are your papers? But people were running for their lives."

Things, she says, are worse for the women. "They are being raped in public. How can human beings behave like animals? I mean, when I talk about this, people assign me all kinds of titles. They say, are you a Christian? I say yes, I'm a Christian, and a Muslim, and every religion." She's paraphrasing Gandhi, when he said, "I am a Muslim, I am a Hindu, I am a Christian, I am a Jew—and so are all of you."

Hers is one of the few Gandhian sentiments I've heard in a while. "I hate Muslims," a teenager spits out when we get to talking at a fair. His face had been boyish in the sideshow light. Now it looks mottled. As the killing continues, at a slower pace but steady, many people here have turned sharply against the Muslims. The complaints they make are the same: Muslims are breeders; they'll overtake Hindus. Muslims living here are not loyal to India; they root for Pakistan in cricket. Muslims think as one. But if that last charge were true, as the author Raj Kamal Jha and others have pointed out, it would, in India, be a supernatural feat. Not just because that would mean 150 million minds had melded, but because it would mean they'd discovered some kind of universal Esperanto. (The 150 million figure is for India alone. The number of Muslims who call India their home is greater than the entire population of Pakistan.)

"A Muslim in Rajasthan who speaks Urdu cannot speak to a Muslim in Tamil Nadu who knows only Tamil," says Jha, who wrote a novel called *Fireproof,* about the violence in Gujarat. "Muslims here don't have a pan-Islamic identity."

Two killed in Gujarat, three, four more. "India is a Hindu country now. Muslims need to leave," a man I've been talking to at a party says angrily, and I recall something else Gandhi said: "An eye for an eye makes the whole world blind." The country, for miles, is in a blind fury.

Dirty Muslims: you cannot trust them. It's horrifying when, in so many of the conversations I have, ugliness cracks veneers. I worry that masks are falling away. I worry that the masks were all along just inventions of mine—projections created in a fog; that my instincts could be this far off; that people I've come to love so deeply could turn out to be this hard.

The fury here is so thick, so very nearly palpable, it never occurs to me that what I'm picking up on is deceptive. There is, in fact, a piece of the puzzle missing, but it'll be years before I'll figure out what it is. I'm simply unable to see even the outlines. Not even the one time the piece appears right in front of me, adamantine, glinting, not even halfway hidden.

LUCKY SINGH PHONES. She asks me over. "Oh, no, Kathy," she says on a terrace edged with flowering bushes. Their sweet scent condenses as the afternoon ebbs. "It has always been a very big problem, the Muslims." Her voice sounds weighted, vowels stretched to hold the sorrows of the world—"Noooo, Kaaathy"—though her voice always does. We stare at the lake across the road as we talk. One lone white bird, skimming the water, pulses with the last of the sun. Noooo, she says, contrary to what I've always heard, the Muslims never coexisted here peacefully. "But the world did not realize they were a problem till something happened in the U.S.," she says, meaning September 11.

"The Muslims are of one mind, to terrorize people," she says, in defense of what's happening in Gujarat. I stare harder, try to keep my tone agreeable. Certainly, Muslims in India have perpetrated terrorist acts, I say; three gunmen in Kashmir just shot thirty-four Hindus to death in an army camp. But she's from Gujarat, I point out. What about how the Muslims there are living: cowed, in squalid camps?

"These people complain about the camps," she says. "But the government is giving them free stay and food. During the day, the people are just playing. Meanwhile, how many Hindu women and girls are being cut up at night and left on the streets by Muslims?" Hindu women? But it's the Muslim women who are being sliced open—"This is not in the papers," Lucky Singh interrupts. Her tone is now frosty, clipped. It's the first time I've heard her sound imperial. "This is from people who were there."

From then on, we're through the looking glass. It's as if she's describing recent history, but with the religious designations reversed. "Kathy, just see how many innocent Hindu children have been tortured. We are angry," she says, even though, in every journalistic report I can come by, it's the Muslim children who've been killed, by Hindu mobs.

The scent from the bushes has grown so sweet it's cloying, is coating the back of my throat. She tells me about the Muslim boy in Gujarat who asked his father for 60 rupees but wouldn't say for what. To buy a dagger, it turned out: "At school, they were learning how to kill Hindus."

"In my father's place, we had Muslims," She says. "As a child, I had a Muslim driver. They are very sweet. These are not Indian Muslims doing this; they are terrorists. They are people who've come across the border." But it's the sweet Indian kind—the good Muslims, let's call them—who are being slaughtered, I start to argue, look over to see her staring at me coldly. Lucky Singh's tender heart is, right now, frozen. What friendship we've had has already cooled on her side. On mine, Lucky Singh's tender heart now seems badly calcified.

HOW COULD SHE—how could so many people there—have believed those things? I'd contemplate that for years. Then I learned Lucky Singh was right about one thing. The reports she was giving me had come from someone who was there: the government. The killings in Gujarat were, by and large, apparently state-sponsored.

Days after the train attack, the newspapers there began running stories about Hindus suffering atrocities at the hands of Muslims. These are the stories that, in some version, had reached Lucky: how Muslim men had snatched Hindu women from the Sabarmati Express and later discarded their horribly mutilated bodies; how the ISI, Pakistan's intelligence agency, had slipped across the border to arm and incite local Muslims.

All hell was breaking loose, the stories implied, and all hell immediately did: the result the government would have had in mind when it likely planted the fabricated articles. The government, in concert with various right-wing groups—the RSS, the Vishwa Hindu Parishad, the Bajrang Dal—then allegedly helped engineer the carnage that followed. Within a day of the train going up in flames, thousands of Hindu villagers were being trucked into the cities and, evidence strongly suggests, equipped with tridents, the symbol of Shiva; with iron rods and rifles and tear gas canisters; with the locations of Muslim homes and businesses; with reminders of the invented atrocities.

"Hanuman went for a walk that day," a speaker at a rally cried in

the days following the fire on the Sabarmati Express. Hanuman, the monkey god, was Rama's majordomo, as everyone in the crowd knew. *"Hanuman got his tail burned. The train was the burnt tail of Hanuman,"* the speaker thundered. *"And who burned it?"*

"Ravana," the crowd shouted. In the Ramayana, Ravana is the demonic king who kidnaps Rama's wife and whom Rama then vanquishes. It was now time, the speaker said, for the Hindus to do the same against their own nefarious Ravana—the Miyan. "Miyan" is a slur for Muslim: roughly, "niggers." It was time, the speaker cajoled, for them to slay Ravana: to kill the Muslims and to dispense with ahimsa, the nonviolence that Gandhi preached. *"Terror was unleashed at the Godhra station because this country follows Gandhi,"* he cried. *"We have to abandon Gandhi."* In truth, they already had.

"We have no orders to save you." The police refrain to the many Muslims who pleaded for help was allegedly made on the orders of the state's chief minister, Narendra Modi, an unsavory character and longtime member of the hate-mongering RSS. In 2005, the United States rejected his request for a visa, citing as the reason his handling of the violence in Gujarat—violence that Modi insists never happened. "It is false propaganda to say that people have died in communal violence. Some one hundred died and all due to police firings," he maintains.

If language is a virus, as one linguistic theory holds, then in Gujarat, it turned malignant. Rhetoric was like contagious prions. It was the external knowledge the neuroscientist Arturo Hernandez had described to me made dangerous. When I read over the reports a human rights organization, the People's Union for Democratic Rights, had filed, which called the events in Gujarat "a systematic attempt to terrorize Muslims," I recalled the point he'd made: "There's language in your head and there's language in the environment. We think of language as ours, but it's not. It's on the news and we speak it with people. We use other people's language all the time. It all makes you question, what is knowledge? What about that—is it in our heads or in our environment?"

If one were to flip through the tenth-grade social studies textbook used in Gujarat schools today, that question takes on a whole other dimension—becomes, for the many Muslims who still live there in reduced circumstances, an urgent one.

"Hitler lent dignity and prestige to the German government," the textbook reads. "He instilled a spirit of adventure in the common people."

IN THE HAVELI, Mrs. Singh and I continue to exempt each other. But then one evening, after I've heard too many bits of stories, I make a caustic remark about Gujarat, can't help it. Neither can she—she shoots her head up, corrects me. *Those Muslims have to leave,*" she says. "*Since Partition, India is a Hindu country. They need to get out. This is not their country.*" Her voice is shot through with iron, like the rough growl a street dog makes if you surprise it. She's unmasked. So is my face, I can feel. After that, whatever friendship had started silently falls away.

· 18 ·

"It is late; let us go home"

 The tourists have returned. The trickle of them that started in the spring is some days now a flood. "No, no, five minutes," one of the young guys who mans my cybercafe says when I stop by late one night and find videshis lined up out the door. "Read the paper. Just five minutes. They will be through then," he says and pushes *Dainik Bhaskar* across the counter. For the next fifteen minutes, I make him translate the parts I can't get. "Heartly," he says—"they celebrated in a heartly way," and I can't even remember the Hindi word now, the next day the concept remains, and how am I going to give this up? I don't care if I'm stiff in this language. It's ozone to the brain, the rarest delight, to be sitting in a late-night cybercafe with a kid who's as amused as you to be reading a newspaper in Hindi together, in the most heartly way.

RUBY AND I DREAM ABOUT how it'll be when we win. "Bring your swimsuits, girls!" I tell her and Priyanka. "There is a swimming

pool at Kumbhalgarh," Ruby clarifies for Priyanka. "And we're going to be in it," I say. Though the truth is, as the date of the contest
approaches, any handicapper of videshi competitions would not be
laying great odds on our team.

The speech, succinct when Ruby first wrote it, now takes years
to say. She can't stop adding to it; neither can half the town. Her latest improvement is a showboating extender, the Hindu New Year's
greeting she composed two months ago, which she's realized she can
get people to listen to now if I say it. This will come right before the
ghazal she recently inserted. The man who runs Ashok Fabrics—our
personal Harry Winston, since he's supplying the outfit—has
thought of a few lines he thinks would be nice. Even Swami-ji has
gotten in on the act. He's proposed the riveting *"I have enrolled in
this contest because I am a student at the institute in Sector Eleven and
because I have seen films there."* Now when I try to say the speech, it
has so many twists and turns, I'm like a folk dancer with ten water
pots on his head and an untied shoelace. I trip, and on the same
lines every time.

"Udaipur, in my next birth I would like to be born here," I'm supposed to declare. The word for "birth" is *janm,* easy enough. But I'll
be flying along, then hit that line and find myself saying, *"Udaipur,
I want to have my next birthday"*—*janmdin*—*"here."* I no sooner
get up than I skid on the unpronounceable *duahuan-ka:* "by your
grace."

"You have not been practicing," Ruby decides whenever she calls
my cell phone to demand a run-through, which she does most
nights. But I have, I have, I tell her. It's just that *janmdin* has become a compulsion: I have to say it.

At a week and a half to go, other complications set in. The tourism board revises the rules. From that date on, no female competi-
tor will be allowed onstage without a male escort. "Maybe Piers
will?" Ruby says hopefully, but Piers won't, even when I beg. Finally,
he comes around when I tell him that Ashok Fabrics will throw in a

maharaja outfit for free. "Okay," he says, "so long as I don't have to say anything," necessitating more rewrites of the speech. *"My humble name, so small and of no consequence, is Kathy Rich, and this guy over here on my left is named Piers Helsen,"* it now begins, after which, it bumps along for another two miles through ghazals, New Year's greetings, and protestations of fervent love for Udaipur.

At one week left, the gods smile, all third of a million. When Ruby calls to demand, "You have been practicing?" I glide through the speech, smoothly, expertly, like a guest with charisma holding forth at a dinner party, a guest who can pronounce *duahuan-ka.* The hours of practice have paid off. I already have the shine of a medalist. "Very good," she says with gruff admiration, and hangs up. Pleased, I start again — *"My humble name, so small and of no consequence"*—when it occurs to me the Singhs don't know anything about the contest, that from downstairs, it must sound like I've been mumbling feverishly to myself for days in my room. Perhaps they think the guy I was sneaking upstairs has thrown me over, and I'm having a fit up here.

"WE ARE HAVING A CHUTTI," Swami-ji says. He and Vidhu need to take a long weekend to go up to Jaipur, scout around for new quarters. The school is clearing out, moving on. This time, the cause isn't cow patty projectiles, but local whispering. Udaipur's the kind of Indian small town where if you so much as talk to the wrong person, your family's reputation is besmirched for the next three generations. Accumulate an institutional record of two death threats and two lawsuits in short order, and you're better off moving.

On the last real chutti we'd had, back at the end of February, I'd wanted to branch out, to take in as much of India as I could. In Benares, the ancient holy city to which I traveled, I saw wondrous things: a dog that was a light frosted blue except for where it had scratched itself pink, a langur scampering among the funeral pyres on the ghats. When I looked back and it was no longer there, I imagined I'd seen a vision of death: a long-tailed, chittering monkey? Made perfect sense.

On this time away, I had no desire to be dazzled. All I wanted now was to burrow farther into Rajasthan, as far in as I still had time for. I made arrangements to stay at a four-hundred-year-old horse estate an hour from town. *"This area is* graam*?"* I asked the driver on the rutted road out. I was surprised to find the word for "rural" coming out of my mouth, even more when he answered, as if I'd made sense. *"Yes, very* graam.*"* As we rumbled by thatched huts still visible in the dusk, I wondered, *What else is in there now?* Worlds within worlds within worlds in my head, none of them convertible.

My room at the estate was over the stables. Mornings I'd wake to the soft nickering of the Marwari stallions, sleek horses with curved ears that touched like lyres. At breakfast, the manager would fan me while I ate. He marveled at how things had changed around here. Ten years ago, the villagers would leave at four in the morning to walk to Udaipur and sell their tomatoes. Now they took the bus. Afterward, I'd return to my room and drift off again in the window seat. Once when I woke, a small, brown owl and a peacock were on a branch outside peering in. A peacock this close-up was shocking: six long feet of vain deep blues and rippling iridescent greens. He soon lost interest in me and fanned his tail for grooming, which had the effect of making the owl look timid and delicate by comparison. The birds were like the two parts of my life as I'd come to define them here, the one in India, the one before: both beautiful, but impossible to think of as related.

I spent afternoons translating Nand's poems into English. Toward dusk, a man in a turban would bring tea. I'd stretch out in the window seat and, for the first time since I'd come, allow myself to fully know how much I missed the States. Before, I couldn't have, it would have sunk me in misery: *still so far to go.* Now I saw that I could leave and come back anytime. I'd proved I could do something like this. I could do it another time, could bust my life open, if I ever had to, if my life ever grew that narrow again.

AT THE DEAF SCHOOL, on my return, the boys are drawing horses. Anukul is absorbed in a book about Hemingway that's written in Hindi. "Ernest Hemingway had many Indian friends," he says.

"He did?"

"Yes, he was friends with the king of Bihar. Once he shot a cigarette out of his mouth." The Dustbin is hunched down in concentration.

"He did?"

"Yes, and he suicided."

"Atmahatya," I said. I'd just learned the word. *Atma:* "soul." *Hatya:* "murder."

"And do you know why he killed himself?"

"Well, because he had a drinking problem—"

"No. Because he had too much royalties." Anukul translates: "'And the publisher gave him too much money for *A Moveable Feast.* Then he couldn't write.' This book, the children gave it to me. It says, 'Don't worry. Be happy.'"

Oh, that would have helped Hemingway, I think. We segue into Hindi. *"My mind is not good because I am alone,"* he says. Rita, as per Indian custom, went to her parents' to have the baby. Anukul now has a son, but a theoretical one. It'll be weeks before she returns.

"Why don't Renee and I take you to a restaurant?" I say. He looks uneasy, wants to know why am I suggesting something like that. Restaurants are suspect here. Because how do you know they're not doing something taboo out of sight, like putting food that was on someone else's plate on yours? I appreciate this position, but it creates a dilemma. In my New York soul, I'm unsure how I'm supposed to make friends with people who won't go to restaurants.

"Okay," Anukul finally agrees. *"But I will not use a knife and fork."*

We continue to catch up while all around, pink, green, cerulean horses form. I am looking *sundar,* "lovely," he says with brotherly regard. It's his opinion I've lost weight at the haveli. And what about him? How does he look? Oh *sundar, sundar,* I reply, and he agrees. "I think I am photogenic," he says. At the end of the hour, a woman, a teacher, appears in the doorway, makes an announcement. "Now we will play," he says.

Out in the courtyard, sunlight is filtering down through the canopy, giving everything the consistency of memory. A volleyball net's been set up for a game. The teachers and I take white plastic chairs. In front of us, on the ground, an excited group of boys is expressing the sincere hope that Australia will get trounced in that night's cricket. Once a kid's written "Australia" on his palm, I have no trouble following the sentences that fly through the air. The boys' hands are balletic, sure; they swing out in graceful arcs. Out here, their hands are so different from the way they are in the classroom, where the signing is determined, exact and choppy; staccato. I'm remarking on that as Anukul looks up from another book he's gotten absorbed in, an illustrated guide to American Sign a friend of mine's just sent over. The two things converge in my head—Anukul, the cricket fans' hands—as he sighs and says with detectable sorrow, "My children do not know grammar, and I cannot teach them." I glance at the kids. No grammar? But grammar is the tracks of a language, and the boys in front of me are speeding on greased rails. No grammar? But the boys, in complicated bullet train sentences, are prophesying Australia's demise.

Players take their places on opposite sides of the net. The cricket fans settle down. I continue thinking about their hands, about something else Anukul said not long ago: "The children have so many words even we don't know. A suspicion has begun to prod me, that the kids have their own language—that they've made one up, are making one up. All year, perhaps, I've been watching a language form and not known it. The idea of a hidden world laid out in plain sight fascinates me, and I'd give anything to know if it's true. But the moment passes. The canopy filters the light but not the heat. In this densely hot afternoon, verification—of anything —seems impossible.

The moment recedes, Australia is trampled, and for weeks, months, long after I return, the question continues to nag at me: But is that what I really saw? Were they?

"OH, POOR DEAF children always do that," a man I'm having a business lunch with is saying. This is now maybe two months after the volleyball game, not long after I'm back in the States. I'm still mute and reduced: my old personality is no longer there to inhabit, and I can't find a new one. I'm gawky and lost when I meet friends, don't get jokes; it's embarrassing. Everything intimidates me, even my old apartment, which looks as if it's been decorated by someone else, someone smarter and more appealing.

"They always create language," the man says, he's read something about it, and I'm amazed to find that any of the mysteries of India are approachable from here. I set out to learn all I can.

The first time anyone documented the fact that deaf children who've grown up isolated will, if they're brought together with other kids like them, begin to invent a language was in Nicaragua, several years after the Sandinista revolution, in 1993. An American linguist named Judy Kegl had gone down to spend time at a deaf school that Hope Somoza, the dictator's wife, had opened sixteen years before, in 1977.

Up until then, education for people who were hearing impaired had been limited in Nicaragua, available only to the few who'd been lucky enough to make their way to the small number of schools for the deaf in existence. When the first kids arrived at this new school, they'd been living, as far as communication went, fairly solitary lives. They'd had, for the most part, no education and minimal contact with other deaf people. They communicated the way children who've been raised like this do: using "home signs." Called *mimicas* in Spanish, these are crude pantomimes that convey basic desires—*eat, ice cream, drink*—the equivalent of pidgin. The signs will get the job done, but they won't develop into a language—not without engagement with another home signer—which means kids forced to get by on these signs alone will, by about age ten, be stranded permanently without full language. Critical periods of language acquisition exist for both the hearing and the deaf. The consequences of this can be grim: a broader life curtailed, intelligence stunted—for the development of cognitive abilities depends on language developing as well.

You can find deaf people who got trapped in that stage in a lot of poor countries. In Managua, they're almost always over age forty-five. "In Managua today, you get the ones, forty-five, fifty years old and above, who can't sign at all," Ann Senghas, head of the Language Acquisition and Development Research Laboratory at Barnard College, was telling me when we met several years after I'd had that lunch. Senghas first went to Nicaragua as Judy Kegl's assistant in 1989, when Kegl visited a vocational training institute for the deaf. Senghas has been back a number of times since. "People that age were all separated when they were young. They still use home signs," she said. She was trying to illustrate for me how, twenty-five years or so after the school opened, you can observe how the collective process of language evolution was pushed ahead with each class. The stages the school's language went through are as profoundly marked as geologic layers.

"Then you find the people who are thirty-five to forty-five today. They were the first pack of children who entered the school in seventy-seven, and they're a huge jump from nonsigners. They have a lot of vocabulary. They have a lot of structure that holds their sentences together.

"Then you go to the twenty-five-year-olds, and suddenly the language they're using becomes an easier one to learn. It's organized. It has nouns and verbs, and it has morphology, and it starts to look like a sign language."

Go to the little kids, she said, and you'll find a language that's really smart and fast. "They have more signs per second, more prepositions per second: they're packing in more information."

Kegl, on her first visit to the school, had begun to make similar comparisons, though without fully understanding what she was seeing. At first it seemed as if everyone at the school was using only the most fragmented, rudimentary signs, but before long she realized that she'd gotten that impression because she'd been talking only to the older kids. Among the youngest, the signing was a whole other creation—far more nuanced, far more dimensions, complete with tense markers and proper word order. She began to question what had caused these differences and soon arrived at an answer: the pidgin of the initial group of students had evolved into a creole among the ones after that, and from there, group by group, it had grown into a full, vibrant language. That was obvious by simply watching the various classes.

All this had happened in only sixteen years, without intervention from the teachers, who'd initially attempted to hold classes in signed Spanish. When word got out of this spontaneous invention of a language, the linguistic community was riveted.

"The Nicaraguan case is absolutely unique in history," the linguist Steven Pinker told a reporter from the *New York Times*. "We've been able to see how it is that children—not adults—generate language, and we have been able to record it happening in great scientific detail. And it's the first and only time that we've actually seen a language being created out of thin air." Senghas, quoted in the same article, likened being there to being present at the big bang.

Inevitably, perhaps, sniping started up in the deaf community.

When Kegl brought some of the Nicaraguan students to tour a prominent American school for the deaf, remarks were made about her "dog-and-pony show." Some people alleged that this wasn't any discovery, that what she'd done was teach them ASL. "Do you know how long it takes to teach someone American sign?" Senghas scoffed when we spoke. She had short, dirty-blond hair and a manner of speaking that was both hip and down-to-earth. What was her name sign in Nicaragua? I asked. "Oh, it's embarrassing." She laughed. "I used to have one of those rat-tail cuts. That's my name sign: 'Rat Tail.'"

Senghas has returned to Managua often to document the language as it has evolved. In the beginning, she says, this was like "trying to hit a moving target. Changes just zoomed through." She recalled how one year, everyone still signed using only intransitive verbs: *"Man give . . . cup . . . woman receive."* By the next time she visited, the sentences had acquired syntax and transitive verbs; the signers had discovered the advantages of transitive objects: *"Man give cup to woman."* Observations could now be more complex.

Some of these changes happened so quickly, it was like watching a language evolve in hypertrophic fast-forward. Once, after a lecture during which Senghas described one change she'd witnessed, a historical linguist told her that "it represented five hundred years of normal change in five years," she said.

Senghas has an ability, perhaps honed from spending so much time around children, to make complex concepts readily accessible. "It's so clear these changes came from the younger children," she said. "Normally, kids are exposed to all kinds of sounds that aren't language—dogs barking, typically—and they won't try to sort those out. But they will try to sort out language." This is, she observed, a natural impulse. "So the new kids come into this world of signers in the school, and they see those kids doing something and they learn it quickly. But it isn't quite sorted out, so each new group continues to organize it. And each year, another fifteen kids enter the school, so each year you get another iteration of learning." She used the analogy of cleaning your room. "You start to put things in boxes, and those boxes start to take on categories. The children build categories."

The categories they build are grammar, a grammar that's entirely different from the one present in the spoken language that surrounds them. Signed grammar is as different from spoken grammar as English is from Navajo. ASL, in fact, has more in common morphologically with Navajo than it does with English.

Often, however, well-meaning teachers in deaf schools will insist that their students use grammar that the instructors recognize as proper: the one they know from the language they speak. This kind of signing is called "manually coded" English or French or Thai, and it is, to deaf people, stilted and artificial. It doesn't come naturally to kids. It doesn't take into account corporal factors, doesn't incorporate the dimension of space. It may even stunt academic growth. In Ireland in the 1960s, deaf students were required to switch from Irish Sign Language to an English-coded system. Immediately after, their literacy rates plummeted.

"It happens everywhere," Senghas said. "It's hard for the teachers to understand that this other sign, the one the kids use—one they're only going to get from a bunch of other kids who may look like scrappy street kids—that it's going to enable them to have cognitive development." I'd just finished telling her about the school in Udaipur, about Anukul's deep dedication to his kids, but also that I suspected he'd been using manual Hindi. That might have explained the discrepancy I'd seen between the more ponderous signing in the classroom and the bullet train gestures outside.

"If the kids' sentences when they were with him followed Hindi word order, that would be a pretty good clue," she said. As far as I could tell, they had.

We talked some more about the Udaipur school, which had been founded about the same time as the one in Managua, and then I asked her a question I'd never come up with an answer for: had those kids, did she think, invented their own language?

She was, she said, logically enough, unable to tell me from so far away. She suggested some questions I could try on Anukul over the phone, inquiries that might provide illumination. Nuanced inquiries that the more I thought about them, the more I was certain wouldn't survive the complications of long-distance and barely matching tongues. I explained that the questions would probably derail before they got to France. Well, then, she said, there was really no other way but to observe firsthand. To go back. I was on the Internet the next day, comparing flights. The decision might have appeared spontaneous, but it was anything but. India, for once, hadn't reached over and pulled me across. For four years, in some part of my mind, this is all I'd been planning every day.

"Yes, why not?" Anukul said when I phoned to try to explain what I wanted to do, when I called to ask if I could barge in and disrupt his classroom one more time. Our conversation was brief. He found it staticky. "You are sounding like an American," he complained.

· 19 ·

"You go on; we are coming"

 The day before the videshi contest, Udaipur is rolling in festivals. Today's, the kickoff to a week's worth to follow, has thrown the institute into another chutti. At 11 A.M., then, I'm free to go to Ruby's. The costumes are in: massive, ten-pound Rajasthani wedding outfits, Piers's request. Mine is spectrally pink, with blinking additions of glitter fringe. His is more sedate, except for the turban, which is a whopper. The costumes and speech are now under control. The only advance work left is styling.

At Ruby's, the kids aren't around. Neither is her husband Rajendra. Cleared of three-quarters of the family, the apartment looks airy. Priyanka and Ruby place me in a chair and, from the black shag couch, coolly appraise my face, my physique, my chances. They trade judgments I can't catch, then every so often Ruby disappears into the back room. One time she reemerges with a stack of shawls; another trip, with silk pouches that contain numberless golden forehead ornaments, miles of bangles, tangles upon tangles of black-threaded pendants. She upends the bags one by one. Damn, no earrings. "The kids were playing with them. They must have put them somewhere," she says, lifting a curtain to see if the earrings might have migrated back there. They haven't, so we give the business of adornments a rest while she decides what she'll wear as festival announcer that night. Hauling suitcases from the bedroom, she turns layer after layer of precisely folded silks into piles of color-burst clouds. "I have two hundred and fifty saris," she says, "and I can never find one to wear."

After the matter of her outfit has been decided, we return to mine. "You put this, and this, and this," she says, loading me up with anklets and head baubles, with waist chains, bangles, bottles of dark nail polish, tubes of lipsticks in shades so severe, they make my *gori*-white face appear shrunken. Once the entire getup is in place, I look like a *hijra,* an Indian cross-dressing eunuch, although Priyanka and Ruby are dazzled. "Oh, so beautiful," they murmur to each other. "Can you believe it?" They demand an immediate dress rehearsal. Standing and balancing myself against the sewing machine, I proclaim my deep hope for rebirth in Udaipur, evade the birthday trap, smoothly round the curve into the ghazal, stop cold, glare. My head coach is laughing so hard at my accent, she's slamming sideways into Priyanka.

"Ruby, you are not advancing the cause," I tell her. "No, no, go on," she says between gasps, and I finish with only two nearly undetectable snags. We are the champions. We relax after that, kick back and gossip. "Don't tell anyone. They will think it's your fault," Ruby warns when I describe how a music teacher made a pass at me, then rushes to tell Priyanka in Hindi.

By lunchtime, the heat has made us stupid. We call it a wrap. When I go out, only the stalwart or desperate are still on the streets. Back in the zenana, I lie on the bed with the air cooler positioned so that it makes my salwar pants billow. Till the heat puts me out, I practice some more. Once again, I cannot say *duahuan-ka*.

THE NEXT MORNING at school, it's just me and the boys. Helaena was supposed to have lined up a weekly guest, but it's now been weeks, and she's never come back. With no one on the docket and an empty hour ahead, I appoint myself the last weekly guest of the year. A student! Swami-ji and Vidhu giggle at this inversion of hierarchy. They sit up straight as I take the teacher's chair and describe in Hindi the life I had before: how I was a writer and before that, an editor, whose work revolved around taking authors to lunch and making investigative forays to island resorts and sometimes bearing witness to the decline of postpubescent models who could not stay away from the beer. Or that's my talk in a nutshell, and all of it's news to the guys. In the formality of the Indian classroom, wide swaths of our backgrounds have never been discussed.

"*Then one time,*" I say, beginning another story from the vaguely louche existence I led, aiming to get them on the edge of their seats, when I see that a blankness has come onto their faces; their bodies are sagging into inattention: *What thing is this?* Although my sentences are lining up in correct Hindi, none of this makes any sense. The world I came from cannot be dragged into Antriksh Flats, so I bring the talk to a close and ask, as a proper weekly guest should, whether they have any questions. Swami-ji has one: "*Kathy-ji. Have you spoken to Helaena?*"

"*Sorry,*" I say with a grin, "*but I don't speak Hindi,*" and as the last weekly guest class winds up, we both chortle till our shoulders shake. It's Swami-ji's kind of joke, even if he's not precisely sure what it means.

ONE LATE AFTERNOON soon after, wedding shawl planted on my head, I creep out the door of the haveli, hoping that, since I'm supposed to look like a Rajasthani woman, I'll make it to a rickshaw unnoticed. Fat chance. Because actually what I look like is not so much that, but a large, motorized confectioner's cake gliding pinkly down the street. I get as far as Lakshmi's General Store next door before I'm spotted.

We've all just recovered, the street and I, from the time last week when I left the house attired, uncustomarily, in a fancy sari. On any given day, my every Western move inspires loud play-by-play commentary from here to the Clock Tower, but now the sight of me attempting to sneak along like this causes busloads of people to appear. My progress is stalled as a crowd forms and onlookers shout out questions. Other bystanders provide live-at-five commentary: *"Yes, she is wearing Rajasthani clothing." "Yes, tonight, at the puppet museum."* I reach up to make adjustments to the shawl, and a beaming woman at the window above Lakshmi's calls down. She flicks her fingers in the air to illustrate her point. *"Yes,"* I shout up, *"I decided to go with nail polish for the big event." "No, I don't usually wear it." "No, you're right."*

I've shaken the crowd, am nearly halfway to the rickshaw stand, when there before me, cresting a hill, is a rabble of festivalgoers, all women dressed vaguely like me, all balancing statues of the goddess Parvati on their heads. We stop dead in our tracks. Their mouths drop. Then shrieking with glee, several women grab my wrists, and as the Parvatis tipple side to side, they pull me along. I'm saved only by the intervention of a quick-thinking rickshaw man. "Madam, you are looking very smart," he says, staring into the mirror as we proceed in the direction of the museum.

Once there, I find Piers moodily wandering the grounds. He looks pained in his wedding suit, as if his curled-back Aladdin shoes are pinching his feet. "Um, yes, well," he says with British reserve when I exclaim over his eyeliner mustache, say he's looking very smart. You can tell he'd like to strangle me for roping him into this.

A man from the tourism board shows us to our seats. We're in the front row of bleachers that were constructed for the evening out of stacked planks and white sheets. We can see everyone up close as they arrive. There's the travel agent's daughter, Tui, who used to answer my India questions. A number of past weekly guests. The guy from the candy shop. Just about everyone I've ever met. Priyanka and Ruby hurry over, so excited they're squeaking. They take the sheeted plank behind us. Renee arrives with her camera and won't stop snapping pictures, which puts Piers further out of sorts. But then accidentally I spill my Coke into the side of his shoe, and that, strangely, improves his mood.

The bleachers fill, all but the competitors' row, which remains empty except for us. Then twenty minutes before showtime, the tourism board guy leads two foreign women in and seats them beside me. One's Canadian; one's English of Indian descent. They're both wearing pink veils. "It was really hard to find these," the Canadian one says. "Where'd you get yours?" We live here, I answer. "Oh. You live here," she says, implying hometown advantage. Hey, where's your male escort? I'm tempted to ask, but I stay collected. The brown-skinned English woman complains that the tourism desk asked twice where she was from, implying she was a ringer. She's not. She's wearing sneakers.

No contest, these two, but at ten minutes and counting, a spectacular double-cross is revealed. Ramesh from Ashok Fabrics—our patron—shows up in a long pink scarf and turban, with a magnificently outfitted Japanese customer in tow, and proceeds brazenly to the videshi section. "Yeah, what country are you from?" I lean across the Canadian to hiss.

The announcer comes on. We tense, ready to take the stage. But no, first, we will all enjoy a long warm-up extravaganza—the broken-glass dance, then the peacock dance, then the interminable fire-shooting-from-the-head dance—while I mumble the speech furiously under my breath and a Mewar channel cameraman stares, unsure whether to film that or not. Priyanka passes me a note.

"Don't do that with your skirt," it reads, meaning clutch one side when you walk, what I'd done when I'd gone to greet Tui.

Then the slinky snake girls salute Shiva, then the announcer says, "Ladies and gentlemen . . ." We're on. I do that with my skirt. The videshis are lined up in order of appearance. Piers and I are at the back. We're last, which is long enough for me to flood my head with oxygen, to feel I've left my body and am riding the lights, to tell myself it hasn't all come down to this one moment. Except it has. Then the announcer is signaling, and without benefit of locomotion, we're in front of the mike. I compose myself and drop the side of my skirt and try not to think of Ruby and Priyanka staring. I calm my breath and begin: *"My humble name, so small and of no consequence . . ."* And the speech bolts, it takes off, the sucker is carrying me, for a miraculous thing has occurred: after hours of listening to Lata Mangeshkar, her grace has somehow transferred over. The New Year's greeting is butter as I glide through it, head high, and after that it's straight on for the ghazal and morning. I'm speeding toward the end, blessed and possessed, the speech now the rushing essence of every sound I've learned here, I'm compressed down into the lights and the Hindi, right up to the moment one tiny lumpen word appears on the track, one small putrefyingly stubborn word, and I'm flipped off course. Sent flying, kicking, through the air.

I blow it.

Right there, right in front of everyone I know, on the home television sets of people who know me and I don't recognize, I blow the whole thing. Because once I've caught on that word, the whole speech falls apart. I stand there and, with a roar in my ears, whir through the same four words, like one monster-size replication of a cake that's got a broken tape recording inside.

This goes on for a while. No one knows what to do. Till some compassionate soul out there on the planks begins to clap, and to my horror, applause spreads through the crowd. Show's over. The announcer is turning toward us. Desperation or the grace of Lata Mangeshkar clears my head. I know what to do.

"No, no, no," I say, smiling, leaning into the mike. *"Now I will sing you a song,"* and I belt out "Yara Seeli Seeli."

All Indian peoples, you better believe, laughed that night. But after the votes were finally tallied, Piers and me, we had the last laugh. For when the verdict came in, we'd taken it by a mile. Kumbhalgarh was Ruby's. We'd won.

"YOU WILL COME DOWN HERE NOW." A week and a half left. The downstairs grandmother and I are alone in the haveli. A marriage proposal for the oldest girl, a sterling offer, has come in. The family's gone off to meet the fiancé's parents, negotiate details of the dowry—get those swindlers to back off their demands for first-class AC bus transport for forty people, that's what Mr. Singh had said. Up until the moment of their departure, the grandmother had been a tiny blur, a shadow with eyes peering out her door whenever I came in. Then the family took off and the main entry door was locked and she immediately emerged onto the second floor as a purple-saried, bucktoothed wrath of god.

"Get down here right now," she's calling huskily up the stairs, using a verb tense I've never heard live before. The second person singular, "used with loved ones and small children," the textbook instructs—also for slapping around daughters-in-law. The grandmother doesn't know how else to address a younger woman who's living in the house. She hasn't left the haveli in fifty years. *You wanted to blend in, be treated like anyone else,* I remind myself as I skid into the hall. *There you go; now you are.*

"Sit," the grandmother commands when I arrive downstairs. I fall into a chair. I'm getting the hang of female hierarchy. When an even older stepgrandmother came to visit last week, I dropped down and brushed the air above her toes, knew to without thinking. The woman was about eighty-five; for the first thirty years of her life, the

Raj was in charge. She was so incredulous to find a foreigner speaking Hindi and behaving normally like this, she expressed her exuberance by banging on my head and punching my arm throughout the conversation. I think we were having a lovefest, though maybe not.

"I thought I lost the dog," the grandmother from the first floor says now with agitation. *"But I looked under the bed, and I found him."* She asks for 100 rupees for the dinner she's cooked, the usual meal charge. I explain that I've made weekly payment arrangements with the family, stand up to go. *"Sit,"* she rasps.

"You will wait till the milkman comes," she says. *"You will go down and fetch the milk."* She bangs a metal bucket for emphasis. I try not to jump. *"My son is gone. We are all alone,"* she says nervously, mostly to herself. She probably went from her father's house to an arranged marriage to living with her son without once spending a night alone. No telling what's lurking outside the front door. Or what variety of stranger she has before her in the house. Up till now, we've never spoken.

I smile to try to calm her. I ask her questions to salve my nerves, and little by little a fast-shuttling discussion in Hindi begins. She's lived here ever since her marriage, for a time on this floor; the upstairs used to be closed; her husband died when he was thirty-nine; that's his picture there; she had to pump water today even though her knees are bad; she came from Gandhinagar in Gujarat; it used to be beautiful there, but now it's spoiled (*bigaad;* there's that word again); so much fighting. So many deaths.

And it's one perfect run; one immaculate conversation. Everything goes through, and she's not adjusting down. I really think I'm there. I want this language to go on forever. I can roll in it. I can slide, I can tumble downhill like there's no tomorrow, even if there is, and it's all just so fine.

"MADAM, I DO NOT see your name here," the man behind the desk at the swank Kumbhalgarh hotel had said when conquering

Team Videshi pulled up. The winner's circle weekend had begun on a low note. Turned out first prize wasn't a night at the fancy resort we'd all just assumed it was, but rather at the place down the street—the one with lackluster staff, the one that looked as if convention-planner architects had whipped it up in their spare time. Beyond the terrace, soaring girders were supported by metal poles strategically placed so they truncated the scenery. Over dinner, you glimpsed the mountains in triangles, but no matter. We were thrilled to be here, Ruby, Priyanka, and I. Piers, who'd been dragged along, was a good sport till he struck up an acquaintance with a member of the staff and disappeared for much of the weekend. Ruby, Priyanka, and I were sharing the spoils-of-victory room down the hall. Lodging for Piers had not been included in the bargain, but I'd happily sprung for it.

Giddiness buoyed my coaches and me through numerous side trips into the cultural discordance zone. "Hope you girls brought your bathing suits!" I exclaimed when we reached our room. But as I struggled into one I'd picked up at Bapu Bazaar that was proportioned like a fat diver's suit, I vaguely registered that they hadn't unlatched their suitcases. I went on ahead, and after twenty minutes in the pool, I looked up and understood why: there were the girls, wading into the water in their street wear, their salwars blowing up around them like flotation devices. It was my gaffe not to have realized that Priyanka and Ruby, good Hindu women that they were, couldn't go prancing around in a bathing suit. It was also my strong suspicion that neither of them had ever been in a swimming pool before.

Priyanka, once in, took to squealing and flicking water, which is how women in Hindi movies behaved in pools. It was slightly annoying, especially since I had to flick back till she got it out of her system. Once she had, the three of us did what people in pools throughout the world do: we stood against the wall and tested water resistance with our arms and talked. "Your teeth are *nakli*?" Priyanka stopped the conversation to ask, staring hard at mine. *Nakli* meant "fake." I flew my hand up to my mouth. "Nakli! No! Why?"

She couldn't take her eyes off my mouth. "I was thinking Americans have false teeth," she said.

I tried to speak without moving my lips. "Why? Does something look wrong with my teeth?"

"*Haan,*" she said. "Because our—how do you say?—gums are pink, and yours are white. That's why I was thinking your teeth are nakli."

"Look," Ruby said, bringing the discussion to a close, "the bearers are coming with chai." We seated ourselves on submerged concrete barstools, and once the men had arranged the tea and samosas on in-pool tables, we asked them to take our pictures. Priyanka made me cover my chest with a towel. We ate samosas, then went for a stroll through the water. When we were back on the stools, I filled them in on swimming pool etiquette. For instance, I told Ruby, it was considered bad form to masticate snacks and swish them out through your teeth. We had more tea and lazily floated our hands with the pampered assurance of maharanis.

The hours continued to spin us into a dream. Up above the terrace that night, one of Nand's ten moons, perhaps the most brilliant, the *nashratn,* "jewel of the night," was shining down as we ate dinner. Piers had joined us, and afterward we all tiptoed down through the dewy grass and arranged lawn chairs in a line by the pool. We told jokes across the various voids of background—Brit, Indian, American—and pretended to laugh at each other's. I told one about an old couple that ended in the punch line "Fuck or drown," and Priyanka laughed hysterically, but when she translated it for Ruby, she made it *"Fuck or down."* Piers and I went all out for Ruby's jokes, even though we couldn't make heads or tails of them, but the mountains were silver in the jeweled moonlight, and we were all feeling heady from the air that smelled like jasmine. The hours spun along, and when we got up to leave, a light flashed on behind the pool. A bearer who'd been stationed on the lawn had been waiting to escort us to our rooms.

The next morning, the female members of Team Videshi elected to hang out in the room. We flipped on Indian MTV the minute we woke up—Macy Gray and Train, back-to-back Bollywood choreographed numbers that blurred into background sound, except when film star Hrithik Roshan appeared and Priyanka went on point, turning up the volume. She was wearing my jeans. Cut loose from home, she'd asked if she could. We'd taken a number of souvenir pictures.

I went into the bathroom to brush my teeth. Ruby's brown salwar kameez was stretched out to dry over half the tub. I climbed back into bed. Ruby and Priyanka were lolling in the other one. We talked and talked, like girls the morning after a slumber party, which is pretty much what we were. *"Hindimein, Hindimein,"* I croaked periodically in my morning voice: let's move this over into Hindi. Priyanka and Ruby were once again speaking it only with each other. *"I can, you know,"* I said with hurt dignity. They capitulated, and it was three-way, slow-going Hindi for twenty minutes, then they switched over on me again, fell into a round of fast talk between themselves. I lay back on the bed and listened. *"Something is wrong with his mind."* Shahid was being his usual annoying self. I nearly made it to the final thought in *"We were in the kitchen, and he wanted me to cook, and . . ."* but then the sentence became static, and I was left hanging. My comprehension continued on like this. I'd get all the way to the end of one of Ruby's shaggy-dog stories, when the listening device in my head would short out, at the precise moment Ruby and Priyanka would shriek and bang the bed. I kept being torn between insisting on Hindi and following an anecdote to the end.

English eventually started up again. Ruby and Priyanka peppered me with questions, aired mystifications over Western habits that had been weighing on them. "How can couples kiss like that in American movies?" "What was the meaning of so many X-rated movies in America?" "Why was Renee's underwear so big?" Frequently, when you went to visit, Renee had a set of undies drying in the bathroom. "Because it's old ladies' underwear," I explained.

"Nachizkanam Kathy Rich hai." Priyanka was standing on the bed in my jeans, unsteadily reprising my winning speech into the pink plastic microphone Ruby had brought as a pool toy. Ruby grabbed the mike, started in on a ghazal, remembered another fact about her marriage she wanted to convey to Priyanka. Midway through, she moaned, "Why can't Indian women live alone?"

"Oh—the World Trade Center," I said sadly. In a Bollywood round-the-world montage that had come onscreen, a couple were dancing in what looked like New Jersey with the Twin Towers rising behind them.

"The World Trade Center," I said softly. "See?" I wondered again what the altered cityscape would look like. An amputation? Or, worse, unremarkable at first, and then you remembered? I wondered whether people who'd lived through the attack chronologically were still flooded with sorrow whenever the World Trade Center appeared unexpectedly in a movie. Here, where this thing had occurred in shuffled time (it had happened, then it hadn't; could be made believably unreal, then you remembered and it happened again), the sight was a fresh shock each time.

Priyanka regained her balance. She bent down to examine the screen. "*That* is New York?" she said with interest. She had her hopes pinned on Chirag. All weekend, Ruby had been starting sentences with "Priyanka, when you go to New York," then crying out, "But *I* want to go there. How do *I* go?" We talked some more. Ruby's attention strayed. "Britney Spears is having very Indian looks," she said, examining the screen.

"Britney Spears?" I frowned at the Britney Spears swingy blond hair and pert American cheerleader nose. "How can you say she looks Indian?"

"Is true," Priyanka concurred. "She is having very Indian looks."

"But how? Why?"

"Haan," Ruby said. "Because her looks are very Indian." End of that discussion. No further explanation forthcoming.

Then we all got back into our bathing attire and went down to the pool, and Ruby trudged away from where we stood in the shallow end. She waded too far out. "Priyanka, I am drowning," she kept calling, till we looked over and saw she was. I swam into the deep end and pushed her to safety. We ate more samosas that we'd won, and drank more chai that we'd earned; we flicked the water a bit, and then it was noon. On the jeep ride home, we were a jumble of legs in the back.

INDIA AND PAKISTAN were teetering on the edge the week I left India. MUSHARRAF WILL UNLEASH A STORM! the newspapers in Delhi were screaming the morning I got to the city. The troops at the border were poised at brinkmanship. Hospitals were gearing up to receive casualties. My brother in Pennsylvania had e-mailed to say the State Department was advising all U.S. citizens to clear out immediately. First I'd learned of that.

"Oh, that's how we always hear about things, too," a diplomat I had dinner with said and laughed. "We only ever know what's happening in India when people in the States write and tell us." She'd looked slightly sheepish at my mention of the State Department communiqué. It had been, um, she said, a mistake. They hadn't meant for it to go out, but when someone accidentally sent it around, everyone just decided to take a holiday and collect the pay. India, the feeling was, was grandstanding, in part to force America to take diplomatic sides. Instead, half the Americans here were quickly packing up and leaving. Panicked businessmen who hadn't heard that the order was the result of a snafu were rushing to get their families onto planes. You couldn't get a flight out now if you tried.

Earlier, I'd been planning to wait to make travel arrangements, was thinking of staying on till my visa ran out, but something had happened the week before that had made me hurry to secure a ticket. The school year had ended. My old life had found me, in the form of a magazine editor who'd e-mailed to see if I'd go on the road with a clothing designer and write a profile. The designer and I were down in Gujarat, where she was talking to fabric makers and I was numbly surveying the aftereffects of the carnage. On the walls of some of the burned-out stalls near the university where we stayed, you could see the claw marks desperate shopkeepers had made after they'd been locked inside and firebombed. I asked students what they had seen. One said coolly that they'd barred the gate to one of the school's Muslim gardeners who was trying to flee a mob. "We didn't want those people inside," she said.

My mood, then, was already somber when my cell phone rang unexpectedly. It was, of all people, the father of Vikram, the Brahmin physicist, the one I'd traveled through the desert with. "Where are you?" his father barked. Before, he'd been soft-spoken. "Your uncle, everyone, has been looking for you everywhere. Your father is not doing well." I hurried off the phone to buy a plane ticket. If Vikram's father hadn't tracked me down, I would have been stranded and missed being with my father in the final week of his life.

My last full day in India, I took a rickshaw out to the Gandhi museum. The designer was launching a line made of khadi, the rough-spun cotton that Gandhi had turned into such an enduring symbol of national independence that for years the Indian flag had at its center a *charkha,* a spinning wheel. Politicians still wear khadi to give speeches as a visual reminder of the transformative self-reliance movement Gandhi set in motion. Learn to spin your own cotton, he'd urged Indians in the days when the British Raj still had them under its thumb. Spinning became a gesture of defiance, an act of nonviolent aggression—a way for people to spurn foreign imports, demonstrate they could stand on their own. This symbolism and history had appealed to the designer, Christina Kim, who applies an archivist's intelligence to her work. So on my last day in India, I headed to the Gandhi museum to get a quote.

Of course I could interview her, the museum's director said when I asked for permission, in Hindi. By now, aside from when I was forced out of it to do my work, that's pretty much all I spoke. She'd be happy to talk, she said, setting aside an antique pen she'd been cataloging. But what about this—she had a better idea. It was Friday afternoon: did I know I was in luck?

As it happened, each Friday, the day Gandhi was killed, a group of freedom fighters, now very old, met on the lawn outside his memorial to spin khadi in his honor. The woman wondered: would I like to meet them? And she stopped what she was doing and walked me a half-hour through Delhi rush-hour traffic. The woman seemed every bit as generous as you'd expect the director of the Gandhi museum to be, but all the same, I had a suspicion she wouldn't have suggested this if I'd approached her in English. Many of the freedom fighters, being the age they were, couldn't speak English, either because theirs had rusted shut, or because they'd never been able to.

We arrived at a great lawn, where under a peepul tree, seven old men and women were seated next to a dozen children—orphans, the director explained. They were all leaning down over charkhas, spinning. The woman escorted me to where they sat. *"This is Kathy-ji,"* she said. *"She speaks very good Hindi. She just has some trouble with gender."* She gave me a teasing smile. Would they mind, she asked, if I joined them and learned to spin?

An old woman in a rough-woven sari patted the space beside her on the mat. She welcomed me in Hindi. A boy handed me a wheel, and without much success, I gave it a try. The woman and I fell to talking. She rocked gently to the motion of the spindle, legs extended. From time to time, she broke into the high, gleeful Indian laugh I'd grown to love. The sound of it made me mournful.

"Yes, oh yes, one time I met Gandhi-ji," she said. *"At this time, I was*

a student. Gandhi-ji came to the university. This was near where I lived. He was giving a speech. I was at the front of the crowd. Afterward I was talking to my friend, and when I looked up, he was beside me. Gandhi-ji put his hand on my head and leaned over, and he said . . ." And of course, at that moment, the listening device went out. I knew enough not to ask her to repeat herself; that never worked. People would always begin at another place in the story. I nodded in time, to keep her going, and tried to piece together what I'd missed. I couldn't. She'd moved along. And this kept happening: she'd lead up to what was surely going to be an extraordinary revelation, then, wham, just roiling sound. It was like watching a television that kept sliding off the channel. It was tormenting.

I hung in, though, and after a while, she told me she'd only ever worn khadi. Partly because by doing that she was fighting pollution, partly because of the spirit it represented, but really, she said, there was a deeper reason. I asked what it was.

"Well," she said, *"it's like if you cook a meal yourself. If someone else does, if a servant or a restaurant cooks it, then the meal is different and useful, but in the end, it's nothing you remember. If someone else prepares it, there's no emotional attachment. No love comes. But if you make the thing yourself, it's from the heart.*

"If someone else has made the cloth, what you have will be perfect, but in time you throw it away." She flipped the manufactured thing away with her hand.

"If someone else has made the cloth, then it won't matter to you," she said. *"But if you make it yourself, it will have knots and imperfections, but you won't care. You will hold on to it."*

I thought of all the loopy sentences I'd constructed that year, all the conversations that had been knotted and imperfect and that, all the same, I'd keep forever. And I was cheered some to realize this, but on this, the very last day, all that was, was consolation. I wanted more than anything I ever had to stay, to just keep on going. The language, in the past week, had gained even more momentum. I could speed now through that translucent green place anytime I wanted.

In that last conversation, on that last day, I kept writing down new words as they came up—*vikriti,* evil; *pavitra,* pure—on reflex, out of stubbornness, with rising anger. All the potential of the words was gone. They filled me with sorrow.

I bent down over my wheel and was uselessly sad. But I'd gotten so close, but the sounds were just forming right.

The woman laughed: I was holding my charkha wrong.

But I'd just learned a new expression that only native speakers used: *Aur nahin to kya?* "If not that, then what?"

Every thread I tried to spin broke.

But language was so ephemeral, this was all going to fade.

A boy readjusted my hands.

But I'd just had one immaculate conversation, but Vidhu had said six months, but I'd only ever dreamed in English and not Hindi.

And the threads began to hold.

Sometimes now, I dream in both.

Epilogue

 Udaipur looked flatter and busier, both, four years on when I returned. The tourists had taken it back. I could see that much, but not much more. There was so little time, only enough for a couple of visits. But then again, most of the people I wanted to see weren't here anymore.

Renee had died two and a half years before, on Valentine's Day. Hindu rites of cremation were performed. She would have been pleased. Afterward, her beloved driver, Gopal, took her ashes the three days to the Ganges. Hindus believe that if someone's earthly remains are placed in the Ganges, they find *moksha,* "release," but I think Renee already had, when she'd found her true home.

The school was long gone from Sector Eleven. They'd all moved north, to Jaipur. Tui, the travel agent's daughter who'd invited me for tea, had, too, when she'd married. Priyanka was married now as well and living in the States. Chirag hadn't come through, this was someone else, in Atlanta, but still, I like to think I got that ball rolling. Helaena wasn't here either, though she was still on the subcontinent. After a stint working at a Motel Six in Pulaski, Tennessee, where the Gujarati owner had her waxing his wife's legs, she'd moved to Washington, D.C., and enrolled in a State Department training program. Now fluent in Tamil as well as Hindi, she was a junior diplomat in Sri Lanka, living, when he was around, with Sumair. Reader, she married him.

I met up with Ruby, briefly, also Nand. Ruby had started her own newspaper. Nand was still going strong. I got to see the Jains. They invited me out to Sector Eleven for dinner. Their driveway was even more intricate than I remembered. The kids were bigger, but Alka and Meena, Rajkumar and Rajesh, looked just the same. So did the grandmother, who now had my old room. Jain Dad 2 assured me I could come back and stay anytime for free, since we were friends, FRIENDS, and that's how friends were. The wives, privately, asked if I'd moved out because of him. I suspect that, perhaps, he might have been spoken to, but it was great, GREAT, all the same, to see him.

One afternoon, I visited Piers. He now lived ten miles out of town, on a serene hilltop estate with the houseboys and their wives; the boys had brought the women down from Nepal. It was one big family out there. Piers had a son now, an orphan he'd adopted from one of the villages and who, when he spoke to me in English, had a bit of a Midlands accent. In the few hours I had, Piers and I sat by his pool and talked about the year I'd been here. What a time! he'd say and laugh. Before long, a man appeared, a gardener. *"Ye ghaas nikaal do,"* Piers told him, pointing to some weeds. I did a double take. For four years, the story in my head had been that Piers would never, ever learn Hindi. But every story, of course, has more than one ending.

What I was mostly here to do, though, was try to figure out what it was I'd seen during my year at the deaf school. My second day in town, I swung by. Boys I didn't recognize were planting trees outside, raising dust clouds in the dirt yard. Inside, Anukul was in the same classroom. He had more gray at the temples now, had grown a bit wider around the waist, but you still would have had to agree he was photogenic. We sat and talked. He could not quite make out the mission I was on. I tried different explanations, which all began: I was here with a plan a linguist had come up with — "a very famous deaf-school professional in the United States." He nodded politely. He'd gotten that part on the phone. At her supervisory suggestion, I told him, I had made videos of friends' kids performing various activities: handing each other a glass of milk, climbing on a table and jumping down. I would now show these videos to children in different grades at the school, and he and I would film them describing the actions to one another in sign. By comparing the descriptions each age group gave, it might be possible to see if the language was evolving and how quickly. That was the plan. So did that make sense?

Anukul stared at me with patience through every explanation. Perhaps it was good he didn't grasp all the nuances, because that night my laptop went permanently black and scotched the video segment of the plan. The video camera also went on the fritz, though just temporarily, and a chutti, out of nowhere, shut down the school. "If you want to make God laugh, tell him your plans," as the saying goes. I'd forgotten that over here, with 333,000 deities to amuse, you could be rendered a comedy special in no time.

Finally, the school reopened. Anukul got the camera up and running; the friend I was traveling with agreed to reenact the video scenes with me live. Kids in all age groups were assembled. Plan on: I was cooking.

The less said about the next four hours, the better. I'll leave it at this: I now count among my video holdings one seasickness-inducing DVD, swaying shots of my friend perched on a child-size desk, muttering, "Is this what she said to do?" while crowds of children, flushed with excitement, point and laugh deliriously. (Whenever I play the DVD, I look again for familiar faces in the crowd, never find a single one. In my four years away, Hemant Patel, Banshi Lal, everyone I knew had moved on, gone to work in the fields, or at Hindustan Lever Factory, or, in the case of the girls, in some-one's house.)

At the end of the school day, my friend went back to the hotel. I went over to Anukul's with a list of backup questions Ann Senghas had compiled for me. I walked into a far different house than the one I'd seen on my first visit. That one had been three plain concrete rooms in a dusty back division. This one teemed with color and life—my second sight had never really gone away. A fat, laughing boy tottered out from the back. "This is Krishanu," Anukul said, grabbing and kissing the son Rita had had when she went to Bihar. A slim, white-haired man was seated on the floor. He had a digni-fied air of self-assurance I recognized; Anukul didn't have to say "This is my father." After his wife had died, he'd come to live here. Rita was demure in a way I'd never seen her, spoke softly, kept her eyes down. But then Anukul picked up the video camera for a group portrait, and she bumped a girl out of the lineup to stand beside me. She stood there beaming. In the spin of time since I'd been gone, I'd proved myself trustworthy.

We crowded together for a bit on the floor, while Krishanu danced and Anukul's father and I spoke in Hindi. I'd been worried the language had evaporated, for I only used it now to startle New York City taxi drivers. But it had started to well up my first night back, well up and spill over, and after that, I was able to talk to people.

Behind the bebopping Krishanu, through the door, potted lemon and guava trees lined a small courtyard. Out along the slopes of the Aravallis, birds were riding currents below the clouds. We pressed together shoulder to shoulder, one compact line, and I was in place, nestled in happiness.

After a while, Anukul inquired, weren't there questions I wanted to ask? He'd spent all day restraining kids in the pursuit of a plan he wasn't quite getting, but if I needed to know more, if it would help the children, well, then he was greedy for his boys.

Rita brought tea, she brought snacks, she brought dinner, as I went through the questions. What about the town's deaf family; could he say if their verbs also came at the end of sentences? Was their language at all like what he used with his kids? Could the family have influenced communication at the school? What about the Bikaner school—how much overlap did he think there was there? Overlap, overlap—oh, he knew: how much was the sign used there like the Udaipur boys'? How much language did his students come in with? And so on. I asked every question I could think of, but by the refresher round of tea, I had to admit I still had no real idea whether the children had invented a language.

I still had no idea because, in fact, I'd asked him every question I might have thought of except one.

We gave up on the list and discussed the day, all the hilarity and jubilation. One kid had held up a toy I'd brought, a bank shaped like a car, and performed some improv that brought down the house. His gestures had been beautifully supple, the way I recalled the boys' had been when they'd described the Australian cricket team's impending trouncing. Hey, I asked, what had that boy said?

"I do not know," Anukul said with a shrug, and I was surprised. When we'd spent Friday afternoons together, he'd nearly always been able to translate conversations for me on the spot, except for occasionally, when he'd gotten thrown by a word. But those Friday afternoons had been structured and under his control, I was forgetting that. Anukul had been leading the discussions then.

"You don't know?" I said.

"No."

"You don't?"

"Maybe something about a car."

"But why not?" I finally thought to ask.

"Oh," Anukul said pleasantly, casually, "because the children have a whole other language, one even we do not understand."

The Cruel Festival Time

by Nand Chaturvedi

One of these days
I'll look at your face and find
The sad detailed imprints
Of the festival days

Now those days
Are useless,
Those days which, like thieves,
Steal residual memory

Who will come for the festival:
Vasantsena, Vasavdutta,
Michael Jackson, Chidambaram,
Or a wild boar?
Won't she come that
Miss World,
What is her name?

In the festival's terror
The village
Has become impoverished, indifferent
Like trees in fall.
On women's shoulders
Naked boys sit,
A little shy,
Hiding their members in their thighs

Where is this Delhi,
Where the festival is?
The nation's president is here,
But where's the nation?
In his eyes are the sun and the moon,
Elongated sad shadows on fields,
A nation in the shape of roti,
Festival of remnant desires

They have become tired
A day before the festival,
On the road, they found the village girl's body
Still clutching the child to her breast.
The day before,
The girls were loaded into the truck
Like young goats
To be taken to the slaughterhouse.

From which festival have you come,
Vasantsena?
Which one is taking place
These days
In the capital of this darkness?

Darling, walk slowly,
For only if you walk
Slow will you see
What walks beside you
In the background,
In this cruel festival time.

Translated by Katherine Russell Rich
and Vidhu Shekhar Chaturvedi

Bibliography

Amunts, K., A. Schleicher, and K. Ziles. "Outstanding Language Competence and Cyber Architecture in Broca's Speech Region." *Brain and Language* 89, May 2004, 346–53.

Becker, A. L. *Beyond Translation*. Ann Arbor: University of Michigan Press, 1995.

Bhatia, Tej K., and William C. Ritchie. *Handbook of Bilingualism*. Oxford: Blackwell, 2006.

Bhatnagar, P. S. *Cambridge Self Hindi Teacher*. Delhi: Pankaj Publications, n.d.

Bhattacharya, Sabyasachi. *The Mahatma and the Poet*. Delhi: National Book Trust, 1997.

Bialystok, Ellen. *Bilingualism in Development*. Cambridge: Cambridge University Press, 2001.

———. *In Other Words*. New York: Basic Books, 1994.

Binder, J. R., D. A. Medler, R. Desai, L. L. Conant, and E. Liebenthal. "Some Neurophysiological Constraints on Models of Word Naming." *Neuroimage* 27, no. 3 (September 2005), 677–93.

Boroditsky, Lera. "Does Language Shape Thought? Mandarin and English Speakers' Conceptions of Time." *Cognitive Psychology* 43, no. 1, August 2001.

Bryant, Edwin. *The Quest for the Origins of Vedic Culture*. New York: Oxford University Press, 2001.

Calvin, William H., and Derek Bickerton. *Lingua Ex Machina.* Cambridge, Mass.: MIT Press, 2000.

Chomsky, Noam. *Language and Problems of Knowledge: The Managua Lectures.* Cambridge, Mass.: MIT Press, 1988.

Cohen, Leah Hager. *Train Go Sorry: Inside a Deaf World.* Boston: Houghton Mifflin, 1994.

Cook, Vivian, and Benedetta Bassetti, eds. *Second Language Writing Systems.* Clevedon, UK: Multilingual Matters, 2005.

Crystal, David. *How Language Works.* Woodstock, N.Y.: Overlook Press, 2006.

Dalrymple, William. "India: The War over History." *New York Review of Books,* April 7, 2005.

———. *White Mughals.* New York: HarperCollins, 2002.

Dijkstra, Ton. "Lexical Processing in Bilinguals and Multilinguals." In *The Multilingual Lexicon,* edited by Jasone Cenoz, Britta Hufeisen, and Ulrike Jessner. Cambridge: Cambridge University Press, 2002.

Dijkstra, Ton, and Walter J. B. van Heuven. "The Architecture of the Bilingual Word Recognition System." *Bilingualism: Language and Cognition* 5, no. 3 (December 2002), 175–97.

Dörnyei, Zoltán. *The Psychology of the Language Learner.* Mahwah, N.J.: Erlbaum, 2005.

Eck, Diana L. *Darsan: Seeing the Divine Image in India.* Chambersburg, Pa.: Anima Books, 1981.

Ellis, Rod. *Second Language Acquisition.* Oxford: Oxford University Press, 1997.

Freed, Stanley A., and Ruth S. Freed. *Hindu Festivals in a North Indian Village.* New York: American Museum of Natural History Anthropological Papers, 1998.

Friese, Kai. "Hijacking India's History." *New York Times.* December 30, 2002.

Gallese, Vitorio. "Mirror Neurons and Intentional Attunement." *Journal of the American Psychoanalytic Association,* 54, no. 1 (Winter 2006).

Gentner, Dedre, and Susan Goldin-Meadow, eds. *Language in Mind.* Cambridge, Mass.: MIT Press, 2003.

Gill, Jerry. *If a Chimpanzee Could Talk.* Tucson: University of Arizona Press, 1997.

Gold, Ann Grodzins. *Fruitful Journeys: The Ways of Rajasthani Pilgrims.* Prospect Heights, Ill.: Waveland Press, 2000.

Goldin-Meadow, Susan. *The Resilience of Language: What Gesture Creation in Deaf Children Can Tell Us About How All Children Learn Language.* New York: Psychology Press, 2003.

Golwalkar, M. S. *We, or, Our Nationhood Defined.* Nagpur, India: Bharat Publications, 1939.

Gopnik, Alison, Andrew N. Meltzoff, and Patricia M. Kuhl. *The Scientist in the Crib.* New York: Morrow, 1999.

Gordon, Raymond G. *Ethnologue: Languages of the World.* Dallas: SIL International, 2005.

Hamilton, Norah Rowan. *Through Wonderful India and Beyond.* London: Holdern & Hardingham, 1915.

Hooper, Rowan. "Spectrum of Empathy Found in the Brain." *New Scientist,* September 18, 2006.

Iacoboni, Marco. "Understanding Others: Imitation, Language, Empathy." In *Perspectives on Imitation: From Neuroscience to Social Science,* edited by Susan L. Hurley and Nick Chater. Cambridge, Mass.: MIT Press, 2005.

Jha, Raj Kamal. *Fireproof.* London: Picador Press, 2008.

Karmiloff-Smith, Annette. "Elementary Dear Watson, the Clue Is in the Genes—or Is It?" *Guardian,* November 6, 2002.

Kathuria, Ramdev P. *Life in the Courts of Rajasthan.* Delhi: S. Chand, 1987.

Kay, Paul, and Terry Regier. "Language, Thought and Color." *Trends in Cognitive Sciences* 1, no. 2 (February 2006), 51–54.

Kecskes, Istvan, and Tünde Papp. *Foreign Language and Mother Tongue.* Mahwah, N.J.: Erlbaum, 2000.

Kenneally, Christine. *The First Word.* New York: Viking, 2007.

King, Christopher R. *One Language, Two Scripts.* Oxford: Oxford University Press, 1994.

Kumar, Amitava. *Husband of a Fanatic.* New York: New Press, 2005.

Lamb, Sydney. *Language and Reality.* New York: Continuum Books, 2004.

Larsen-Freeman, Diane, and Michael H. Long. *An Introduction to Second Language Acquisition Research.* Essex, UK: Addison Wesley Longman, 1991.

Lavery, David. "The Mind of Benjamin Whorf." Paper presented at the South Atlantic Modern Language Association, Atlanta, October 1995.

Lightbown, Patsy M., and Nina Spada. *How Languages Are Learned.* Oxford: Oxford University Press, 1999.

Luce, Edward. *In Spite of the Gods.* New York: Doubleday, 2007.

Lynch, Owen M. *Divine Passions: The Social Construction of Emotion in India.* Berkeley: University of California Press, 1990.

"Maaro! Kaapo! Baalo! State, Society, and Communalism in Gujarat." Report, People's Union for Democratic Rights, Delhi, May 2002. http://www.onlinevolunteers.org/gujarat/reports/pudr.

MacFarquhar, Larissa. "The Strong Man: Where Is Hindu-Nationalist Violence Leading?" *The New Yorker,* May 26, 2003.

Macleod, Mairi. "Mindless Imitation Teaches Us to Be Human." *New Scientist,* April 1, 2006.

Malgady, Robert G., and Giuseppe Costantino. "Symptom Severity in Bilingual Hispanics as a Function of Clinician Ethnicity and Language of Interview." *Psychological Assessment* 2, June 1998, 120–27.

McLaughlin, Judith, Lee Osterhout, and Albert Kim. "Neural Correlates of Second-Language Word Learning: Minimal Instruction Produces Rapid Change." *Nature Neuroscience* 7, no. 7 (July 2004), 703–4.

Mehta, Suketu. *Maximum City: Bombay Lost and Found.* New York: Knopf, 2004.

Miller, Greg. "Waiter, There Is a Fly in Meiner Suppe." *ScienceNOW,* June 8, 2006.

Mishra, Pankaj. "Impasse in India." *New York Review of Books,* June 28, 2007.

Morrow, Ann. *The Maharajas of India.* Delhi: Srishti, 1998.

Oberman, Lindsay M., Edward M. Hubbard, Joseph P. McCleery, Eric L. Altschuler, Vilayanur S. Ramachandran, and Jaime A. Pineda. "EEG Evidence for Mirror Neuron Dysfunction in Autism Spectrum Disorders." *Cognitive Brain Research* 24, no. 2 (2005), 190–98.

Osborne, Lawrence. "A Linguistic Big Bang." *New York Times,* November 28, 1999.

Paradis, Michel. "Linguistic Parameters in the Diagnosis of Dyslexia in Japanese and Chinese." In *Reading and Writing Disorders in Different Orthographic Systems* edited by P. G. Aaron and R. Malatesha Joshi. Dordrecht, Netherlands: Kluwer Academic, 1989.

———. *Neurolinguistic Theory of Bilingualism.* Amsterdam: John Benjamins, 2004.

———, ed. *Readings on Aphasia in Bilinguals and Polyglots.* Montreal: Didier, 1983.

Pavlenko, Aneta. "Autobiographic Narratives as Data in Applied Linguistics." *Applied Linguistics* 28, no. 2 (June 1, 2007), 163–88.

———. *Emotions and Multilingualism.* Cambridge: Cambridge University Press, 2006.

———. "Second Language Learning by Adults: Testimonies of Bilingual Writers." *Issues in Applied Linguistics* 9, no. 1 (June 1998), 3–19.

Paz, Octavio. *In Light of India.* New York: Harcourt, 1997.

Perfetti, Charles A., Ying Liu, and Li-Hai Tan. "How the Mind Can Meet the Brain in Reading: A Comparative Writing Systems Approach." In *Cognitive Neuroscience Studies of the Chinese Language,* edited by H.S.R. Kao et al. Hong Kong: Hong Kong University Press, 2002.

Phillips, Webb, and Boroditsky, Lera. "Can Quirks of Grammar Affect the Way You Think? Grammatical Gender and Object Concepts." In *Proceedings of the 25th Annual Meeting of the Cognitive Science Society.* Boston: Cognitive Science Society, 2003.

Pinker, Steven. *How the Mind Works.* New York: Norton, 1997.

———. *The Language Instinct.* New York: Morrow, 1994.

———. *The Stuff of Thought.* New York: Viking, 2007.

Polich, Laura. *The Emergence of the Deaf Community in Nicaragua.* Washington, D.C.: Gallaudet University Press, 2002.

Ratey, John J. *A User's Guide to the Brain.* New York: Vintage, 2002.

Ratner, Carl. "A Cultural-Psychological Analysis of Emotions." In *Culture and Psychology Journal* 6, no. 1 (March 2000), 5–39.

Roy, Arundhati. "India's Shame." *Guardian,* December 15, 2006.

———, ed. *13 Dec: A Reader.* Delhi: Penguin, 2006.

Russo, Francine. "Hidden Secrets of the Creative Mind." *Time,* January 8, 2006.

Rymer, Russ. *Genie.* New York: HarperCollins, 1993.

Sacks, Oliver W. *Seeing Voices: A Journey into the World of the Deaf.* Berkeley: University of California Press, 1989.

Schmidt, Richard W. "The Role of Consciousness in Second Language Learning." *Applied Linguistics* 11, no. 2 (June 1990), 129–58.

Schumann, John H. *The Neurobiology of Affect in Language.* Malden, Mass.: Wiley-Blackwell, 1999.

Schumann, John H., Sheila E. Crowell, Nancy E. Jones, Namhee Lee, Sara Ann Schuchert, and Lee Alexandra Wood. *The Neurobiology of Learning: Perspectives from Second Language Acquisition.* Mahwah, N.J.: Erlbaum, 2004.

Seidenberg, Mark S. "Connectionist Models of Word Reading." *Current Directions in Psychological Science* 14, no. 5 (October 2005), 238–42.

Sen, Amartya. *The Argumentative Indian.* New York: Farrar, Straus and Giroux, 2005.

Sharma, Pandit Vishnu. *Panchatantra.* Delhi: Rupa, 1991.

Sharma, Rakesh. *Final Solution.* Documentary about Gujarat. Available from Rakesh Sharma, P.O. Box 12023, Azad Nagar Post Office, Mumbai-400053, India.

Smith, Neil, and Ianthi-Maria Tsimpli. *The Mind of a Savant.* Oxford: Blackwell, 1995.

Snell, Rupert, with Simon Weightman. *Teach Yourself Hindi.* Lincolnwood, Ill.: NTC, 2000.

Sousa, David A. *How the Brain Learns to Read.* Thousand Oaks, Calif.: Corwin Press, 2005.

Sternberg, Robert J., and Li-Fang Zhang. *Perspectives on Thinking, Learning, and Cognitive Styles.* Hillsdale, N.J.: Erlbaum, 2001.

Stille, Alexander. "Speak, Cultural Memory: A Dead-Language Debate." *New York Times,* September 30, 2000.

Tan, L. H., et al. "Brain Activation in the Processing of Chinese Characters and Words: A Functional MRI Study." *Human Brain Mapping* 10, no. 1 (May 2000), 16–27.

Tannen, Deborah. *Talking Voices.* Cambridge: Cambridge University Press, 1989.

Tharoor, Shashi. *The Elephant, the Tiger, and the Cell Phone.* New York: Arcade, 2007.

———. *India: From Midnight to the Millennium.* New York: Arcade, 1997.

Tillotson, G.H.R. *The Rajput Palaces.* New Haven, Conn.: Yale University Press, 1987.

Toro, Juan M., Josep B. Trobolan, and Nuria Sebastian-Galles. "Effects of Backward Speech and Speaker Variability in Language Discrimination by Rats: Animal Behavior Processes." *Journal of Experimental Psychology* 31, no. 1. (January 2005), 95–100.

Turner, Mark. *The Literary Mind.* New York: Oxford University Press, 1996.

Vaid, Jyotsna. "Exploring Word Recognition in a Semi-Alphabetic Script: The Case of Devanagari." *Brain and Language* 8, nos. 1–3 (April 2007), 679–90.

Varadarajan, Siddarth, ed. *Gujarat: The Making of a Tragedy.* Delhi: Penguin, 2002.

Vatsyayan, Kapila, ed. *Concepts of Time, Ancient and Modern.* Delhi: Sterling, 1996.

Weller, Anthony. *Days and Nights on the Grand Trunk Road.* New York: Marlowe, 1997.

Whorf, Benjamin Lee. *Language, Thought, and Reality: Selected Writing.* Cambridge, Mass.: Technology Press of MIT, 1956.

Wierzbicka, Anna. "Bilingual Lives, Bilingual Experience." *Journal of Multilingual and Multicultural Development* 25, nos. 2 and 3 (2004), 94–104.

———. *Emotions Across Languages and Culture.* Cambridge: Cambridge University Press, 1999.

Williams, Marion. "Motivation in Foreign and Second Language Learning." *Educational and Child Psychology* 11, no. 2 (1994), 77.

Wittgenstein, Ludwig. *Philosophical Investigations.* Oxford: Blackwell, 1967.

Wright, David. *Deafness.* London: Faber & Faber, 1991.

Acknowledgments

My first week studying in India, at loose ends one afternoon, I took a rickshaw downtown and settled in at a café. I was copying Hindi social phrases in Devanagari script, hoping to inscribe the words in my brain, when a jostling sound made me look up. "Excuse me," said one of the three waiters who'd been standing at attention. "You close this here" — and he pointed to one of the letters in *"I am much obliged for your kindness"* — "or otherwise it answers the other." All three grinned as I made the correction, then resumed their straight-backed pose. Midway through *"I am very much pleased to meet you,"* however, a shadow fell across the page.

"Miss, miss," the man said, tapping a letter with his finger. "This same like that one, also closed." On completion of *"After a time I have the honor of seeing you,"* I checked to see how it had gone. The men nodded. *"Please sit down comfortably,"* I started to write, reaching for my lassi, which in the heat had baked to sludge. I asked for water. Then I asked for love. Guffaws went up all around. Not *pyar,* "love," the waiter said, shaking his finger. *Pyala,* "cup," he said, and disappeared, returning with a Dixie cup, which he set in front of me. "Here's your love!" he cried, and I joined in the chortling. That was a good one, for sure.

So many people helped shape this book, I don't know how to begin to acknowledge them all, so I figure I'll start with the crack team of de facto Hindi teachers who prowled the streets of the Indian town where I lived—all the bank clerks, restaurant personnel, cybercafe owners, and rickshaw drivers who, unbidden, jumped in to fine-tune my Hindi every time I turned around and who, in the process, made me love the country even more than I already did.

There are a number of people, too, whose names I do know and whom I'd like to thank as well for their kindnesses and instruction:

Bindishwari Aggrawal, Susham Bedi, Tej Bhatia, Wendy Doniger, Neha Jain, Raj Kamal Jha, Amitava Kumar, Joel Lee, Suketu Mehta, Prassananshu, Rakesh Ranjan, Tulasi Srinivas, Salil Tripathi, and Michael Witzel, all of whom expanded my knowledge of India and saved me from making any number of foolish errors.

Priyanka Sharma, who exhibited noteworthy patience when it came to answering my everlasting slew of questions about India and Hindi. I'm grateful to her for not changing her e-mail and for the gracious reflection she gave to each inquiry.

The linguist Alton Becker, for helping me make sense of what, at times, was a fiercely puzzling map. Michel Paradis, for his cheerful and unwavering willingness to illuminate the brain for me. Nancy Isenberg, for hours of fascinating conversations in Princeton, New Jersey, about autism, mirror neurons, and culture shocks. Martha Young-Scholten, for her enthusiasm and the overview of linguistics she provided.

Ellen Bialystok, Derek Bickerton, Jeffrey R. Binder, Andrew Cohen, Vivian Cook, Marie Coppola, Ton Dijkstra, Chris Frith, David Green, Arturo Hernandez, Marco Iacoboni, Dora Johnson, Judith Kroll, Sydney Lamb, Brian MacWhinney, Gaurav Mathur, Istvan Molnar-Szakacs, Lorraine K. Obler, Lee Osterhout, Aneta Pavlenko,

Charles Perfetti, Kenneth Pugh, John Rassias, Terry Regier, Jenny Saffran, John H. Schumann, Annie Senghas, Ragnar Steingrimsson, Deborah Tannen, Jyotsna Vaid, Michael Vitevitch, and Anna Wierzbicka were all enormously helpful in elucidating scientific theories that appear in this book.

Early on in the writing, the Dorothy and Lewis B. Cullman Center for Scholars and Writers at the New York Public Library gave me the extraordinary opportunity to spend a year surrounded by books and uncommon fellowship. Many thanks to the library's Rebecca Federman, Pamela Leo, and Jean Strouse; ace researcher and writers' friend David Smith; and Usha Bhaskar and Sunita Vaze.

The Corporation of Yaddo, where the book first came together. The MacDowell Colony, where I finished it.

Deb Baker, Martha Barnette, Jo Ann Beard, Betsy Carter, John Catalinotto, Jill Ciment, Greg Gibson, Sue Halpern, Amy Hempel, Margaret Jaworski, Patricia Lear, Rachel Manley, Sara Nelson, Diego Olivé, Martha Ann Overland, Leslie Savan, Judith Stone, Peter Trachtenberg, and Lindsy Van Gelder read all or parts of the book and offered valuable suggestions.

Delphine Blue; Dennis Nurkse; George Raptis, M.D.; and Syd Straw, for the joy of their insights and support.

All the members of the Invisible Institute, beginning with Chris Kenneally, Annie Murphy Paul, and Alissa Quart.

Arun Krishnan vetted the final draft and also made me laugh every time I downloaded his "Learn Hindi from Bollywood Movies" podcasts — the place to go when you need to know how to say "In the next twenty-four hours, I will make twenty-four pieces out of you" in Hindi.

Gabriela Ilieva, for her friendship and her scared-straight approach to Hindi language study. She's a superb teacher, for she has the rare ability to make you, during the time you spend with her, smarter than you are.

My agent, Betsy Lerner, was a djinn. She sowed the seed, provided counsel that got me over numerous hurdles, knew when to step in and when to hang back.

And: Sasheem Silkiss-Hero, a pleasure to work with, at Houghton Mifflin Harcourt. The elegant Pat Strahan, who acquired the book. Eamon Dolan, who with wit and sharp intelligence guided it through. Anjali Singh, who came in at the end and proved to be a writer's dream: deeply respectful, able to see the best in the work, and indefatigable in her arguments when she's absolutely right. Which, as it turned out, was much of the time.